THE
FACE
OF
WAR

MARTHA GELLHORN

THE
FACE
OF
WAR

ATLANTIC
MONTHLY
PRESS

To my son Sandy

The Face of War was first published in 1959 in the United States by Simon & Schuster and in Great Britain by Hart Davis; revised in 1967 and published in Great Britain by Sphere; and revised in 1986 and published in Great Britain by Virago. The Atlantic Monthly Press edition is a revised and updated edition of the one published by Virago.

Atlantic Monthly Press edition first published in the United States of America in March 1988.

Published simultaneously in Canada
Printed in the United States of America

Library of Congress Cataloging-in-Publication Data

Gellhorn, Martha, 1908–
   The face of war / Martha Gellhorn.
   ISBN 0-87113-211-7
   1. Military history, Modern—20th century. I. Title.
D431.G4   1988   87-30801
904'.7—dc 19

Design by Laura Hough

The Atlantic Monthly Press
19 Union Square West
New York, NY 10003

FIRST PRINTING

Contents

THE SECOND WORLD WAR, 85

THE WAR IN JAVA, 187

INTERIM, 201

THE WAR IN VIETNAM, 221

Author's Note

The structure of this book needs explaining. It has grown by addition and subtraction through four versions over almost thirty years. All the reports are reprinted as originally published. When the titles had not been my choice and I disliked them, I have changed them. The first version, 1959, began with an introduction and ended with Dachau. I deleted six reports from the second version, 1967, to make room for the sections called the War in Java and Interim, and The War in Vietnam; and added a short introduction and conclusion. Through all versions, I have not altered my prefatory comments on each war though by the third version, 1986, some sentences written in 1959 were happily outdated. The 1986 version attached a new introduction, included the entire 1967 version, and added later comment on the Vietnam War, the Six Day War, and war in Central America. This fourth and final version deletes the superfluous 1967 introduction and conclusion, and the 1986 comment on the Vietnam War: I wrote a new one, I hope a better one. I have added one report, "Three Poles," to the Second World War, one article, "Suffer the Little Children," to the Vietnam War and a Conclusion.

Introduction
1959

When I was young I believed in the perfectibility of man, and in progress, and thought of journalism as a guiding light. If people were told the truth, if dishonor and injustice were clearly shown to them, they would at once demand the saving action, punishment of wrong-doers, and care for the innocent. How people were to accomplish these reforms, I did not know. That was their job. A journalist's job was to bring news, to be eyes for their conscience. I think I must have imagined public opinion as a solid force, something like a tornado, always ready to blow on the side of the angels.

During the years of my energetic hope, I blamed the leaders when history regularly went wrong, when cruelty and violence were tolerated or abetted, and the innocent never got anything except the dirty end of the stick. The leaders were a vague interlocking directorate of politicians, industrialists, newspaper owners, financiers: unseen, cold, ambitious men. "People" were good, by definition; if they failed to behave well, that was because of ignorance or helplessness.

It took nine years, and a great depression, and two wars ending in defeat, and one surrender without war, to break my faith in the benign power of the press. Gradually I came to realize that people will more readily swallow lies than truth, as if the taste of lies was homey, appetizing: a habit. (There were also liars in my trade, and leaders have always used facts as relative and malleable. The supply of lies was unlimited.) Good people, those who opposed evil wherever they saw it, never increased beyond a gallant minority. The manipulated millions could be aroused or soothed

1

by any lies. The guiding light of journalism was no stronger than a glow-worm.

I belonged to a Federation of Cassandras, my colleagues the foreign correspondents, whom I met at every disaster. They had been reporting the rise of Fascism, its horrors and its sure menace, for years. If anyone listened to them, no one acted on their warnings. The doom they had long prophesied arrived on time, bit by bit, as scheduled. In the end we became solitary stretcher-bearers, trying to pull individuals free from the wreckage. If a life could be saved from the first of the Gestapo in Prague, or another from behind the barbed wire on the sands at Argelès, that was a comfort but it was hardly journalism. Drag, scheming, bullying and dollars occasionally preserved one human being at a time. For all the good our articles did, they might have been written in invisible ink, printed on leaves, and loosed to the wind.

After the war in Finland, I thought of journalism as a passport. You needed proper papers and a job to get a ringside seat at the spectacle of history in the making. In the Second World War, all I did was praise the good, brave and generous people I saw, knowing this to be a perfectly useless performance. When occasion presented, I reviled the devils whose mission was to deny the dignity of man; also useless. I took an absurd professional pride in getting where I intended to go and in sending my copy to New York on time; but I could not fool myself that my war correspondent's work mattered a hoot. War is a malignant disease, an idiocy, a prison, and the pain it causes is beyond telling or imagining; but war was our condition and our history, the place we had to live in. I was a special type of war profiteer; I was physically lucky, and was paid to spend my time with magnificent people.

After the victory in World War II, I hung on in the climate of war for another year, since peace was uneasy and unconvincing. At last in Java I saw the postwar new-style little war, and knew I never wanted to see any more of it again anywhere. Probably that pathetic murderous mess in the East Indies was inevitable. The tall white men had been conquered and debased by short yellow men; why should anyone accept the white man as master again? The Dutchmen of the Indies returned, like skeletons and ghosts, from Japanese prisons and from building the Japanese death railway through the jungle; their sick, starved women and children emerged from years in Japanese concentration camps on Java; and immediately they were set upon by the natives they had tried to rule with care and decency. Both the Indonesians and the Dutch needed time to heal from the war and find a just plan for their lives. There was no time. Nothing anybody wrote was going to shorten this torment, nor save one victim, white or brown.

Journalism at its best and most effective is education. Apparently people would not learn for themselves, nor from others. If the agony of the Second World War did not teach them, whatever would? Surely the postwar world is a mockery of hope and an insult to all those who died so that we should survive.

As civilization seemed determined to grope its way towards suicide, the sane occupation for a private citizen, while waiting, was to cultivate his own garden with a view to making it as clean and merry and pleasant as possible. I devised a life which seemed to me good because it was harmless, behind high garden walls.

Now I have different ideas. I must always, before, have expected results. There was an obtainable end, called victory or defeat. One could hope for victory, despair over defeat. At this stage in my life, I think that I think this is nonsense.

Until the invention of the A-bomb, the H-bomb, the Cobalt bomb, or whatever next, we could reasonably consider human history to be a giant interminable roller coaster, going up and down. The ceaseless but temporary riders on the roller coaster changed their clothes, carried new luggage, talked in varying jargons, yet remained men, women and children, constant in their humanity. The unique possession anyone on the roller coaster had, as far as I could see, was his own behavior while making the mysterious journey. For his own behavior each one is responsible, but no behavior is final. It shapes human destiny—any behavior, all behavior—but it makes no last decision. Victory and defeat are both passing moments. There are no ends; there are only means.

Journalism is a means; and I now think that the act of keeping the record straight is valuable in itself. Serious, careful, honest journalism is essential, not because it is a guiding light but because it is a form of honorable behavior, involving the reporter and the reader. I am no longer a journalist; like all other private citizens, the only record I have to keep straight is my own.

Despite official drivel about clean bombs and tactical nuclear weapons, anyone who can read a newspaper or listen to a radio knows that some of us mortals have the power to destroy the human race and man's home on earth. We need not even make war; only by preparing, by playing with our new weapons, we poison the air, the water, the soil of our planet, damage the health of the living, and weaken the chances of the unborn. How can anyone, anywhere, discount the irreversible folly of testing our nuclear bombs, or the promise of extinction if we use them in war?

The world's leaders seem strangely engaged in private feuds. They hurtle in airplanes on their Olympian business; they meet each other, always each other; or they deliberate in the various palaces of government; and they talk and talk, incessantly, for publication. Their talk sounds as if they believed nuclear war to be a thing that can be won or lost, and probable; any minute now, without warning, we may find ourselves in it. (Be calm. We will slay the enemy with our superspace, supersonic, triple-intercontinental, X-ray-guided, anti-offensive-defensive missiles. Do not fear. We will burn the foe with our best smallest deadliest fission-unfission-defission-profission bombs. Meanwhile, my comrades, my people, fellow citizens, loyal subjects, your service is civil defense; dig a little blast proof hole in your back yard and wait for the Apocalypse.)

The world's leaders appear to have lost touch with life down here on the ground, to have forgotten the human beings they lead. Or perhaps the led—so numerous and so mute—have ceased to be quite real, not living people but calculated casualties. For we are led and must follow whether we want to or not; there is no place to secede to. But we need not follow in silence; we still have the right and duty, as private citizens, to keep our own records straight. As one of the millions of the led, I will not be herded any farther along this imbecile road to nothingness without raising my voice in protest. My *NO* will be as effective as one cricket chirp. My *NO* is this book.

It is hard not to sound like a harangue, not to boom or squeak. And very hard (for me, certainly) to make one-two-three sense, logical paragraph piled on logical paragraph. I see mysteries and complications wherever I look, and I have never met a steadily logical person. Still one can sometimes say what one means, with immense effort.

4

No one need point out my contradictions; I know them and feel them. I thought that 1939 was at least three years too late to start fighting Hitler and all his cohorts and everything they did and stood for. Our victory spared us temporarily from unbearable evil; it solved nothing. War, when it has any purpose, is an operation which removes, at a specific time, a specific cancer. The cancer reappears in different shapes, in different parts of the human race; we have learned no preventive medicine for the body of the nations. We fall back, again and again, on nearly fatal surgery. But the human race has always survived the operation and lived.

I do not hope for a world at peace, all of it, all the time. I do not believe in the perfectibility of man, which is what would be required for universal peace; I only believe in the human race. I believe that the human race must continue. Our leaders are not wise enough, nor brave enough, nor noble enough, for their jobs. We, the led, are largely either sheep or tigers; we are all guilty of stupidity, the ruling human sin. This being so, we can expect wars; we have never been free of them. I hate this fact and accept it.

But nuclear war is unlike any other kind of war that has threatened mankind, and cannot be thought of in the old known terms. Nuclear war reaches a dimension unseen before in history. That dimension is towering, maniacal conceit.

We hardly remember who fought the Wars of the Roses or why, yet those wars lasted for thirty years and must have been a deep dark night for the combatants and civilians trapped in them. Still, we are here: the natural world remained healthy, nourishing and lovely; the race continued, uninfected in its bones, its blood, its minds. From the earliest wars of men to our last heart-breaking world-wide effort, all we could do was kill ourselves. Now we are able to kill the future. And we are so arrogant that we dare to prepare for this, insane pygmies menacing the very existence of nature. Five hundred years from now our East-West quarrel will seem as meaningless as the Wars of the Roses. Who are we that we presume to *end* anything?

At this point I hear loud and angry voices, as passionate as mine, saying: survival is not all. If men will not fight against tyrants and slavery, life is worthless and civilization should perish. Et cetera. I cannot understand this argument, although I have tried. I do not see how the human spirit, housed in the human body, will

5

be able to cherish freedom, revere the rights of others, and practice its highest talent, love, when the earth is sterile from man-made poisons, the air tainted, and the race sick and dying. I do not see what human values can be defended when all humanity is lost, the good and the evil together.

If we make or allow war, we deserve it; but we must limit our weapons and our locales, and keep our crime under control. We will have to satisfy the madness that is in human nature with small non-nuclear wars of a type we are getting more and more used to. It is in our ancient tradition to murder each other; but only we, in the present, should pay the price for our abominable stupidity. Nothing that concerns us, in our brief moment of history, gives us the right to stop time, to blot out the future, to end the continuing miracles and glories and tragedies and wretchedness of the human race.

This book is a selection from the reporting I did on wars in progress during eight years in eight countries. The people in these articles are ordinary people, anyone; what happened to them happened to uncounted others. The pictures are small but there are many, and it seems to me that they merge finally into one crowded appalling picture.

There is a single plot in war; action is based on hunger, homelessness, fear, pain and death. Starving wounded children, in Barcelona in 1938 and in Nijmegen in 1944, were the same. Refugees, dragging themselves and whatever they could carry away from war to no safety, were one people all over the globe. The shapeless bundle of a dead American soldier in the snow of Luxembourg was like any other soldier's corpse in any other country. War is a horrible repetition.

I wrote very fast, as I had to; and I was always afraid that I would forget the exact sound, smell, words, gestures which were special to this moment and this place. I hope I learned to write a bit better as the years passed. The point of these articles is that they are true; they tell what I saw. Perhaps they will remind others, as they remind me, of the face of war. We can hardly be reminded too much or too often. I believe that memory and imagination, not nuclear weapons, are the great deterrents.

Introduction
1986

The first report in this book was written forty-nine years ago. After a lifetime of war-watching, I see war as an endemic human disease, and governments are the carriers. Only governments prepare, declare and prosecute wars. There is no record of hordes of citizens, on their own, mobbing the seat of government to clamor for war. They must be infected with hate and fear before they catch war fever. They have to be taught that they are endangered by an enemy, and that the vital interests of their state are threatened. The vital interests of the state, which are always about power, have nothing to do with the vital interests of the citizens, which are private and simple and are always about a better life for themselves and their children. You do not kill for such interests, you work for them.

I am suspicious of governments—with a few admirable exceptions—and their version of vital interests. If they were doing their jobs properly, governments would concentrate on seeing that their countries functioned well, to the best advantage of the largest number of citizens: they would not lavish huge chunks of the communal wealth on armaments and economize on the needs of the people. Whether rich or poor or middling, all governments have money for war and every year, more and more, all governments have enormous sums of money to stockpile the weapons of war. And all of them, democratic or despotic, existing on their people's earnings, grudge money for services to the people. We live in an overarmed, underfed world.

To get a war started, you need an aggressor, a government so ambitious, so greedy that the vital interests of its state require foreign conquest. But an aggressor government sells its people the project of war as a defensive measure: they are being threatened, encircled, pushed around; enemies are poised to attack them. It is sadly easy to make people believe any lies; people are pitifully gullible, subject to instant flag-waving and misguided patriotism. And once a war has started, the government is in total control: the people must obey the orders of their government even if their early induced enthusiasm has waned. They also see that however needlessly the war started, it would be better not to lose it.

The nation or nations that are attacked have no choice except to fight the aggressor. But would not competent governments have seen the menace and taken early action to prevent the aggressor from completing preparations for war? It is probable that Hitler could have been stopped in 1936, when he reoccupied the Rhineland in violation of the Locarno Pact. Surely the Falklands war could have been avoided by intelligent foresight? Governments are more competent at waging war than preventing it. And, when you get right down to it, war is not so terrible for governments, the people at the top, the people in charge. Their power increases, and governments thrive on power; they have the excitement, the enhanced importance and none of the hardships. They are not ordered to fight or work in factories; miraculously they are not wounded or killed like ordinary people; they are too valuable to live on pinched rations. Until the Second World War, when its unique monstrousness changed the rules, governments paid no more grievous penalty for losing a war than losing their jobs. The Kaiser simply retired to a small rural palace.

Yet ten million men died in the Great War of 1914–18, because of the vital interests of the Kaiser's government which no one now can remember. Progressing from trench warfare to total war and genocide, 35 million human beings died in World War II because of the insane vital interests of Hitler's state, and the vital interests of the government of the Emperor of Japan, who survived unscathed. Since 1945, people have been dying every year in wars large and small, due to the vital interests of some state.

Perhaps the Kremlin, if not the uninformed Russian people, is having anxious second thoughts about the vital interests of the state that were protected by invading Afghanistan. I never saw what vital interests of the state obliged the U.S. government to launch America into its longest, and undeclared, war in Vietnam, and clearly no vital interests were involved, since losing the war left America intact, business proceeding as usual. Though the U.S. government did make an effective statement, at the cost of its citizens' blood and treasure: it is wiser for small Asian nations to be amiable about whatever the U.S. government deems its vital interests. And maybe that is what the Kremlin thinks it is accomplishing in Afghanistan: serving notice that, on the frontiers of the Soviet Union, you behave or else.

For those of us who have a merely human, not geopolitical, view of the world, the vital interests of the Soviet state in Afghanistan, the vital interests of the American state in Vietnam look like madness, and a cruel disaster for other humans, Russians, Afghans, Vietnamese, Americans. It would be wonderful if ordinary people learned to be wary and distrustful of the virus carried by governments: the vital interests of the state.

Wonderful but unlikely. Our amazing species is programmed from childhood in my-country-right-or-wrong patriotism. I wonder how that sounds in Urdu or Chinese. It is a nonsense phrase, despite its compelling power. My country is a fact, not right or wrong, a land, language, customs, culture. Invoked for the purpose of rallying citizens to war, the correct phrase should be my-government-right-or-wrong. That would be a salutary change, causing citizens to ask questions and decide whether their government was right or fatally wrong. I always liked Tolstoi's crusty remark that "governments are a collection of men who do violence to the rest of us," but now I think the old Russian was a prophet. Since the advent of nuclear weapons, the entire human race is at the mercy of those governments which own and control these world-killing weapons. Violence of such final magnitude was never before entrusted to the fallible people who are governments.

Of course we are told that nuclear weapons are purely defensive: they are deterrents. Due to them, our governments inform us, we have had forty years of peace, which is visibly false. What they mean is that we have not had a war between the Superpowers. Even describing nuclear weapons as deterrents is a lie. Since the Superpowers long ago had enough nuclear weapons to destroy each other (and everyone else) once, it is hardly necessary to go on manufacturing more and more of these weapons so that they can destroy everyone forty times. Nuclear weapons have become Big Business, probably the biggest business there is.

Tens of thousands of people are very gainfully employed in our nuclear weapons industry; colossal profits are made in the capitalist world. Star Wars is a giant pork barrel, as well as a giant folly. In the Soviet Union I presume that thousands of Soviet citizens are well rewarded for their work in this important field. The expense is borne by the Soviet people who are deprived because there isn't enough money for everything and nuclear weapons come first. The minor French and British nuclear arsenals are pointless; governmental snobbery, dues paid for membership in the Nuclear Club, dues paid by the French and British people who need that tax money to improve the condition of their lives.

The richest state in the world, the U.S.A., dispenses military money on a breathtaking scale. In 1986, the Pentagon will be spending $1 billion a day, $41 million an hour, $700,000 a minute. From 1983 to 1989, $450 billion is allotted for nuclear weapons alone. It is impossible to imagine money in that amount, but worth noting that in America there are charity soup kitchens for the destitute and rat-infested slums, and 35 million Americans live below the poverty line and no officials make a connection between epidemic drug addiction and crime among the workless, outcast young and the misery of their homes.

It costs £1 million a day to run Britain's Polaris submarines and who knows how many millions to replace them with the stylish Tridents. Think what £365 million a year would do for housing in the worst of Britain's inner cities: housing and recreation centers for the young, and trees and green space: an environment to cherish, not burn. There is never enough money for life, though money can always be found for armaments, nuclear and conventional, and for our immense military establishments.

But our governments know best; it is the supreme vital interest of the state to protect us from attack by the Soviet Union. Our governments talk freely of "the enemy," which is the other name for the Soviet Union. All maneuvers—even the recent rather charming home-guard maneuvers in Britain to defend the country against Soviet parachutists—are planned and carried out against "the enemy." It is assumed as fact, as if it were a certainty like the sun rising in the east, that the Soviet Union intends to attack western Europe; and all the thousands of nuclear weapons scattered in Europe, spread over the United States, all the war games, plans, dispositions, are based on that assumption. We must be constantly, ruinously prepared, for the Reds would come if we were not.

No one ever answers this question: *why should they?* For what reason, to what purpose would the Soviet Union wish to attack western Europe and start the Third World War, with or without nuclear weapons? What do they need from western Europe? What would they gain by trying to hold down 300 million hostile people? The present American government has entirely forgotten, though the Russians have not, that Russia was invaded and devastated almost to Moscow and twenty million Russians lost their lives. The Great Patriotic War is not ancient history to the Russian people. No one who has ever been to Russia has not heard Russians speak with terror of another war, with passionate longing for peace.

I blame our governments, supposedly the most enlightened, experienced and powerful, for the sick and ominous pass to which they have brought us. Above all, I blame the governments of the Superpowers, temporary men behaving as if the rivalry between the United States and the Soviet Union were the most momentous episode in the long history of mankind. We cannot live with the insanity of nuclear weapons. It must stop. A fragile détente now and again is not enough, nor a deal to limit these weapons, scrap those, while retaining thousands of new and improved models. We can and should start with a freeze, then go on to rid ourselves entirely of the evil nuclear arsenals, theirs and ours. We might keep one megaton murderer targeted on Moscow, one on Washington, to remind the governments of the Superpowers that they must act like responsible adults and negotiate their differences.

Governments are here today and gone in a few years; even dictators are transient. The quarrels between nations are impermanent. Enemies turn into allies and vice versa. No wars, in the war-logged record of our species, have been terminal. Until now, when we know that nuclear war would be the death of our planet. It is beyond belief that any governments—those brief political figures—arrogate to themselves the right to stop history, at their discretion. In case of Armageddon, governments are provided the best possible shelters, built with public money. Do they believe that they could or should survive nuclear war? Do they expect to sit out the

11

agony in some underground bunker and emerge to take charge again? Of what? Those shelters prey on my mind. I cannot decide which is worse, the moral imbecility or the mindless lack of imagination.

Meanwhile we exist under threat of annihilation and waste our wealth on nuclear weapons because They would attack western Europe if They dared. They exist under threat of annihilation and waste their wealth on nuclear weapons because We would attack the Soviet Union if We dared. We say Their fear of us is paranoia. What about our fear of Them? Two paranoias facing each other, poisoning the present, destabilizing life, since for the first time ever the human race cannot be sure it will continue. An intolerable way to run the world. Intolerable for every one of us, all the people who live here.

THE WAR IN SPAIN

In the summer of 1936, I was checking background material for a novel, in the Weltkriegsbibliothek of Stuttgart. The Nazi newspapers began to speak of fighting in Spain. They did not talk of war; the impression I got was of a bloodthirsty rabble, attacking the forces of decency and order. This Spanish rabble, which was the duly elected Republic of Spain, was always referred to as "Red Swine-dogs." The Nazi papers had one solid value: Whatever they were against, you could be for.

Shortly after I was twenty-one I had gone to France to work and there became one of a group of young French pacifists. We had in common our poverty and our passion. Our aim in life was to kick out the evil old, who were clearly leading us into another war. We believed that there could be no peace in Europe without Franco-German rapprochement. We had the right idea, but the Nazis arrived.

13

In 1934 we met the young Nazis in Berlin. At the frontier, German police had come through the train, paused in our third-class carriage, and confiscated our newspapers. Although we represented no one except ourselves, we read and disagreed on all opinions, ranging from Monarchist to Socialist to Liberal-reformer (me). We united, for once, in thinking this newspaper seizure an outrage. When we got off the train, in our usual shabby argumentative huddle, we were greeted by the young Nazis in clean blond khaki-clad formation. They proved to have one parrot brain among the lot and we did not care for them. We tried very hard to excuse them; we tried to agree that they were Socialists, as they kept assuring us, not National Socialists. Being sorry for the defeated Germans was a condition of mind of many people, after both world wars; I had it then. Also, I was a pacifist and it interfered with my principles to use my eyes. By 1936, no amount of clinging to principles helped me; I saw what these bullying Nazi louts were like and were up to.

But there I was, working with miserable determination on a novel about young pacifists in France. I stayed some months in Germany discussing, with anyone who still dared to discuss, the freedom of the mind, the rights of the individual, and the Red Swine-dogs of Spain. Then I went back to America, finished my novel, shoved it forever into a desk drawer, and started to get myself to Spain. I had stopped being a pacifist and become an anti-fascist.

By the winter of 1937, the Western democracies had proclaimed the doctrine of non-intervention, which meant simply that neither people nor supplies could pass freely to the Republican territory of Spain. I went to the French authorities in Paris to get whatever stamps or papers were required to leave the country. The French fonctionnaire, as all know who have dealt with him, is a certified brute. He sits, unlistening, behind a grille, scratching away with a sharp governmental pen and pallid ink. I cannot have come out well with this type, as I only remember studying a map, taking a train, getting off at a station nearest to the Andorran–Spanish border, walking a short distance from one country to another, and taking a second train—ancient cold little carriages, full of the soldiers of the Spanish Republic who were returning to Barcelona on leave.

They hardly looked like soldiers, being dressed however they were able, and obviously this was an army in which you fed yourself, since the government could not attend to that. I was in a wooden carriage with six boys who were eating garlic sausage and bread made of powdered stone. They offered me their food, they laughed, they sang. Whenever the train stopped, another young man, perhaps their officer, stuck his head in the carriage and exhorted them. I gathered that he was exhorting them to behave beautifully. They did behave beautifully, but I do not know what they said, as I spoke no Spanish.

Barcelona was bright with sun and gay with red banners, and the taxi driver refused money; apparently everything was free. Apparently everyone was everyone else's brother too. Since few people have lived in such an atmosphere, even for a minute, I can report that it is the loveliest atmosphere going. I was handed around like a package, with jollity and kindness; I rode on trucks and in jammed cars. And finally, by way of Valencia, we came at night to Madrid, which was cold, enormous and pitch-black, and the streets were silent and perilous with shell holes. That was on March 27, 1937, a date I have found somewhere in notes. I had not felt as if I were at a war until now, but now I knew I was. It was a feeling I cannot describe; a whole city was a battlefield, waiting in the dark. There was certianly fear in that feeling, and courage. It made you walk carefully and listen hard and it lifted the heart.

In New York a friendly and spirited man, then an editor of *Collier's*, had given me a letter. The letter said, to whom it might concern, that the bearer, Martha Gellhorn, was a special correspondent for *Collier's* in Spain. This letter was intended to help me with any authorities who wondered what I was doing in Spain, or why I was trying to get there; otherwise it meant nothing. I had no connection with a newspaper or magazine, and I believed that all one did about a war was go to it, as a gesture of solidarity, and get killed, or survive if lucky until the war was over. That was what happened in the trenches of France, as I had read; everyone was dead or wounded badly enough to be sent away. I had no idea you could be what I became, an unscathed tourist of wars. A knapsack and approximately fifty dollars were my equipment for Spain; anything more seemed unnecessary.

I tagged along behind the war correspondents, experienced men who had serious work to do. Since the authorities gave them transport and military passes (transport was far harder to come by than permission to see everything; it was an open, intimate war) I went with them to the fronts in and around Madrid. Still I did nothing except learn a little Spanish and a little about war, and visit the wounded, trying to amuse or distract them. It was a poor effort and one day, weeks after I had come to Madrid, a journalist friend observed that I ought to write; it was the only way I could serve the *Causa,* as the Spaniards solemnly and we lovingly called the war in the Spanish Republic. After all, I was a writer, was I not? But how could I write about war, what did I know, and for whom would I write? What made a story, to begin with? Didn't something gigantic and conclusive have to happen before one could write an article? My journalist friend suggested that I write about Madrid. Why would that interest anyone? I asked. It was daily life. He pointed out that it was not everybody's daily life.

I mailed my first Madrid article to *Collier's,* not expecting them to publish it; but I did have that letter, so I knew *Collier's* address. *Collier's* accepted the piece and after my next article put my name on the masthead. I learned this by accident. Once on the masthead, I was evidently a war correspondent. It began like that.

This is the place to express my gratitude to a vanished magazine and to Charles Colebaugh, the editor who then ran it. Thanks to *Collier's,* I had the chance to see the life of my time, which was war. They never cut or altered anything I wrote. They did, however, invent their own titles for most of my articles. I did not like their titles and am not using them here, but they were a trifling price to pay for the freedom *Collier's* gave me; for eight years, I could go where I wanted, when I wanted, and write what I saw.

What was new and prophetic about the war in Spain was the life of the civilians, who stayed at home and had war brought to them. I have selected three reports on this twentieth-century war in the city. The people of the Republic of

Spain were the first to suffer the relentless totality of modern war.

I have praised the *Causa* of the Republic of Spain on the slightest provocation for twenty years, and I am tired of explaining that the Spanish Republic was neither a collection of blood-slathering Reds nor a cat's-paw of Russia. Long ago I also gave up repeating that the men who fought and those who died for the Republic, whatever their nationality and whether they were Communists, anarchists, Socialists, poets, plumbers, middle-class professional men, or the one Abyssinian prince, were brave and disinterested, as there were no rewards in Spain. They were fighting for us all, against the combined force of European fascism. They deserved our thanks and our respect and got neither.

I felt then (and still do) that the Western democracies had two commanding obligations: they must save their honor by assisting a young, attacked fellow democracy, and they must save their skin, by fighting Hitler and Mussolini, at once, in Spain, instead of waiting until later, when the cost in human suffering would be unimaginably greater. Arguments were useless during the Spanish War and ever after; the carefully fostered prejudice against the Republic of Spain remains impervious to time and facts.

All of us who believed in the *Causa* of the Republic will mourn the Republic's defeat and the death of its defenders, forever, and will continue to love the land of Spain and the beautiful people, who are among the noblest and unluckiest on earth.

High Explosive for Everyone

July 1937

At first the shells went over: you could hear the thud as they left the Fascists' guns, a sort of groaning cough; then you heard them fluttering toward you. As they came closer the sound went faster and straighter and sharper and then, very fast, you heard the great booming noise when they hit.

But now, for I don't know how long—because time didn't mean much—they had been hitting on the street in front of the hotel, and on the corner, and to the left in the side street. When the shells hit that close, it was a different sound. The shells whistled toward you—it was as if they whirled at you—faster than you could imagine speed, and, spinning that way, they whined: the whine rose higher and quicker and was a close scream—and then they hit and it was like granite thunder. There wasn't anything to do, or anywhere to go: you could only wait. But waiting alone in a room that got dustier and dustier as the powdered cobblestones of the street floated into it was pretty bad.

I went downstairs into the lobby, practicing on the way how to breathe. You couldn't help breathing strangely, just taking the air into your throat and not being able to inhale it.

It seemed a little crazy to be living in a hotel, like a hotel in Des Moines or New Orleans, with a lobby and wicker chairs in the lounge, and signs on the door of your room telling you that they would press your clothes immediately and that meals served privately cost ten percent more, and meantime it was like a trench

19

when they lay down an artillery barrage. The whole place trembled to the explosion of the shells.

The concierge was in the lobby and he said, apologetically, "I regret this, Mademoiselle. It is not pleasant. I can guarantee you that the bombing in November was worse. However, it is regrettable."

I said yes, indeed, it was not very nice, was it? He said that perhaps I had better take a room in the back of the house, which might be safer. On the other hand, the rooms were not so agreeable; there was less air. I said of course there wouldn't be so much air. Then we stood in the lobby and listened.

You could only wait. All over Madrid, for fifteen days now, people had been waiting. You waited for the shelling to start, and for it to end, and for it to start again. It came from three directions, at any time, without warning and without purpose. Looking out the door, I saw people standing in doorways all around the square, just standing there patiently, and then suddenly a shell landed, and there was a fountain of granite cobblestones flying up into the air, and the silver lyddite smoke floated off softly.

A little Spaniard with a lavender shirt, a ready-made bow tie and bright brown eyes was standing in the door watching this with interest. There was also no reason for the shells to stay out of the hotel. They could land inside that door as well as anywhere else. Another shell hit, halfway across the street, and a window broke gently and airily, making a lovely tinkling musical sound.

I was watching the people in the other doorways, as best I could, watching those immensely quiet, stretched faces. You had a feeling you had been waiting here forever, and yesterday you felt the same way. The little Spaniard said to me, "You don't like it?"

"No."

"Nothing," he said. "It is nothing. It will pass. In any case, you can only die once."

"Yes," I said, but without enthusiasm.

We stood there a moment, and there was silence. Before this the shells had been falling one a minute.

"Well," he said, "I think that is all. I have work to do. I am a serious man. I cannot spend my time waiting for shells. *Salud,*" he said, and walked out calmly into the street, and calmly crossed it.

Seeing him, some other men decided the shelling was finished too, and presently people were crossing that square, which now was pock-marked with great round holes, and littered with broken cobblestones and glass. An old woman with a market basket on her arm hurried down a side street. And two boys came around the corner, arm in arm, singing.

I went back to my room, and again suddenly there came that whistle-whine-scream-roar and the noise was in your throat and you couldn't feel or hear or think and the building shook and seemed to settle. Outside in the hall, the maids were calling to one another, like birds, in high excited voices. The concierge ran upstairs looking concerned and shaking his head. On the floor above, we went into a room in which the lyddite smoke still hung mistily. There was nothing left in that room, the furniture was kindling wood, the walls were stripped and in places torn open, a great hole led into the next room and the bed was twisted iron and stood upright and silly against the wall.

"Oh, my," the concierge said miserably.

"Look, Conchita," one of the maids said to the other; "look at the hole there is in 219 too."

"Oh," one of the youngest maids said, "imagine, it has also spoiled the bathroom in 218."

The journalist who lived in that room had left for London the day before.

"Well," the concierge said, "there is nothing to do. It is very regrettable."

The maids went back to work. An aviator came down from the fifth floor. He said it was disgusting; he had two days leave and this sort of thing went on. Moreover, he said, a shell fragment had hit his room and broken all his toilet articles. It was inconsiderate; it wasn't right. He would now go out and have a beer. He waited at the door for a shell to land, and ran across the square, reaching the café across the street just before the next shell. You couldn't wait forever; you couldn't be careful all day.

Later, you could see people around Madrid examining the new shell holes with curiosity and wonder. Otherwise they went on with the routine of their lives, as if they had been interrupted by a heavy rainstorm but nothing more. In a café which was hit in the morning, where three men were killed sitting at a table reading their morning papers and drinking coffee, the clients came back in the afternoon. You went to Chicote's bar at the end of the day, walking up the street which was No Man's Land, where you could hear the shells whistling even when there was silence, and the bar was crowded as always. On the way you had passed a dead horse and a very dead mule, chopped with shell fragments, and you had passed crisscrossing trails of human blood on the pavement.

You would be walking down a street, hearing only the city noises of streetcars and automobiles and people calling to one another, and suddenly, crushing it all out, would be the huge stony deep booming of a falling shell, at the corner. There was no place to run, because how did you know that the next shell would not be behind you, or ahead, or to the left or right? And going indoors was fairly silly too, considering what shells can do to a house.

So perhaps you went into a store because that was what you had intended doing before all this started. Inside a shoe shop, five women are trying on shoes. Two girls are buying summery sandals, sitting by the front window of the shop. After the third explosion, the salesman says politely: "I think we had better move farther back into the shop. The window might break and cut you."

Women are standing in line, as they do all over Madrid, quiet women, dressed usually in black, with market baskets on their arms, waiting to buy food. A shell falls across the square. They turn their heads to look, and move a little closer to the house, but no one leaves her place in line.

After all, they have been waiting there for three hours and the children expect food at home.

In the Plaza Major, the shoeblacks stand around the edges of the square, with their little boxes of creams and brushes, and passers-by stop and have their shoes polished as they read a paper or gossip together. When the shells fall too heavily, the shoeblacks pick up their boxes and retreat a little way into a side street.

So now the square is empty, though people are leaning close against the houses around it, and the shells are falling so fast that there is almost no time between them to hear them coming, only the steady roaring as they land on the granite cobblestones.

Then for a moment it stops. An old woman, with a shawl over her shoulders, holding a terrified thin little boy by the hand, runs out into the square. You know what she is thinking: she is thinking she must get the child home, you are always safer in your own place, with the things you know. Somehow you do not believe you can get killed when you are sitting in your own parlor, you never think that. She is in the middle of the square when the next one comes.

A small piece of twisted steel, hot and very sharp, sprays off from the shell; it takes the little boy in the throat. The old woman stands there, holding the hand of the dead child, looking at him stupidly, not saying anything, and men run out toward her to carry the child. At their left, at the side of the square, is a huge brilliant sign which says: GET OUT OF MADRID.

No one lived here anymore because there was nothing left to live in, and besides the trenches were only two blocks away, and there was another front, in the Casa de Campo, down to the left. Stray bullets droned over the streets, and a stray is just as dangerous as any other kind of bullet if it hits you. You walked past the street barricades, past the ruined houses and the only sound you heard was a machine gun hammering in University City, and a bird.

It was a little like walking in the country, over gutted country roads, and the street barricades made it all seem very strange, and the houses were like scenery in a war movie; it seemed impossible that houses could really be like that.

We were going to visit a janitor who lived in this section; he and his family. They were the only people here, except the soldiers who guarded the barricades. His name was Pedro.

Pedro lived in a fine apartment house; he had been the janitor and caretaker for eight years. In November a bomb fell on the roof; Pedro and his family had been in their tiny basement apartment when the bomb hit, and they were all safe. They saw no reason to move. They were used to living there, and in time of war a basement is more desirable than in time of peace.

They showed us their building with pride. We went into a marble hall, past an elevator, through a mahogany front door, and were in a room that was all dust and broken plaster. Looking up, for eight stories, you could see the insides of all the apartments in that building. The bomb had fallen squarely, and now only the outside walls remained. There was a very fine bathroom on the seventh floor, and the tub was hanging into space by its pipes. A cabinet with china in it stood on the fourth floor, and all the china was in neat unbroken piles. The concierge's two little daughters played in this destruction as children play in an empty lot, or in caves they have found beside a river.

We sat in their underground apartment, with the lights burning, and talked. They said yes, of course, it was difficult to get food,

23

but then it was difficult for everyone and they had never really been hungry. Yes, the bombing had been very bad, but they had just waited in the basement and finally it had stopped. The only trouble, they said, was that the children couldn't go to school because the school had been bombed, and it was impossible to let the children go all the way across Madrid to another school, because bullets whined up past the street barricades at the end of their block and they couldn't risk having the children hurt.

Juanita remarked that she didn't like school anyhow very much, she wanted to be an artist and it was better to sit at home and paint. She had been copying a picture—with crayons on wrapping paper—of a very elegant Spanish gentleman whose portrait hung on the wall of a ruined first-floor apartment in their building.

Mrs. Pedro said it was wonderful now, women could have careers in Spain, did I know about that? That was since the Republic. "We are very in favor of the Republic," she said. "I think Maria may be able to get training as a doctor. Isn't it fine? Can women be doctors in North America?"

I always got a shock from the Palace Hotel, because it had a concierge's desk and a sign saying "Coiffeur on the First Floor," and another sign saying how beautiful Majorca was and they had a hotel to recommend there. The Palace Hotel had its old furniture, but it smelled of ether and was crowded with bandaged men. It is the first military hospital of Madrid now. I went around to the operating room, which used to be the reading room.

There were bloody stretchers piled in the hall, but it was quiet this afternoon. The Empire bookcases, where they used to keep dull reading for the hotel guests, were now used for bandages and hypodermic needles and surgical instruments, and there were brilliant lights in the cut-glass chandeliers to make operating easier. The nurse on duty told me about the men on the sixth floor and I went up to see them.

The room was full of sun. There were four men. One of them was sitting with his leg up on a chair; it was in plaster. He had on a red blouse and was sitting in profile. Beside him, a man with a beret was working quietly, drawing his portrait in pastels. The two other men were in bed. One of them I tried not to look at. The other one was quiet and pale and looked tired. Once or twice he smiled, but did not speak. He had a bad chest wound.

The man in the red blouse was a Hungarian; his knee had been smashed by a piece of shell. He was handsome and very polite and refused politely to talk about his wound because it was of no importance. He was alive, he was very lucky, the doctors were fine and his knee would probably get well. At any rate, he would be able to limp. He wanted to talk about his friend who was making his portrait. "Jaime," he said, "is a fine artist. Look how well he works. He always wanted to be an artist but he never had so much time before."

Jaime smiled and went on; he was working very close to the paper, stopping now and again and peering at the man in the red blouse. His eyes looked a little strange, filmed over and dim. I said it was a fine portrait, a great likeness, and he thanked me. A little later someone called him and he left and then the man in the red blouse said, "He was wounded in the head; he covers it with the beret. His eyes are not very good; they are very bad, really. He does not see much. We ask him to paint pictures of us to keep him busy and make him think he still sees well. Jaime never complains about it."

I said, softly, "What happened to that boy over there."

"He's an aviator."

He was blond and young, with a round face. There was nothing left except the eyes. He had been shot down in his plane and burned, but he had been wearing goggles and that saved his sight. His face and hands were a hard brown thick scab, and his hands were enormous; there were no lips, only the scab. The worst was that his pain was so great he couldn't sleep.

Then a soldier I knew, a Pole, came in, and said, "Listen, Dominie in room 507 has some mimosa. A whole big branch of it. Do you want to come up and see it? He says it grows all around where he lives in Marseille. I never saw any flowers like that before."

Every once in a while the actors would stop talking and wait; shells were exploding down the street in the Plaza Major and to the right of the Gran Via and when they hit too close you couldn't hear the lines of the play, so they waited. It was a benefit performance on Sunday morning; it was to make money for the hospitals.

An amateur had written the play and amateurs directed, costumed and acted it; it couldn't have been more amateur. The audience was delighted; it was a dramatic play, all about the moral and psychological crisis of a young man who decided not to enter the priesthood. The audience thought it was terribly funny and laughed with great good will at the emotional places.

The hero came out, after the curtain rang down, and said he was sorry he'd forgotten his lines that way but he hadn't had time to memorize them. He'd been in the trenches near Garabitas until just a few hours ago (everyone knew an attack had been going on there for two days), and so he couldn't memorize things.

The audience applauded and shouted that it was quite all right; they didn't care anyhow. Then he said he had written a poem up there in the trenches and he would like to recite it. He did. It rolled and tossed and was full of enormous big words and remarkable rhymes and his gestures were excellent and when he was through the audience cheered him and he looked very happy. He was a nice boy, if not a brilliant poet, and they knew he had been in a bad piece of trench, and they liked plays and theaters, even bad plays and even theaters just down the street from where the shells were landing.

Every night, lying in bed, you can hear the machine guns in University City, just ten blocks away. Every once in a while you can hear the dull, heavy explosion of a trench mortar. When the shells wake you, you think first that it is thunder. If they are not too close, you do not really wake.

You know that in November there were black Junker planes flying over and dropping bombs, that all winter long there was no fuel and the days were cold and the nights were colder, you know that food is scarce, and that all these people have sons and husbands and sweethearts at the front somewhere. And now they are living in a city where you take your chances and hope your chances are good. You have seen no panic, no hysteria, you have heard no hate talk. You know they have the kind of faith which makes courage and a fine future. You have no right to be disturbed. There are no lights anywhere and the city itself is quiet. The sensible thing is to go back to sleep.

The Besieged City

November 1937

At the end of the day the wind swooped down from the mountains into Madrid and blew the broken glass from the windows of the shelled houses. It rained steadily and the streets were mustard-colored with mud. It rained and people talked about the coming offensive, wondering when, when . . . Someone said he knew that food and munitions were being moved; someone else said that Campesino's outfit was in the south or in the north; villages (forty of them, in this direction, in that direction) had been evacuated; the transport unit was ready to go; have you heard? All front passes have been recalled, leaves are cancelled. Who told you, does he know? What, what did you say? So it went, and then the rain would start again. And everyone waited. Waiting is a big part of war and it is hard to do.

Finally it was someone's birthday, or a national holiday (and still cold and nothing happening, only the rain and the rumors), so we decided to have a party. There were two of us who lived in this hotel in Madrid and the third was a visiting friend, an American soldier from the Abraham Lincoln Brigade. A machine-gun bullet had smashed his hip and he had come to the city on his first leave from the brigade hospital. We took the entire hoard of cans from the bottom bureau drawer—canned soup, canned sardines, canned spinach, canned corned beef and two bottles of new red wine—and planned to eat ourselves warm and talk about something else, not

27

the offensive. We would talk about movie stars and pretty places we had seen and have a proper party. It went perfectly until the coffee (one teaspoonful in a cup of hot water and stir). Then the first shell plunged into the building next door, brought down a shower of glass on the inner courtyard and rattled the typewriter on the table.

The boy with the splintered hip moved his heavy plaster-encased leg and said, "Anybody seen my crutches?" He found his crutches and shifted to the place between the windows, and we opened the windows so that we could hear better and so that they wouldn't break, turned off the lights and waited.

We knew this well: the whirling scream of the shells as they came, the huge round roar as they hit, guessing where they went, where they came from, timing them with a stop watch, counting, betting on the size of the shells. The boy was sad. He was used to war at the front where you could do something about it, not to this helpless war in the city; but he would never go to any front again, as his leg would always be too short, and you can't be an infantryman with a cane. There was smoke in the room and the hotel had been hit several times, so we took our wine glasses next door, on the agreeable and traditional theory that if a shell came in the front room it would not bother to come as far as the back room, passing through the bathroom on its way.

We counted six hundred shells and got tired of it, and an hour later it was all over. We said to one another, "Well, that was a nice little shelling." Then we said, "Maybe that means the offensive will start." On the strength of this, we ate up the last bar of chocolate and called it a night.

The next day it rained again, and Madrid picked itself up as it had done before. Streetcars clanked slowly through the streets, collecting the fallen bricks, the broken glass, the odd bits of wood and furniture. People stopped on their way to work, looking at the new shell holes. The front of the hotel gaped a little more. The elevator man, who worked in bronze for his pleasure, hunted for unexploded shells in the rooms, to make lamps from them. His friend, the night concierge, painted warlike scenes on parchment for the lamp shades, and they were both busy all the time. The maid said, "Come and see the room you used to have," and we went merrily in to where nothing remained except the dressing table, with the mirror uncracked, and I found the nosecap of the shell in the broken wood of the bureau. On the fourth floor, lying against the staircase railing, was a long heavy shell that had not exploded. It had only ripped out half a wall and chopped up the furniture of room 409, pulled down the door, and come to rest there in the hall, where everyone admired it because it had a new shape. Some friends telephoned and remarked, "Ah, so you aren't dead." It was just like before. Like the last time and time before and all the other times. Everybody wondered why the Fascists shelled last night and not some other night; does it mean anything? What do you think?

In Madrid there is not only first-aid service for wounded people, but there is also a first-aid service for wounded houses. The men who manage this are architects and engineers and bricklayers and electricians, and some workers are employed only to dig bodies from the collapsed houses. This staff is always active because when they are not propping up, repairing, plugging holes and cleaning off debris, they make plans for a beautiful new city, which they will build in place of what has been destroyed, when the war is over. So that morning in the rain, I went about with them to see what had happened during the night and what could be done.

In the best residential section, at one street corner, police were telling people not to crowd and to move on. A shell had burst through the top floor of a fine new apartment house, blown the iron balcony railing onto the roof of a house across the way, and now the top floor stood without support, ready to fall into the street. Farther up, a water main had been cracked by a shell and the street was rapidly flooding. One of the architects had with him, wrapped in a newspaper, his day's ration of bread. He was very careful all morning, climbing through ruins, jumping flooded gutters, not to drop the bread; he had to take it home—there were two small children there, and come death and destruction and anything else, the bread mattered.

We climbed to the top floor, moving gently into a room where half the floor hung in space. We shook hands with all the friends and visitors who had come to see also. Two women lived here, an old woman and her daughter. They had been in the back of the apartment when the front of it blew out. They were picking up what they could save: a cup that had no saucer left, a sofa pillow, two pictures with the glass broken. They were chatty and glad to be alive and they said everything was quite all right—look, the whole back of the apartment could still be lived in, three rooms, not as bright or as nice as the rooms that had been destroyed, but still they were not without a home. If only the front part didn't fall into the street and hurt someone.

A mud road, behind the bull ring on the other side of Madrid, led into a square where there was a trough for the women of that place to wash clothes. There were ten little houses, huddled together, with cloth tacked over the windows and newspapers stuck in the walls to keep the wind out. Women with quiet, pale faces and quiet children stood by the trough and looked at one house, or what was left of it. The men stood a little nearer. A shell had landed directly on one flimsy shack, where five people were keeping warm, talking with one another for comfort and for gaiety, and now there was only a mound of clay and kindling wood, and they had dug out the five dead bodies as soon as it was light. The people standing there knew the dead. A woman reached down suddenly for her child and took it in her arms, and held it close to her.

Disaster had swung like a compass needle, aimlessly, all over the city. Near the station, the architect asked a concierge if everyone was all right in her house. Four shells had come that way. Yes, she said, do you want to see it? Upstairs the family, including the husband's sister and mother, and the wife's niece, and her baby, were standing in their living room, getting used to what had happened. The front wall was gone. The china was broken, and the chairs.

The wife said to me, "What a shame for the sewing machine; it will never work again."

The husband picked a thin, dead canary off the sideboard, showed it to me sadly, shrugged and said nothing.

I asked where they would live now. (The wind coming in, looking down five flights into the street, the broken furniture and all of them crowded into one room and the kitchen. It is bad enough to be cold, never to eat enough, to wait for the sound of the shells, but at least one must have four walls, at least four solid walls, to keep the rain out.)

The woman was surprised. "But we will live here," she said. "Where else shall we go? This is our home, we have always lived here."

The architect said to me, miserably, "No, I cannot patch up the walls; we must save the wood for essentials. The walls are not going to fall out; there is no danger from them."

"But the cold," I said.

"Ah, the cold," he said. "What can we do?" He said to them, Good luck, and they said to him, Thank you, we are all right, and then we walked silently down the steep, unlighted stairs.

It was night now. Streetcars, with people sticking like ivy on the steps and bumpers, burned muffled blue lights. People hurried, with their heads down against the rain, through the dark streets to their homes, where they would cook whatever they had and try to keep warm and wait for tomorrow and be surprised at nothing. A man walked along by himself, singing. Two children sat on a doorstep having a long, serious conversation. A shop window showed a bargain in silk stockings. We were tired, but there was a house near here that the architect had to see. A man brought a candle and we found our way up the stairs. It was hardly worth while going inside the apartment. There was nothing left at all, nothing to save; the the walls were gored, and the ceiling and the floor. What had been a place to live was now a collection of old rags and paper, pieces of plaster and broken wood, twisted wires and slivers of glass. The man held the candle above his head so that we could see, and the shadows crawled over chaos.

An old woman had been standing by the door. She came in now. She took my arm and pulled at me to come closer to hear her. She said, very softly, as if she were telling me a secret, "Look at that, look at that, do you see, that is my home, that's where I live, there, what you see there." She looked at me as if I should deny it, with wide, puzzled, frightened eyes. I did not know what to say. "I cannot understand," she said slowly, hoping I would understand and explain; after all I was a foreigner, I was younger than she, I had probably been to school, surely I could explain. "I do not understand," she said. "You see, it is my home."

And all the time it was cold. Madrid flowed with rain, rain everywhere; oh, the cold and, oh, the wet feet, and the thick smell of wet wool overcoats. And we waited for the offensive. The rumors grew each day; they rushed and swayed over the town. People looked wise or sly or happy or worried or anything, and you wondered, What do they know about the offensive? We knew it was to be an important offensive; everyone had confidence in its success whenever it came; everyone was waiting. But there was nothing to do.

31

And so, to fill the days, we went visiting at the nearest fronts (ten blocks from the hotel, fifteen blocks, a good brisk walk in the rain, something to circulate your blood). There were always funny people in the trenches, new faces, always something to talk about. So we strolled to University City and Usera, to the Parque del Oeste, to those trenches that are a part of the city and that we knew so well. No matter how often you do it, it is surprising just to walk to war, easily, from your own bedroom where you have been reading a detective story or a life of Byron, or listening to the phonograph, or chatting with your friends.

It was as usual cold, and that day we walked through all the trenches in that particular park. In these trenches, in this once fine Madrid park, the mud was like chewing gum. We admired the dug-outs smelling of fresh wood and of wood smoke from the little stoves, the bright blankets over the machine guns, the pictures of movie stars on the walls, the curious serenity—and, after all, there was no news in it. But on the other hand, it was different at night. Every night, clearly, you could hear from the hotel the machine guns hammering, and the echoing thud of mortars, and what was normal in the daytime became a strange business at night.

So the next evening, when the sky turned blue-purple, we presented ourselves at staff headquarters, in a bombed apartment house. It was a homelike spot: there were three women, the wives of officers, shrill as birds. A five-months-old baby slept on the plush sofa and his mother told us all about him breathlessly, with astonishment, as women will. The Major was tired but very courteous. The staff cook wandered in, laughing like Ophelia and a little mad, and asked when they wanted dinner. The soldier who would be our guide was at a dance given by another battalion. They had been making war here for over a year; it was right in the city and the dance was within ten minutes' walk, and a man wants a change now and again. Presently he came, a boy with fantastic eyelashes and an easy laugh, and we walked a block, went down some slippery steps and were in the trenches.

The flashlight was fading, and the mud pulled at our shoes, and we had to walk bent over to avoid hitting the low beams that held up the trench, and it was very cold. In the third line we leaned against the mud walls and looked at the thin, stripped trees of what had once been a city park, and listened. We had come to hear the loud-speakers. At night, one side or the other presents the soldiers in those trenches with a program of propaganda and music. The loud-speakers were hidden near the front line, and you could hear everything, as you can hear a telephone conversation. Tonight the enemy was speaking. A careful, pompous radio voice began: "The chief of Spain, the only chief, is willing to give his blood for you . . . Franco, Franco . . ."

Another solider had come up and he and our guide lighted cigarettes, and our guide, who was anxious for us to enjoy our- selves, said, "This talking part is very tiresome, but it won't last long; afterward comes music."

Suddenly, blaring across that narrow no man's land, we heard "Kitten on the Keys," played seven times too fast. "Ah," said our guide, "that is very pretty, that is American music."

Then the smooth, careful voice came back: "Your leaders live well in the rear guard while you are given guns to go out and die." There was a burst of irritated machine-gun fire after his remark. "He is too stupid," the soldier guide said, with disgust. "Usually we do not listen to him. Why doesn't he stop talking and play the music? The music is very nice. We all enjoy the music. It helps pass the time."

At this point the music started: *Valencia, deedle-deedle-deedle- dee* . . . It went on for about an hour. We were moving forward with some difficulty because the flashlight had worn out, feeling our way through covered trenches with our hands out, touching both walls, bending beneath the beams of tunnels, slipping on the duckboards when they were any, or stumbling in mud. At one point a mortar exploded, flashing through the trees, and the ma- chine guns clattered an answer. The radio voice said, *"Viva, Franco! Arriba España!";* and we could hear from up ahead in the first line, the jeers of the government troops. Then we heard the voice but not the words of a soldier who was answering that remote radio orator.

The guide explained, "The fight will now start. Now it is mainly a joke, but that loud-speaker used to make us angry. We have heard it so much, and we know it is so silly, and sometimes it announces a great victory right here where we have been all day and seen nothing, and we do not pay attention to it. But it is the custom to answer back."

Very thin and high, and through the trees, we could still hear the soldier's voice, shouting.

"He says," the guide said, after listening, "that it is useless to talk to them in Spanish because they are all Moors over there."

We waited but could not make out any other words. The guide went on: "One of our boys usually tells them they are liars and are destroying Spain, and they tell him he is a murderous Red, and later they will get angry and throw mortars at one another. Their loudspeaker is a waste of time, but the music is agreeable."

"You seem very much at home here," I said, because it suddenly struck me that we were as casual as people at an outdoor concert in any peacetime city in the summer. (The stadium in New York with all the stars, that place in a park in St. Louis, with the two great trees growing from the stage, the little brass bands in the little squares in Europe. I thought, it takes something to be so calm about war.)

"These trenches are good," the soldier said. "You can see that for yourself. And we have been here a long time." The machine guns down by the Puente de los Franceses echoed over the black land. "If necessary," the boy said quietly, "we can stay here forever."

I asked where the government loud-speaker was. He said probably up the line somewhere, toward the Clinical Hospital; they didn't always work at the same place at the same time.

"You should come and hear ours some night," the guide said. "We have very pretty music, too, but only Spanish songs. You would like it."

We were by this time in a communicating trench, on our way to the first line. A mortar shook the walls of the trench and scattered mud over us, and did not explode, to everyone's delight. The guide said to the other soldier, "It is scarcely worthwhile to kill foreign journalists for a little music." He told us he could not take us farther and, as we could see, both the music and the speaking were finished, and now there were only mortars. We argued it, bracing ourselves against the walls of the trench, but he said, "No, the Major would be very angry with me and I will get in trouble."

So we went back as we had come.

"Well," the major said, "how did you enjoy it?"

"Very much."

"How was the music?"

"A little too fast."

"I have here something that will interest you," the Major said.

He took a rocket, like a Fourth of July rocket, from the table. "The Fascists send these over with propaganda in them, and sometimes I write an answer and we send them back. It is quite a discussion."

He now showed us the propaganda. "It is too much," he said. "It makes you laugh. They think we know nothing. Look at this."

He thumbed through the little booklet quickly, dismissing statements he had seen before and arguments he considered either too boring or too ridiculous. One page started: "What are you fighting for?" The Major smiled and said, "That's something we all know."

He then read us his reply, all very careful, very dull. And we said, "That is fine."

A lieutenant offered me some acorns and the talk turned to America. The guide said he knew a great deal about America because he had read Zane Grey and also James Oliver Curwood, although he realized that was about Canada. Aragon must be very much like Arizona, no? Yes, that's right.

The Major said when the war was over he would like to visit America, but he was a poor man. "I am a worker," he said gently and yet proudly. "Would I ever have enough money to go to America?"

"Certainly," we said. Well, then, how much? Ah, now, that was difficult, in the cities it was more, in the small towns less, travel by bus was not expensive.

"Well, it's hard to say how much it would cost, *Commandante*."

"How about two dollars? Could you do it with two dollars a day?"

"That depends," I said.

"Well, three dollars."

"Oh, surely with three dollars."

They were all quiet. The Major looked at his adjutant. "*Hombre*," he said, "thirty-six pesetas a day. Something." And then to me, "Ah, well, there is much work to do here and we are all needed. But America must be so beautiful. I would like all the same to see it."

At the end of the cold wet waiting days, Chicote's is the place to go in search of company and conversation and more rumors about the offensive. Chicote's used to be a bar where the elegant young men

35

of Madrid came to drink a few cocktails before dinner. Now it is like a dugout on the Gran Via, that wide rich street where you can hear the shells, even when there is silence. Chicote's is not in a safe locality at all, and every day it is so crowded that you remember, comfortably, the subway at five o'clock, Times Square and the Grand Central Station.

A group of us were sitting in Chicote's wondering whether to drink the sherry, which was tasteless, or the gin, which was frankly fatal. The English girl, who looked like a small, good-humored boy, drove an ambulance for a base hospital. One of the men, a German, wrote for a Spanish newspaper and was now talking rapid French about politics. There were two American soldiers, the two wonderfully funny ones, so young, and so much braver and gayer than people usually are. The smoke from black tobacco was choking, the noise deafening; soldiers at other tables shouted their news; the indomitable girls with dyed hair and amazing high heels waved and smiled; people walked in through the sandbagged door and stared and saw no one they knew or nothing they liked and walked out again. In this crowded din, one could be entirely alone and quiet, and think one's own thoughts about Spain and the war and the people.

How it is going to be possible ever to explain what this is really like? All you can say is, "This happened; that happened; he did this; she did that." But this does not tell how the land looks on the way to the Guadarrama, the smooth brown land, with olive trees and scrub oak growing beside the dry stream beds, and the handsome mountains curving against the sky. Nor does this tell of Sanchez and Ausino, and the others with them, those calm young men who were once photographers or doctors or bank clerks or law students, and who now shape and train their troops so that one day they can be citizens instead of soldiers. And there is no time to write of the school where the children were making little houses of clay, and dolls from cardboard, and learning to recite poetry and missed school only when the shelling was too bad. And what about all the rest, and all the others? How can I explain that you feel safe at this war, knowing that the people around you are good people?

The Third Winter

November 1938

In Barcelona, it was perfect bombing weather. The cafés along the Ramblas were crowded. There was nothing much to drink; a sweet fizzy poison called orangeade and a horrible liquid supposed to be sherry. There was, of course, nothing to eat. Everyone was out enjoying the cold afternoon sunlight. No bombers had come over for at least two hours.

The flower stalls looked bright and pretty along the promenade. "The flowers are all sold, Señores. For the funerals of those who were killed in the eleven o'clock bombing, poor souls."

It had been clear and cold all day yesterday and probably would be fair from now on. "What beautiful weather," a woman said, and she stood, holding her shawl around her, staring at the sky. "And the nights are as fine as the days. A catastrophe," she said, and walked with her husband toward a café.

It was cold but really too lovely and everyone listened for the sirens all the time, and when we saw the bombers they were like tiny silver bullets moving forever up, across the sky.

It gets dark suddenly and no street lights are allowed in Barcelona, and at night the old town is rough going. It would be a silly end, I thought, to fall into a bomb hole, like the one I saw yesterday, that opens right down to the sewers. Everything you do in war is odd, I thought; why should I be plowing around after dark, looking for a carpenter in order to call for a picture frame for a friend? I found Hernández' house in a back street and I held my cigarette lighter above my head to see my way down the hall and up

37

the stairs and then I was knocking on the door and old Mrs. Hernández opened the door and asked me to come in, to be welcome, her house was mine.

"How are you?" I said.

"As you see," old Hernández said, and he pushed his cap back on his forehead and smiled, "alive."

It wasn't much of a home but they looked very handsome in it. A wick floating in a cup of oil lighted the place. There were four chairs and a big table and some shelves tacked on the wall. The ten-year-old grandson was reading close to the burning wick. The daughter-in-law, the wife of their youngest son, played quietly with her baby in a corner. Old Mrs. Hernández had been working over the stove, and the room was smoky. What they would have to eat would be greens, a mound of cabbage leaves the size of your fist, and some dry bread. The women start cooking greens long in advance because they want to get them soft at least. Boiled flavorless greens go down better if they are soft.

The picture frame was not ready, Hernández could not get the wood. Wood is for dugouts and trenches, bridges, railroad ties, to prop up bombed houses, to make artificial arms and legs, for coffins. He used to collect the fragments from destroyed houses, he said, not to work with, but for firewood, but now that is all saved for the hospitals. It was hard to be a carpenter, there wasn't much wood or much work any more.

"Not that it matters about me," Hernández said, "I am very old."

The little boy had been listening. His grandmother kept looking at him, ready to silence him if he interrupted while his elders spoke.

"What do you do all day?" I said.

"I stand in the food line."

"Miguel is a good boy," Mrs. Hernández said. "He does what he can to help his old grandmother."

"Do you like doing that?" I said.

"When they fight," he said, laughing to himself, "it is fun."

His grandmother looked shocked. "He does not understand," she said. "He is only ten. The poor people—they are so hungry, sometimes they quarrel among themselves, not knowing what they do."

*　*　*

(They put up a sign on the shop door, and word flies through the neighborhood that you can get food today. Then the lines form. Sometimes they are five blocks long. Sometimes you wait all that time but just before your turn comes the shop closes. There is no more food. The women wait in line and talk or knit, the children invent games that they can play standing in one place. Everyone is very thin. They know perfectly, by the sound of the first explosion, where the bombs are falling. If the first bomb sounds hollow and muffled, they do not move from their places, because they know there is no immediate danger. If they can hear the drone of the planes too clearly or the first explosion is jagged and harsh, they scatter for doorways or refuges. They do this professionally, like soldiers.

The pinched women file into the shop and hand their food cards over the high bare counter. The girls behind the counter look healthy because they are wearing rouge. Then the food is doled out in little gray paper sacks. A sack the size of a cigarette package, full of rice: that will have to do two people for two weeks. A sack half that big, full of dried peas: for one person for two weeks. Wait, there's some codfish too. The girl behind the counter pulls out a slab of the gray-white flat fish and cuts off a little piece with a pair of scissors. She cuts it with scissors, not a knife, because scissors are more accurate. A piece as long as your finger and twice as thick is the ration for one person for two weeks. The woman with gray hair and a gray frozen face and exhausted eyes reaches out to get her piece of fish. She holds it a minute in her hand, looking at it. They all look at it, and say nothing. Then she turns and pushes her way through the crowd and out the door.

Now she will wait every day to hear whether the store in her neighborhood is open again, whether you can trade anything, whether a farmer she knows is coming to town with a dozen eggs and four cabbages and some potatoes. Whether somewhere, somehow, she can get food for her family. Sometimes when the shop runs out of food before everyone is served, the women are wild with grief, afraid to go home with nothing. Then there's trouble. The little boys don't understand the trouble, all they know is that a quarrel brightens the long hours of waiting.)

"You don't go to school?" I said.

"Not now."

"He did very well at school," his grandmother said.

"I want to be a mechanic," the child said, in a voice that was almost weeping. "I want to be a mechanic."

"We do not let him go to school," Mrs. Hernández said, stroking the child's black head. "Because of the bombs. We cannot have him walking about alone."

"The bombs," I said, and smiled at the boy. "What do you do about the bombs?"

"I hide," he said, and he was shy about it, telling me a secret. "I hide so they won't kill me."

"Where do you hide?"

"Under the bed," he said.

The daughter-in-law, who is very young, laughed at this, but the old people treated the child seriously. They know that you must have safety in something; if the child believes he is safe under the bed it is better for him.

"When will the war end?" the daughter-in-law asked suddenly.

"Now, now," said the old man. "It will end when we have won it. You know that, Lola. Have patience and do not be silly."

"I have not seen my husband for five months," the girl explained, as if this were the very worst thing that could ever happen to anyone. Old Mrs. Hernández nodded her head, which was like a fine worn wood carving, and made a little sympathetic noise.

"You understand, Señora," Mr. Hernández said to me, "I am so old that perhaps I shall not live to see the end of the war. Things do not make any difference to me any longer. But it will be better for the children afterward. That is what I tell Lola. Spain will be better for her and Federico afterward. Besides," he said, "Federico is learning a great deal in the Army."

(The Internationals had left the lines and were waiting to go home, or were already gone.* There was a parade for them, down the Diagonal, and women threw flowers and wept, and all the Spanish people thanked them somehow, sometimes only by the way they

*In September 1938 the Republican government of Spain, no doubt hoping to shame Franco into a similar gesture, withdrew the International Brigade from the fronts. Four of Mussolini's Italian divisions stayed and fought for Franco until the end of the war. Hitler's artillerymen and pilots also remained. Italian planes were bombing Barcelona when this article was written.

watched the parade passing. The Internationals looked very dirty and weary and young, and many of them had no country to go back to. The German and Italian anti-Fascists were already refugees; the Hungarians had no home either. Leaving Spain, for most of the European volunteers, was to go into exile. I wonder what happened to the German who was the best man for night patrols in the 11th International Brigade. He was a somber man, whose teeth were irregularly broken, whose fingertips were nailless pulp; the first graduate of Gestapo torture I had known.

The Spanish Republican Army, which had been growing and shaping itself through two winters, now dug in for the third winter of war. They were proud and self-confident soldiers. They had started out as militia companies, citizens carrying any sort of rifle, and had become an army and looked like an army and acted like one.

They were always a pleasure to see and often a surprise. On a clear night, coming back very tired from the Segre front, we stopped at divisional headquarters to look at maps and get some dinner too, if lucky. We were received by the Lieutenant Colonel, who commanded ten thousand men. He was twenty-six years old and had been an electrician at Lerida. He was blond and looked American and he had grown up with the war. The chief of operations was twenty-three and a former medical student from Galicia. The chief of staff was twenty-seven, a lawyer, a Madrid aristocrat who spoke good French and English. Modesto, commanding the Army of the Ebro and a great soldier, was thirty-five. All the new corps commanders were in their late twenties and early thirties. Everybody you saw knew what he was doing and why; it was a cheerful army. The winter is the worst time of all in war and the third winter is long, cold and desperate; but you couldn't feel sorry for that army.)

"Both my boys are soldiers," Mrs. Hernández said. "Miguel's father is the oldest, Tomás, he is at Tortosa; and Federico is up toward Lerida somewhere. Tomás was here only last week."

"What did he say of the war?" I asked.

"We do not speak of the war," she said. "He says to me, 'You are like all the other mothers in Spain. You must be brave like all the others.' And sometimes he speaks of the dead."

"Yes?"

"He said, 'I have seen many dead.' He says that so I will understand, but we do not speak of the war. My sons are always close to the bombs," she said in her blurred old voice. "If my children are in danger, it is not well that I should be safe."

The girl Lola had started to sing to her child, to keep it quiet, and now she brought the baby over near the lighted wick, for me to see. She turned down a grayish blanket showing the child's head and sang, "Pretty little child, my pretty little girl."

The face seemed shrunken and faded, and bluish eyelids rested lightly shut on the eyes. The child was too weak to cry. It fretted softly, with closed eyes, and we all watched it, and suddenly Lola pulled the cover back over the bundle in her arms and said, coldly and proudly, "She does not have the right food to eat and therefore she is not well. But she is a fine child."

(The hospital was huge and ornate, the way all modern buildings are in Catalonia. This one was built of orange bricks and was a real horror to look at. It was new and well equipped and had a garden. The buildings, called pavilions, were placed around this garden. The children's pavilion was off to the right and we followed a lanky, quiet boy who was showing us the way. I did not want to come, really. I knew the statistics, the statistics were enough for me. In Catalonia alone, there were approximately 870,000 children up to school age. Of these, the statistics announced, more than 100,000 suffered from bad nutrition, more than 200,000 suffered from under-nourishment, more than 100,000 were in a state of pre-famine. I thought the statistics were no doubt mild, and I did not want to think at all about Madrid, about the swift dark laughing children in Madrid. I did not want to imagine how hunger had deformed them.

There were two great wards, the surgical ward and the medical ward, and it was almost suppertime and the surgical ward was brightly lit. Small beds lined the walls. It was very cold, between the stone floors and the plaster walls; there is no heat anywhere. The children looked like toys until you came closer—tiny white figures propped up with pillows, swathed in bandages, the little pale faces showing, the great black eyes staring at you, the small hands playing over the sheets. There was not one child in the hospital for any peacetime reason, tonsils or adenoids or mastoid or appendicitis. These children were all wounded.

A little boy named Paco sat up in his bed with great dignity. He was four and beautiful and had a bad head wound. He had been crossing a square to meet a little girl on the other side—he played with her in the afternoons. Then a bomb fell. Many people were killed and he was wounded in the head. He had gone through his pain quietly, the nurse said. The wound was five months old. He had always been patient with it, and as the months wore on he grew solemner and more elderly every day. Sometimes he cried to himself, but without making a sound, and if anyone noticed he tried to stop. We stood by his bed and he watched us gravely but he did not want to talk.

I asked if they had anything to play with and the nurse said, Well, little things, not much. No, not really, she said. Just once in a while someone brings a present for one of them. A jolly little girl, with pigtails and only one leg, was having a nice time making paper balls out of an old newspaper.

There were three little boys with shaved heads and various splints on them; one of them had his leg held up on a rope from the ceiling. They lived in a corner by themselves; they were not only wounded, but they had tuberculosis. The nurse said they had fever and that made them gay, particularly at this hour. They would not live, she didn't think they would live even if there was food to give them, or a sanatorium to send them to. The sanatoriums were all full. Anyhow, they were too far gone. It works very fast on them, the nurse said. The little boys had a sort of Meccano toy, it was on the bed of the boy who had a broken arm. A bomb fragment broke his arm, the nurse said; he did not suffer as much as some but he used to scream at night. The other two were now shouting instructions to their friend, how to play with the toy. They were building a bridge. When we stopped beside them, they grew shy and gave up their game. All the children were the color of their pillows except the little ones with t.b., who looked quite rosy. They were unbelievably thin.

"No," the nurse said, almost impatiently, as if it hurt and angered her to talk about it. "Of course we haven't enough food to give them. What do you think? If only they didn't bomb all the time," she said, "it would help. When the children hear the siren they go crazy, they try to get out of their beds and run. We are only four nurses in these two rooms and we have a hard time with them. At night it is worse. They all remember what happened to them and they go crazy."

We went into the second room. A little boy was crying noisily and the other children were listening to him, frightened by his grief. The nurse explained that he had been wounded today, in one of the morning raids, and of course he was in pain but mainly he was homesick. He wanted his mother. He was also hungry. We stood by his bed helplessly and promised to bring him some food tomorrow if only he would stop crying and we promised that his mother would come right away, only please stop crying. He twisted on the bed and sobbed for his mother. Then she came. She was a dark witch of a woman, outdone by life. Her hair straggled from a knot on top of her head, and her bedroom slippers were worn through and her coat was pinned together with two safety pins. She looked gaunt and a little mad and her voice was as harsh as stone scraping on stone. She sat on the bed [we had been careful not to touch the bed, not to move or shake the small aching wounded child] and talked to him in her shrill voice, telling him of the family's catastrophes.

Their house had been destroyed by the bomb that wounded him, though he was the only one hurt. But now they had no home, no furniture, nothing to cook with, no blankets, no place to go. She told the round-eyed child the story of woe and he listened with interest and sympathy and wasn't homesick anymore. Then she took a pot from some pocket, it materialized like a rabbit from a hat, and gave it to the child, and said, "Here, eat." He began to scoop up cold rice from the pot, just cold rice boiled in water. He ate it, his face close to the pot, spilling a little on the bedclothes and stopping only to collect the grayish rice grains with his fingers. He seemed happy then and at home. His mother was now talking with another woman, in her hard tormented voice, and presently the little boy went to sleep.

"Would you like to see the medical ward?" the tall lanky boy said.

"Well," I said. Well, no, I thought.

"I like the children."

So we went.

Three blue lights were burning and the ward was in shadow. The children sat up in bed, silent and waiting. We stepped aside to let the dinner wagon pass. It made a metal clanking sound on the floor, and I watched their eyes follow the wagon down the ward. There was the seven-months-old baby with tuberculosis who did not notice and there was another child, like an old-faced doll against the pillows, who turned away her head. On the wagon were four lumps of something green and cooked, four shrunken lettuces, I think, and a great cauldron of soup. The nurse went over to the cauldron and lifted a ladleful and let it spill back into the pot. It was clear pale-beige water. That was supper. "The children cry for food most of the time," she said, looking at the thin soup with hate.

"What is the matter with them?" I asked. She evidently thought I was not very sound in the head.

"There are only two things the matter with them. Tuberculosis and rickets."

The old-faced doll reached out a tiny white hand. I walked over to her and her hand curled around my fingers and she smiled. She was, the nurse said, seventeen months old and her name was Manuela.

Manuela let go my fingers and began to cry. Had I done something bad? "Only hungry," the nurse said. She picked the child up, lightly and gently, and tossed it in her arms. The child laughed aloud with pleasure at this lovely game. As the nurse held her you saw the rope-thin legs and the swollen stomach of rickets.

"Will she be all right?" I said.

"Certainly," the nurse said and she was lying, you could see that in her face. "Certainly she'll get well. She has to. Somehow.")

"Yes, she's a fine child," I said to Lola Hernández, but I thought, Maybe we can stop looking at the child, when we all know she's sick with hunger and probably will not live until summer. Let's talk about something else, now, just for a change.

"Have you been to the opera?" I said to Lola.

"I went once," she said, "but I do not like to go. All the time I was there, I kept thinking, What if this minute my husband is wounded, or what if he is coming home on leave. I almost thought he had come home and then I would have missed an hour with him. So now I stay home."

"We all stay home," the old man said, "I like the house. We have been here for twenty-five years."

"Do you go often?" Lola asked.

"I've been," I said. "It's wonderful."

(The opera is not as funny as the movies, though the people of Barcelona don't think the movies are funny. But you can't help laughing when go go to see *Jane Eyre,* and it is all about a life that none of the audience ever knew or imagined, and then in the middle the film flickers off and you hear the bombs falling somewhere, while the audience groans with irritation, knowing it will take half an hour before the current comes on again, and they are dying to see what happens to Jane and her handsome gentleman friend, and they are fascinated by the madwoman and the burning house. I particularly liked the Westerns, and seeing the horse stopped in midleap for an air alarm, knowing that the dangerous activities of the hero and his horse were much more thrilling to the audience than a mere covey of bombers flying at a great safe height and sending down indiscriminate, expensive steel-encased death and destruction.

It costs about two pesetas for the best seats at any show, and nobody earns less than ten pesetas a day. The only thing you want to spend money on is food, and there is no food, so you might as well go to the opera or to the movies. It would be very stupid to save up to buy furniture, the way the city gets bombed. Besides, it's warm inside the big overdecorated theaters, because there are so many people, and it's friendly, and sitting there with something to look at on the stage you forget for a while that you aren't really safe, you aren't really safe at all. And also you might even forget how hungry you are.

But the opera was a wonder. Some afternoons there was opera and some afternoons there was the symphony orchestra. The people of Barcelona crowded to both. The opera house was far too near the port for comfort, and bombs had ruined much of the neighborhood. It was surprising that the singers had energy to sing, considering how little they eat. It was surprising to see such thin singers. The women were any age at all, wearing the prewar costumes, a little mussed now but still brilliant and romantic. All the men were old. The young men were at the war. The opera house was full every day and everyone enjoyed the music immensely, and roared with laughter at the stale formal opera jokes, and sighed audibly at the amorous moments and shouted *"Olé!"* at each curtain. We used to sit and scratch, because everyone had fleas this winter, there was no soap any more and everyone was very dirty and malodorous indeed. But we loved the music and loved not thinking about the war.)

The Hernández' only daughter now came home from her job, and there was much loud gay talk as if they had not seen each other for weeks, with everyone reporting on the day's air raids. She wore her dark hair in braids around her head and was glowing with rouge, and quite well dressed. She earned plenty of money because she worked in a munitions factory.

(You never know exactly where the munitions factories are, and are not intended to know. We drove over many streets I had not seen before and stopped before a great grille gateway, somewhere at the edge of town. The factory looked like a series of cement barns, not connected particularly, and shining and clean and cheerful in the winter sun. We walked across the courtyard and into the first open door. The woman in charge of this room came forward; she had a nice smile and was timid and behaved as if I had come to tea unexpectedly.

The women were working at long tables, heaped with shining black squares and oblongs, they looked like trays full of sequins. There were other trays full of shining little leads, like short fillers for an automatic pencil. The woman picked up a handful of the sequins and let them slip through her hands. "They're pretty, aren't they?" she said.

"Very pretty," I said, mystified. "What are they?"

"Powder," she said, "explosive. What makes the shells go off."

At the other end of the room women worked at sewing machines, the old-fashioned kind that you pump with your feet. There was cloth for summer dresses, a lovely pink linen, a nice gray-and-white stripe that would have made handsome shirts, a thick white silk for a bridal gown. They were sewing little bags, and bigger bags, like sacks for sachet. A girl came around and collected them and took them to the front of the room where they were filled with the explosive that looked like sequins. Then the little pink sachet bag of sequins was dropped into a shell base.

Other women carefully and daintily glued together tiny cellophane horseshoes; in these horseshoes was black powder, and this skilled elegant work served to make a mortar the thing it is.

Two barns farther down were the great guns, home for repair. The place looked like a museum full of prehistoric animals, huge gray strangely shaped animals come to rest in this smoky room. Men worked beside each gun, with a little fire to heat the tools and for keeping warm. The room twinkled with light from the charcoal burners. The guns all wore their small name tags: Vickers Armstrong, Schneider, Skoda. We had seen them and watched them being fired day after day and month after month at the front. The grooved rifling inside the barrels had been worn smooth from the many thousand rounds they had fired, and the barrels were being rebored. There were few guns in Republican Spain now that had the same caliber they started with, and with each reboring the size of the shells had to be changed.

"Would you like to see the shells?" the foreman asked. He was obviously proud of them.

He led me out in the sun and around two buildings and then into a vast storeroom. Used shell cases the color of old gold were stacked neatly against one wall; they would be hammered into shape and used again. In the center of the building and against the right wall the new shells were piled in squares and oblongs and pyramids; they were painted black and yellow. There were 75s looking neat and not really harmful at all. And there were the tall shells, the 155s, that frighten one more when they are coming in.

We admired the shells and at this moment, like a dream or a nightmare or a joke, the siren whined out over Barcelona. I think that one of the worst features of an air raid is the siren. The howling whining whistle rises and screams and wails over the city, and almost at once you hear, somewhere, the deep *hud-boom* of the bombs. I looked at my companion and he looked at me and smiled (I thinking, foolishly, never forget your manners, walk do not run) and we sauntered out of doors. I could not see the planes but I heard them; on a clear day they fly high for safety, so you rarely see them. I thought, anyhow, in case a bomb falls around here we won't even know it.

"What do the workers do?" I said.

"Nothing," he said. "They wait."

The planes now showed themselves clear and silver just a little way down the sky, the sky dotted with a few small white smoke bubbles from anti-aircraft shells. The men came out of the factory and walked across the courtyard and leaned against a wall where they could get a better view, and smoked. Some played an innocent game, pitching a coin. The women dragged out empty packing cases, in which bullets would be shipped later, and sat down in the sunshine and started knitting. They did not bother to look up. Everyone knew that the electricity was turned off for half an hour, so there would be no more work for a time. They knitted and gossiped, and watching the sky I saw the silver planes wheel and circle and fly back out to sea.

They all like working in a munitions factory because they get two rolls of bread each day as a bonus.)

"I must leave," I said. "Please forgive me for staying so long. Goodbye, Miguel, after the war you'll be a mechanic."

"After we have won the war," old Mrs. Hernández corrected me. "We will invite you to come here and eat a big supper with us."

They were all delighted, delighted with winning the war and delighted with eating a big supper.

"You will see Federico too," Lola said.

"Yes," I said, "that will be a great pleasure. Goodbye, goodbye," I said, shaking hands all around, "and many thanks."

We were standing up now, and looking at them I suddenly said, "The third winter is the hardest."

Then I felt ashamed. They were strong brave people and didn't need me to say cheering words for them.

"We are all right, Señora," Mrs. Hernández said, making it clear at once, saying the last word in her home about her family. "We are Spaniards and we have faith in our Republic."

THE WAR IN FINLAND

People may correctly remember the events of twenty years ago (a remarkable feat), but who remembers his fears, his disgusts, his tone of voice? It is like trying to bring back the weather of that time.

When the Second World War officially started, in September 1939, it must have seemed to me so expected, so on schedule, that I have no memory of the occasion. I think I stopped reading newspapers or listening to the radio. The rapid patriotic fervor of the Johnny-come-lately anti-Fascists was revolting. It was easy enough, and unbearable, to imagine what the real war was like in Poland.

Beginning with Hitler's occupation of the Rhineland, repeated chances to prevent this war had been lost, and so had the chances to make a war in the name of honor. This was the war to save our skins. It must absolutely be won; it was an overdue

51

police operation, a war *against*, too late to be a war *for*. Now one could only ally one's mind and heart to the innocents—the various unknown people who would be paying for war, with all they had to love and lose.

Early in November, Charles Colebaugh suggested Finland; he thought something was about to happen there. I looked Finland up on a map. Further inquiry revealed that the Finns were a highly literate nation who looked after each other's needs and rights, with justice: a good democracy. I was eager to go. No one makes fancy speeches in the midst of danger, and whatever happened Finland would surely not be the aggressor.

I did think, professionally, that it was unusual timing to arrive in a strange frozen country one dark afternoon and be waked the next morning at nine o'clock by the first bombs, the declaration of war. But before the bombs, there were the sea and the mines. Looking back, nearly twenty years, it seems to me that my thinking or feeling about war changed again on that curious ocean journey.

In Spain I had understood the meaning of the war; I saw clearly what the Spanish war was for and what it was against. On the boat, going first to England, I was in on the beginning of a great war of greed, started by a madman; and it felt different. It felt unreal, yet obviously nothing about high explosive is unreal. But this war was a total madness: one criminal lunatic and his followers wanted what they could never get, domination over their time, and they grabbed for it; other grabbers joined them; and the world slid into a six-year-long dream of hell. The sense of the insanity and wickedness of this war grew in me until, for purposes of mental hygiene, I gave up trying to think or judge, and turned myself into a walking tape recorder with eyes. The way people stay half sane in war, I imagine, is to suspend a large part of their reasoning minds, lose most of their sensitivity, laugh when they get the smallest chance, and go a bit, but increasingly, crazy.

Bombs on Helsinki

December 1939

War started at nine o'clock promptly. The people of Helsinki stood in the streets and listened to the painful rising and falling and always louder wail of the siren. For the first time in history they heard the sound of bombs falling on their city. This is the modern way of declaring war. The people moved unhurriedly to bomb shelters or took cover in doorways and waited.

That morning Helsinki was a frozen city inhabited by sleep-walkers. The war had come too fast and all the faces and all the eyes looked stunned and unbelieving.

The sky had been slate-colored all day, with a low blanket of cloud folding over the city. The second air raid came at three o'clock. No siren gave the alarm; there was only the swift breath-taking roar of the bombs. The Russian planes flew high and unseen and dived to within two hundred meters of the ground to dump their bombs in heavy loads. The raid lasted one minute. It was the longest minute anyone in Helsinki had ever lived through.

There were five great explosions and afterward the stillness itself was dreadful. Then a rumor flew through the quiet, broken streets: poison gas. Anything was believed now. Guided by the tremendous sound of the bombs, we could see in that direction a high, round, gray cloud of smoke blowing slowly between the buildings. We had no gas masks.

They shut the doors of the hotel, but as the hall skylight had already been broken by concussion this seemed feeble protection.

From a fifth-floor window I saw the light of fire, pink around the sky. "Not gas yet," we said to one another, greatly cheered. "Just incendiary bombs."

We shuffled through broken glass in the streets. The gray afternoon was darker with smoke. The bombed houses on this block were so shrouded in flames that you could not see through into the ruins. Turning left, we ran toward the light of another fire. The Technical School, a vast granite square of buildings, had been hit. The houses around it and on the next street were gutted clean, with flames leaping out of all the empty windows. Firemen worked fast and silently but there was nothing much to do except try to put out the fire. Later they could dig for the bodies.

At a street corner, in the early oncoming night, a woman flagged a bus and put her child on it. She did not have time to kiss the child goodbye and no one said anything. The woman turned and walked back into the bombed street. The bus was collecting children to take them away, anywhere, no one knew where but out of the city. A curious migration started that afternoon and went on all night. Lost children, whose parents were gone in the burning buildings or separated in the confusion of that sudden attack, straggled out alone or in twos and threes, taking any road that led away from what they had seen. Days later the state radio was still calling their names, trying to find their families for them.

Close to a big filling station a bus lay on its side, already burned out, and beside it in the street was the first dead man I saw in this war. On my first morning in Madrid, three winters ago, I saw a man like this one. Now as then there was no identification left except the shoes, since the head and the arms had been destroyed. In Spain the small, dark, deformed bundle wore the rope-soled shoes of the poor, and here the used leather soles were carefully patched. Otherwise the two remnants of bodies were tragically the same. I thought it would be fine if the ones who order the bombing and the ones who do the bombing would walk on the ground some time and see what it is like.

In Finland it is black night at four o'clock in the winter afternoon, but people stayed in the streets as if to take comfort from one another. Women clustered in doorways and did not speak, and nowhere was anyone crying, nowhere was there the wild grief and panic that could be expected. That freezing night the roads out of Helsinki were dark with silent people, carrying knapsacks or light suitcases or carrying nothing, walking to the forest for safety.

Next morning, the street-clearing department shoveled broken glass off the streets around the Technical School with snow shovels. The great buildings were holed through from roof to cellar and burned black inside. A fireman took me into an apartment house next door. We waded in water from the fire hoses and climbed two flights of stairs and went through a hanging door into a home that had once been comfortable and sweet. Now the white-painted furniture of the bedroom was half splintered and the voile curtains hung in damp rags and the family photographs and all the small, useless, ornamental things people collect and cherish were blown about like rubbish on the floor. All night the firemen had been digging out bodies in this flat and the next one, and a week later they were still finding the buried dead. This fireman had worked in San Francisco and Trenton, years ago, and we talked about those cities and how lucky the people were who live there. We stood in the street and watched a fire that was still burning and looked at the ruins of the high school and the shattered homes, and the firemen said quietly, but not to joke, "Nice fellas, these Roosians."

There was a woman in one of the hospitals who had been pinned under the wreckage of her home and was now waiting to die, pushing the blankets from her body because any weight was intolerable. Her child was dead but she did not know it, and her husband lay in another ward staring in front of him with fixed, mad eyes. The husband was a house painter. In the bed beside him a handsome dark boy with a bright face of fever held himself very still because with a hole like that in his back even breathing was torture. He had been a plumber.

The Russian planes came over again at one o'clock on the second day of the war, and the machine guns, on the roofs of the office buildings and apartment houses that line the main street, hammered up at them into the thick gray sky. The planes turned and dumped their bombs over the workers' quarters at the outskirts of the city. The florists sent flowers to the hospitals and made wreaths for the coffins, and little processions of unweeping people followed the pretty coffins to the cemetery.

They went on evacuating children in hearses and cattle cars, in anything that would run on wheels or rails. People had been hiding

55

in the freezing woods for three days and nights without shelter or food, and now they were beginning to find their way into the villages. Then a truck would come to a village to move some of them to a country station, where they could catch a train going farther north. A driver put a ladder up against his truck and seven little old ladies, carrying small satchels, clambered up the ladder twittering like birds. They spoke the neat, stilted English of governesses and laughed because they were so awkward and said yes, they were going to take a train now, and no, they didn't know where they were going but it would be all right, they would find some place to stay. It had been rather hard in the woods, they said, but now everything would be quite all right. A well-dressed young woman with two small children and a baby had walked from the city, the children's nurse pushing the baby carriage and she leading and carrying the other children. She had left everything behind, as had all the others. But the baby had a fur rug in his carriage to keep him warm, so she was not complaining. In a neighboring village a fine big woman with red cheeks was buying cough medicine for her ten-year-old daughter. Her child was ill from three nights in the open woods. The mother said they slept ten in a one-room hut now, but that way, of course, they were warm. "We wait and we hope," she said. "Why should we be afraid? We have done nothing wrong."

Rumors, the inevitable by-product of war, circulated through the countryside and in the city, saying that the Russians were planning a giant air attack—they were going to flatten Helsinki. Nothing and no one would be left. In the midst of all this the Russians bombarded the city with propaganda by leaflets and by radio. The Finns reacted with bitter amusement. With the bombs came badly printed pamphlets saying, "You know we have bread, why do you starve?"

Since the Finns eat as well as any people in the world, this was not convincing. They were told repeatedly by the Moscow radio that the Finns were brothers and this war was not the work of the real Finnish people but only the devilish machination of a small band of Finnish revolutionaries. These singular statements became the best joke in Helsinki. There is less than one per cent illiteracy in Finland and the people are well and constantly informed. They believe the Russian bombs but not the Russian propaganda.

As you neared the southern frontier and the battle zone, the tide of refugees thickened on the roads. The refugees traveled by sledge in this white, deadly-cold country, mostly old people huddled over their bags and bundles, with a horse or two tied on and following behind. The war was five days old and the first shock had worn off. There had been no panic at any time but only a stony determination to defend the country, and already it seemed as if people knew exactly where they had to go, and as if each person had some special work that was essential to all. An Italian journalist had remarked in Helsinki that anyone who could survive the Finnish climate could survive anything and we decided with admiration that the Finns were a tough and unrelenting race, seeing them take this war as if there were nothing very remarkable in three million people fighting against a nation of one hundred and eighty million.

Driving in Finland is one of the worst features of the war. In towns and villages you are constantly muffled in darkness, and the roads through the countryside are narrow and iced like a skating rink. It is also horribly cold. Late at night we stopped at a farmhouse to thaw out before continuing. The farm belonged to President Szinhuszue, first *regius* of Finland and third President, a greatly loved man whom all the Finns call Peter.

We were welcomed into the house by the President, a tall old man wearing a lumberjacket shirt and high boots. His wife, a bright-eyed, small dark woman almost as old as he, joined us in the living room. Sixteen soldiers, whom they treated as their children, were quartered in their house. The old President had spent two and a half years of his life in Siberia because he refused to violate Finnish law at the dictate of Russia, and during those years his wife went three times to the prison camp to take care of him. Their loyalty to each other and to Finland is legendary, and now this faithful old couple seemed symbolic of their people. Like all other Finns they hate war. Like all other Finns they know what this war means.

But they have been a long time building their country, and though nothing is perfect they know that Finland is a place where men do not suffer from unemployment or hunger, where health and the disabilities of old age are a state concern, where schools are available to all, where co-operatives, and widespread state ownership of industry and transport, and cheap land guarantee a fair division of wealth, where all men may believe what they like, talk as they see fit and read anything they desire. They are not going to give up easily, and though this war is disaster they accept it calmly because they have no choice.

President Szinhuszue offered us small apples from his orchard and told us how beautiful Finland was in the summer, and his wife asked us to come back and see them when the war is won. "We will not have moved," she said. "This is our home."

The Army of possibly half a million, backed by a unified and unfrightened civil population of two and a half million, have decided to fight a defensive war rather than lose their country, their republic and their hard-working, unaggressive, decent way of life. A nation of brave people is a good thing to see.

A boy of nine stood outside his home in Helsinki and watched the Russian bombers. He was blond and plump and he stood with his hands on his hips and with his feet apart and looked at the sky with a stubborn, serious face. He held himself stiffly so as not to shrink from the noise. When the air was quiet again he said, "Little by little, I am getting really angry."

The Karelian Front

December 1939

The road was just wide enough for the car and here it narrowed at a bridge. The blued lamps of the car only dimly lighted the frozen snow four feet ahead. "Be careful," the soldier guide said to our driver.

We had been driving in first gear and now we seemed barely to move. Suddenly our dimmed lights showed a red-painted pole to the left, marking the bridge. The bridge felt different from the road, smoother and even more slippery. When we were across, the soldier let out his breath. "That's dangerous," he explained, "those mined bridges—if you skid, I mean. One of our men hit such a mine and we couldn't even find him. There's another to cross now." The car had cleared the side of the bridge by less than a foot.

Our civilian driver turned on his full lights; he wasn't crossing any more of those bridges in the dark. The black, close-growing pine forest stood out against the snow, and the ice on the road flickered. We crossed the second bridge and the driver sighed and the soldier offered me a cigarette. Ahead of us a staff car painted dead-white—the camouflage color here—blinked its lights twice, turned a corner and suddenly sped along a narrow road past an open snow-covered field. We followed with full lights at a more sensible pace. The soldier muttered something, then the forest closed in again and the soldier spoke in a pleasant conversational voice to the driver. The driver answered quickly. I asked what they were talking about. Finnish is not a language you can pick up in a short time. "He says," the driver translated, "that I should not have kept my lights on going past that field, or else I should have gone faster. The Russians can see you from there, but he says they are poor marksmen and they have not managed to hit the road yet."

Our soldier guide, a lieutenant, wore a gray astrakhan cap and a romantic-looking but practical coat with astrakhan collar and trimming, and high, over-the-knee leather boots with turned-up toes, and he was twenty-one and answered to the nickname of Viskey. I had no idea where we were or where we were going because we had been driving for three hours, since leaving Viipuri, on these unmarked glassy roads.

Now Viskey said stop, and we piled out and joined the four staff officers from the car ahead. We spoke in whispers. Gun flashes from the Finnish batteries burned like summer lightning against the sky, and the noise of the outgoing shells was very loud and blurred; and, like an echo, the explosion could be heard as they landed. For an hour I had been waiting to hear the Russian batteries reply and still they were silent.

Ahead of us a line of soldiers loaded the small lightweight sledges the Finns use for transport. Sledges are the nearest you can come to mechanized efficiency in these forests and on these roads. The line of soldiers stretched far forward into the darkness. I thought it was probably a company of 150 men but couldn't be sure; most of them, wearing white overalls over their uniforms, seemed part of the snow, and the dark-dressed ones were lost against the dark trunks of the trees. They moved fast but in absolute silence, and from time to time the gun flashes would light up a man bending to fix his boots or another slapping his hands for warmth.

Then a clear, crackling word was shouted down the line. It came from the leading officer commanding this action and was passed on by every twentieth man, and now it sang out over the road, and the sledges and the men began to move forward. "Follow!" called a voice from the darkness. "Follow!" the other voices echoed.

This was the first big night operation of the war. The Russians were less than three quarters of a kilometer ahead, and all that day they had been maneuvered into a trap. The Finnish colonel in command of this sector believed there was an entire Russian division caught in the pocket.

Two battalions of Finnish soldiers, moving into the darkness, were to circle and pass the Russian lines and attack from the rear while other mobile units attacked from the front. Now we watched these go, and we heard behind us the rumble of trucks and stepped back into the ditches to leave the road clear as heavy ammunition trucks, burning cat's-eye lights, drove up and stopped. The road seemed to be blocked with incoming supplies.

An officer I had known for three hours, and who was therefore an old friend, loomed up and said, in German, "Get in your car. You must go back. This is the height of stupidity—and besides, your cars are in the way." He said something sharply to Viskey, who laughed and took my arm.

The officer who ordered us back had been an assistant professor of sociology at the University of Helsinki. He had a puckered thoughtful face and wore glases and took his responsibilities seriously. We returned as we came, following the almost invisible white staff car. We drove on the slant toward the ditch, to let more trucks pass, and behind them came more caravans of supply sledges, and three Red Cross sledges that would serve as ambulances. We brought Viskey to what seemed nothing more than one pine tree out of many but was actually the point of entry into the clearing where his tent stood. Later we drove slowly alongside a company of soldiers returning from the front. Their light field guns were on horse-drawn caissons; their sledges were piled high with bicycles and skis, the cavalrymen slept on their horses, the wagon cookstove smoked faintly, and in two large trucks men slept rolled up together, dark and shapeless.

Half frozen and very tired, we reached the bombed city of Viipuri at five-thirty in the morning. We had left Helsinki at five-thirty the morning before. That was the end of the day and night but all of it had been strange enough.

At eight o'clock, in the beginning of the preceding night, we had arrived at GHQ for the Karelian front. GHQ was in a large, rambling country estate with many barns, stables and outbuildings. We found staff headquarters and were ushered into a ballroom with pale-blue walls, lace curtains, cut-glass chandeliers and a grand piano. From this we were led into a small, equally elegant salon where scale maps were pinned on the wall and a long, businesslike table was the only furnishing. The Commanding General, a gray, slender, shy man, came in presently from a trip to the front.

The talk was friendly and formal and unrevealing, as it always is with high army officers, and at last I asked for permission to go to the front. The General said that it would be impossible—I would have to walk eight kilometers through these forests where every inch of ground seems taken up by either a tree or a granite boulder, and where between rocks and trees the snow drifts as high as your neck. I said, from French to Finnish via the aide-de-camp, that I was perfectly prepared to try to walk through anything. I had argued with generals before and knew it was a losing game.

Nothing was decided, as far as I could make out, though a rapid discussion went on in Finnish. We shook hands with the General, and a sentry guided us across the grounds to a remodeled church where supper was being served. You helped yourself from a side table. Piles of butter over a foot high stood on the table, and there was macaroni with cheese and meat in a creamy brown sauce, and every kind of bread and many pitchers of milk and lemonade. This is the sort of extraordinary food that is given to the Army everywhere. The entire Army—officers, men and even pilots—functions on total prohibition, which is a comment on the Army's discipline and the excellent state of its nerves. After dinner we were told to get in our cars. I still did not know where we were going. It took us two hours to drive twenty-five miles. We stopped at a farmhouse and picked up a guide. After a few minutes we stopped again and followed our guide into the forest and almost stumbled on a large round tent. The troops, who had been fighting a retreating guerrilla action for five days, giving the Army time to get in its present position, were now encamped invisibly in these woods and catching up on their sleep.

We crawled through the tent opening, and twelve soldiers woke in surprise. They were all very young—boys who were doing their regular military service and had got a war instead of academic practice. They came mostly from central Finland and were farmers' sons. The tent was the warmest place I had been in that day. Their officer, a young man with Prince Albert sideburns, spoke English and translated as they recounted how they had stopped tanks at twenty meters and how Russian infantry attacked.

Here, as everywhere else, I heard the same story about the Russian infantry column. The Russians attacked en masse in line, and the hidden and dispersed Finns mowed them down with machine-gun fire. And here, as everywhere else, I heard soldiers and officers express regret that other men should have to die stupidly and wastefully like slaughtered animals.

We connected with Viskey here, and the next stop was field headquarters, another tent equally warm and comfortable and lost in the woods. The Colonel showed us positions on his scale map and answered questions and joked, and all this time an attack was starting. It is not usual to find a field headquarters so calm and good-humored when real business is under way. Only once division headquarters telephoned to ask how things were going, and the answer was "Fine!" Meanwhile the Finnish batteries, scattered through these woods, were preparing for the attack with a fairly heavy bombardment.

The Finnish batteries, eighteen guns here, were using three- and six-inch shells. The Colonel said that the Russians used ten-inch shells but that the firing was inaccurate, there were many duds, and the shells had a low explosive value. He also said that the Russians used 150- to 250-kilo bombs on this front, and despite low flying they were inaccurate in their work. He showed me on a map how his men, divided into small, swift units, attacked in five different places over a fifty-kilometer radius in one day. They can and do fight like Indians, in woods which they know as well as we know the orderly streets of our own neighborhoods. The weather now was not the best for them, as it was too snowy for bicycles and too early for skis, but the new snow had started and the whole army would soon change to skis, which gives them a tremendous advantage of speed. Every Finn moves on skis as other people walk.

From this place we could see the sky marked with fire from burning villages, and we had passed on the road numerous small fires reflected in a lake. These small fires were from burning hay; the Finns systematically destroy anything that may be of use to the enemy, and the burning villages in front of the lines were fired either by occasional Russian shells or by the retreating villagers themselves or by the Finnish Army. The Russians come to a bare and unfriendly country where there is nothing to eat and little or no shelter.

Also in the dark, we had passed the Mannerheim Line; the Finnish Army was still in front of its own fortifications.

The Mannerheim Line crosses the bottleneck of the Karelian

Isthmus in a triplicate defense of granite tank traps, barbed wire and trenches. But nature itself has provided the Finns with the best defense—the forest studded with rocks and broken by lakes, icy weather and a gray cloud-thick sky. I don't know what is going on in the north, where it is no more than 125 miles from the Russian border to the Finnish coast of the Gulf of Bothnia and the vital railway line that connects Finland with Sweden. Nor does anyone know what the Russian Army has in store or what the Russian aviators can produce. But, those days on the southern front, the Russians were being outfought and liquidated.

At eight-thirty in the morning, after three hours' sleep, we heard the siren wail over Viipuri and we descended to the concrete-walled hotel garage. Nothing happened. Then the snow started to fall, soft and steady, and the day promised to be safe.

We went to the Viipuri prison to visit the captured Russians. The chief warden of this prison was a spare gray man with pince-nez and a stammer and the gentle manner of a professor. He was talking in Russian with a Soviet flier. The flier was thirty-two years old and had a sad, tired face and two days' growth of beard, and he stood as straight as his fatigue would let him and answered questions in a humble, soft voice. I asked whether he had any family. He did not move and his voice did not change, but tears rolled down his face, and the warden and the jailers turned away because they did not want to look. The flier said in the same soft voice that he had two children, one so high and the other so high, and his beloved wife had another child on the way. He simply stated these facts, not asking for pity, but his loneliness was terrible to see.

We walked down stone steps into the cellar and two Russian soldiers were let out of barred cells. They also stood in this tight, rigid manner, and I thought probably every time they were called out of their cells they expected to be shot. One was a tall man of thirty-seven and the other a boy of twenty-three. They had had two and three months' military training respectively. They were very thin, their clothes were the crudest cotton pants and coats—in this desperate climate—and the Finns were shocked because they were so louse-infested. These prisoners answered questions shiveringly also, and they repeated what all the others had said: they were told Finland was attacking them, and so they were fighting to save Russia. The individual man, in trouble and alone and lost, is pitiful, and these were as pitiful as any I had ever seen. The warden allowed me to give them cigarettes, thus breaking a prison rule of seventeen years' standing and proving also that he was a kind, unhating old man.

The roads are as ghastly by day as by night. Cars spin like coins, skidding on ice and gently descending into ditches. We arrived in the dark at the town where we were to sleep, and the next morning we were treated to a fine imitation of the best London fog. The Finns seemed very lucky in these matters. This town was a bombing objective for the enemy and an unhealthy place to be in clear weather.

I was taken to the great airfield of this sector, where fighter planes were stationed. Not much can be written about it. Even when you were on the field you could see nothing. The planes were hidden in the woods and in their own dugouts. All the vastly complicated organization work was carried on in dugouts which looked from the ground like snowdrifts. Most of the planes—fast single-seater pursuits—were imported from Holland; some were copies made in Finnish factories.

We stepped over sweet-smelling pine boughs that camouflaged a dugout where the crack pursuit squadron of Finland has its quarters. As always, one is astounded by the age of the pilots; they ought to be going to college dances, you feel, or cheering at football games. Their dugout was warm and cheerful and one of the pilots played a guitar. The squadron commander, a new hero of Finland, answered questions for a time politely and then said, "Do you want to hear a sad Finnish love song?" I said I would be delighted, and a pilot sang to the accompaniment of the guitar, and the squadron commander, when it was over, remarked with a delicious quick smile, *"Paris et l'amour."*

This officer, a tall man of thirty with a beautifully chiseled face, had brought down two planes in one day. The second one, at a distance of thirty meters, splashed him with oil as it fell. All these men were modest and jolly, the way brave men are. They go up, alone or in twos, to fight off any number of oncoming bombers. The squadron commander, on his big day, had been fighting alone against thirteen Russian bombers. He told me, in passing, that some years ago he tried to get a job flying transport between New York and Boston but he failed because the American company didn't think he was good enough. He said of course it was much easier to fly pursuit planes in war.

The Colonel of this air regiment said he thought the Russian bombers were good planes but slow. The Finnish fighter planes have a greater speed at low altitudes and their speed increases with height. The Russians' have been flying low, not above 16,000 feet, throughout this war, both over the cities and over military objectives.

A Russian squadron is nine planes, and bombers are flown without any accompanying protective pursuit planes. The Colonel believed the Russians were flying now from their field at Novgorod, which is several hundred kilometers inland from the Russian coast, and their pursuits did not have enough fuel capacity to convoy the bombers, fight and return. The bomb load of these Russian planes is approximately a thousand kilos and they carry their light incendiary bombs in barrel containers. At this field all the captured Russian pilots were interviewed and the Finns were surprised that such inexperienced men had been sent against them. The Russian pilots said they had received only ten hours of combat flying training, and one Soviet flier stated that in Russia the aviators were told the Finns had neither anti-aircraft nor pursuit planes. The Finns have both, in small quantity but splendidly manned.

One cannot know what will happen in a war from one day to the next, and certainly guessing is even more hazardous in a war between such unequal forces, but it is safe to say that the Finns have a trained army, helped by knowledge of the terrain; the soldiers are well equipped and wonderfully fed and the pilots are apparently, from results already shown, superior. The Army has the sound and comforting gaiety of good troops. It has confidence in its leaders. And it has the determination of those who fight on their own soil. The squadron commander spoke for them all when he said, "They will not get us as a present."

THE WAR IN CHINA

Nineteen forty must have been the most ominous year of the war, for our side. Far off, safe in the sun, I listened to the radio, a daily funeral bell. The defeat of Finland; the Nazi invasion of Denmark and Norway; the Nazi invasion of Holland, Belgium and Luxembourg; the Nazi terror raid on Rotterdam; the surrender of the Dutch and Belgian armies; the Dunkirk evacuation; the Battle of France, immediately followed by the parade of the Nazi army down the Champs-Elysées; Italy's entry into the war; the French armistice with Germany and Italy; the Battle of Britain and from then on, through the blitz, through the winter, the awful mounting toll of the civilian dead; the pact between Germany, Italy and Japan, called horribly "The New Order"; the Italian attack on Greece; the start of the war in the Western Desert.

There was no confusion of mind in hating and fearing the enemy. If that had been the only problem, it would have been a simple war, for the enemy was entirely profoundly evil. But there was also our side, and our record was not all shining and admirable, and one could not give one's undivided loyalty to our leaders, not by a long shot. We were guilty of the dishonest abandonment of Spain and the quick cheap betrayal of Czechoslovakia. We niggled and refused asylum to doomed Jews; we inspected and rejected anti-Fascists fleeing for their lives from Hitler; we were full of shames and ugly expediencies. In the immortal words of E. M. Forster, "Two cheers for democracy." Two cheers was all one could manage.

I learned my last lesson in what is called political reality during a visit I made to Paris at Christmastime in 1939, on my way home from Finland. It was an important lesson for me because I decided I had learned the same thing over and over, for long enough; political reality and political morality have nothing to do with each other. Politics really must be a rotten profession considering what awful moral cowards most politicians become as soon as they get a job. It is pointless to heap blame on leaders in a democracy, since we put them where they are in the first place and once there, they are subject to the law: power corrupts. But I see no need to hero-worship any of them.

In the early winter of 1939, Paris was the Sleeping Beauty. Blue dim-out lights shone on the snow in the empty Place de la Concorde. People moved quietly about the unscathed city, as if walking in a lovely white countryside. There were no crowds, few cars, no sense of haste or disaster. Paris had never been more at peace. I felt that I was looking at this grace for the last time. In my experience cities were bombed; that was what they could count on.

The only work I had to do in Paris was to try to rescue some friends who were imprisoned with the defeated Spanish army beside the Mediterranean, in holes dug on the beach at Argelès. This project interested no one at all. As a successful politician said to me, while we were both stuffed *foie gras:* My dear girl, a German and a former Communist, really, what do you expect? It was useless to point out that these men, forgotten behind barbed wire, had been fighting Hitler long before anyone else thought of doing so, or had been forced to do so. I realized finally how unwise it was to be "prematurely anti-Fascist."

The people of France, who have so many rare talents, apparently have no talent for self-government, which is after all a question of choosing your leaders to suit your real needs and keeping a stern eye on their actions. I knew many of the Frenchmen then in power, from the days of my youth; I knew all of their records. The ruling class did not seem to take this war very seriously; it was a brand-new witty type of war: you declared it and sat down in your fortifications and no doubt in time the whole disagreeable mess would clear up.

I said goodbye, with love, to the French people I knew who were so fine that they were sure to be killed; and I bolted from Europe. I didn't think there would be a battle; I thought there would be a massacre, and I could not bear to witness another, to watch helplessly while the innocent were destroyed. Worse than destroyed, I thought, and still made futile last-minute pleas for my imprisoned friends. War and death could be borne; what was beyond one's imagination, and the root of all fear, was the tortures of the Gestapo. So in 1940 Europe was lost and the Gestapo hunted over the Continent, searching for the best and bravest.

No one then knew or cared much about the war in China, but Japan had become an Axis partner and what Japan did held a new menace. I wanted to see the Orient before I died; and the Orient was across the world from what I loved and feared for. Journalism now turned into an escape route. My assignment was to report on the defenses of Hong Kong, Singapore and the Dutch East Indies, take a look at the Burma Road, and find out how the Sino-Japanese War was getting on. I am reprinting only one of the reports written on this long journey.

My China articles were not entirely candid. They did not say all I thought, and nothing of what I felt. There was a severe censorship in China, but I was more troubled by an interior censorship, which made it impossible for me to write properly. I had been included, twice, in luncheon parties given by the Chiangs. They struck me as the two most determined people I had met in my life. Their will to power was a thing like stone; it was a solid separate object which you felt in the room. They were also immensely intelligent, gracious and I thought inhuman. But I had accepted their hospitality, and since they owned China, it would be as if I had visited them as a guest and thanked them by writing unpleasant revelations about their house. I have never again accepted hampering hospitality.

The notion that China was a democracy under the Generalissimo is the sort of joke politicians invent and journalists perpetuate. The local men-in-office, whenever the absence of democracy became embarrassing, explained these conditions by saying that any country, in the midst of a long terrible war, must abandon some of its domestic liberties; and this is a sad fact, as we can all testify. But I do not believe that China ever was a democracy, nor will be, in our lifetime. How could it be? For democracy, or even the pretense of democracy, you need a fair percentage of literacy among the population, free communication—not only by speech and print but by road and rail, and enough time out, from struggling desperately for survival, to vote.

I thought a good six-point program for China during the next hundred years would be: clean drinking water—at least at stated places; sewage disposal everywhere; a government-issued birth-control pill; and an agricultural scheme which would guarantee the bare minimum of rice required to prevent the death by starvation of any Chinese. With these matters attended to, they could begin on a universal health service, attacking cholera, typhoid, typhus, leprosy, amoebic dysentery, malaria (malignant and benign), and all the other ills the flesh is heir to, but more heir to in China than in any other country I know. After that, it would be time to build schools and fill them. And then, finally, but how far in the future, the moment might have come to say a word about democracy.

I felt that it was pure doom to be Chinese; no worse luck could befall a human being than to be born and live there, unless by some golden chance you happened to be born one of the .00000099 per cent who had power, money, privilege (and even then, even then). I pitied them all, I saw no tolerable future for them, and I longed to escape away from what I had escaped into: the age-old misery, filth, hopelessness and my own claustrophobia inside the enormous country.

The Canton Front

March 1941

We climbed up the riverbank, slipping in the mud. A platoon of Chinese soldiers stood in the rain alongside a bamboo shelter. Eight men were lined up facing the platoon. They wore large conical straw hats which served as umbrellas, yellow oilcloth jackets, shorts and straw sandals. These were the stable coolies. Seven of them held the bridles of seven horses slightly larger than Shetland ponies. The eighth coolie held the bridle of a former Hong Kong race horse; it had been captured from the Japanese. It was horse-size. The soldiers, the coolies and the horses shivered with cold, and water dripped from them onto the mushy field.

We took the salute of the waterlogged platoon and mounted our horses. My horse, kicking like a baby with a tantrum, knocked down our interpreter, who landed in the mud. Whenever these miniature horses misbehave, the coolies hit them on the nose and scream at them and the horses squeal and try to bite the coolies. In the midst of this a bugle brassed out something unrecognizable. We set off in single file on a path seemingly made of a mixture of grease and glue. Each coolie ran ahead of the horse he had been holding. The gait of the horses was like the bucking, jerking movement of an electrical-horse machine in a gymnasium. The rain came down in sheets, soaking through our clothes. It swelled the mountain creeks, which looked as if they had been used to rinse out all the dirty laundry in that part of China. We followed the path around the side of a hill, leaning away from the wet bushes, ducking under low branches, and hauling up our legs so that they would not hang in the water when we forded streams. The procession jolted forward in sodden silence. We were starting for the Canton front.

Five days earlier, in the dark, we had gone to the airfield at Hong Kong. We waited there for three hours, listening to the wind. They canceled the flight when the final weather report came in, saying that at Namyung the ceiling was zero and the visibility nil. The next day we took off into a low cloud-covered sky, flew for an hour and a half over the mountains and the Japanese lines, and landed blind on a mud field inside China. There we got into a very old small Chevrolet, together with five Chinese, and jolted over a yellow mud road until we reached Shaokwan at dark.

Our hotel was called the Light of Shaokwan. We had a small sitting room, furnished with bamboo chairs and a table, two weak kerosene lamps and a spittoon. Behind this were windowless cubbyholes with two boards nailed together and raised about a foot from the floor; each of these narrow platforms was meant for a bed. A slit in the wall was the bathroom, holding one enamel washbowl but no pitcher, one spittoon and one mirror. We unpacked blankets and mosquito nets (it was very cold but there were plenty of mosquitoes, that frail slow-moving kind with the curled-up hind legs, the malarial mosquito) and settled down in this palace.

The next day, the General in command of this war zone invited us to lunch. He looked like a cheerful Buddha. Sitting around a table in a dim stone-walled room, we drank the inevitable tea, exchanged the usual compliments and made a few sad, polite jokes. This formality finished, we joined the general staff in a marvelous meal, composed of twelve different dishes ranging from shark's-fin soup to ancient black eggs.

It is an old Chinese custom to drink guests under the table. The host has the right to stop a drinking contest by announcing regretfully that he has run out of liquor. Even in a prohibition army, there is always rice wine for visitors. So now the General and the officers proposed one *gambai* (bottoms up) toast after another. We drank to China and America, the Generalissimo and the President, to health and happiness, the success of our trip; and finally a simple nod would pass for a toast. The General began to sweat profusely and two staff officers turned a beautiful mulberry color and the interpreter stammered and swayed and found it hard to translate a toast about glorious armies and final victory. By the time the General announced that he was plumb out of liquor, people were laughing heartily at any remark whatever. The luncheon drew to a brilliant close and still no business had been transacted.

We wanted to visit the Canton front, which is the back door to Hong Kong. Potentially it is one of the most important fronts in China. If the Japanese ever succeeded, having already made two big offensives, in driving north from Canton, they could cut free China in two. If the Chinese ever recaptured and held Canton they could open up a direct practicable line of communication with the outside world. There would then be an adequate route into China for all the aid America has promised. But many Seventh Zone staff officers have never traveled down the North River from Shaokwan to the front, and no foreigners of any description have been through this roadless portion of Kwantung province. The General agreed to let us go, as soon as our transport could be arranged. It took an hour and a half by air to get from Hong Kong to Namyung in free China, and it took four days' travel to go straight back from Namyung to within seventy-five miles of Hong Kong.

Army Transport sent a truck to call for us at the Light of Shaokwan. In China two men are necessary to handle a car, the driver and the mechanic. The mechanic is the one who raises the hood to start the motor, who springs out to put a block of wood behind the rear wheels when you start to roll downhill backwards, and who argues with anyone blocking the road. There were four of us in the front seat of a not large truck and the battery was on the floor alongside the gearshift. The mechanic had t.b. and his dry cough mingled rhythmically with the catarrhal bark of the driver, who had only the worst possible cold. In the rear end of the truck they stowed the luggage and three officers who were accompanying us and our bodyguard of four slim silent soldiers in faded cotton uniforms. Our bodyguard carried rifles, hand grenades and Mauser pistols in wooden holsters. They all looked twelve years old and were probably nineteen.

The road was bright-brown mud under the misty rain. We passed villages with square stone towers where the peasants had formerly taken refuge from bandits, but which would now be no shelter from bombs. We passed the gray mud water of the rice fields, where barelegged men plow behind the gray, almost hairless water buffaloes. There were beautiful trees and sharp mountains and a flowering bush that looked like honeysuckle. After two hours of average bumping we hit the section of the road that was, as they said, not so good. The driver clung to the wheel and was racked by his cough. We braced ourselves with one hand against the windshield and one against the roof. The truck ground through mud or leaped in great shaking jumps from hole to hole. The driver and the mechanic hawked and spat and muttered together. We had by now rubbed raw places in the small of our backs and were a little winded. Then we jolted down a hill and stopped at the edge of a village. We had come thirty-five miles in three hours and after this there was no road at all.

We followed the baggage coolies down the mud bank to the river. Sitting on boat hooks and coiled ropes, we made ourselves comfortable on the roof of the motorboat. This was a venerable twenty-four-foot Chris-Craft which had to be pumped out every two hours to keep it from sinking. The hull was so rotten that you could poke into it with your hand, and the cabin looked and smelled as could be expected. It was the only motorboat on the river and its important feature was that it ran.

Everything and everyone being stowed aboard, we chugged out into the river, towing behind us a sampan almost twice our size. On this sampan, separated from each other by bamboo partitions, were our bodyguard, our escort of three officers, and the sampan family—two men, two boys, two women, and a very new baby who cried steadily. The mother strapped the baby on her back when she cooked the meals. It cried even better in that position.

The North River looks like the Missouri, broad and mud-colored and with a heavy current. Bamboo and pine and banyan grow along the high banks, and sand flats stretch out like fingers into the stream. Behind and ahead the mountains rose smooth and dark blue in the fading afternoon light. Now, standing like gateposts on either side of the river, straight stone palisades reared up. A Buddhist shrine was cut into the side of the rock forty feet above the water. Last year the Japanese drove this far, trying to take Shaokwan.

Sampans with square brown patched sails moved downstream, and others, fully loaded, were being pulled or poled upstream against the current. In China every other person is either bowed under great weights suspended from a pole across the shoulders or bent over, pulling or pushing other terrific weights. A line of men, women and children, like dark, straining statues, pulled the tow-rope of their sampan and slowly moved the heavy barge forward. They chanted to time their effort, and the sound came as a rising and falling wail across the water. The North River is one of the three water highways to this roadless front, and the sampan is what the Army uses instead of trucks.

The pilot of the motorboat was a very old man with a sparse white beard, a few yellow teeth, a black knitted stocking cap and a bamboo pipe. He sat cross-legged on the high chair by the wheel and shoveled rice into his mouth with chopsticks, then sucked down a bowl of soup, belched to show that everything was good, and spat out the window. His grandson brought him his pipe. His grandson was a tiny mysterious boy, like a Chinese version of Jackie Coogan in *The Kid,* with the same cap and the same enchant-ing, wistful face. He slept on a shelf in the small, evil-smelling forward toilet and spent most of his time pumping out the boat. The old man's son did all the other work on board. Now he was crouched alongside the charcoal cooking fire in the stern, eating his dinner with the loud smacking and sucking noises, belching and spitting, that are common to China. At this point the towrope to our sampan, a rope suitable for tying up parcels, snapped. It was time for dinner and anyhow, being four-thirty in the afternoon, so the sampan poled alongside, we climbed aboard, sat on the floor, rinsed our chopsticks in boiling water, and began the first meal of the day.

By six it was dark and the bodyguard went to sleep and the officers, wearing their long underwear, tucked themselves in cosily on the floor of the sampan. We returned to the clean air of the motorboat roof. We ran without lights, and when the starless night really closed in, the Chris-Craft began going aground. The pilot's son stood in the bow, taking soundings with a boat hook. He called in the singsong Chinese voice to the pilot, "Two feet, two and a half, two feet," calling steadily until we scraped another sandbar. We ran aground five times and finally were all mixed up, with the sampan out ahead of us. Our course had been a constant circle for the last hour. The pilot accepted defeat and took us inshore, where we anchored in the midst of a floating village of sampans. As we came up to them we received at once their noise, their smell and their mosquitoes.

We ran for five more hours in the morning, and the downriver trip was over. We had left the Light of Shaokwan twenty-four hours ago, and there was still much rain and two days' riding between us and the front.

There are no Maginot or Mannerheim lines in China—there are mountains. The Canton front, which is typical, consists in mountain strong points, lightly fortified and held by machine guns. In case of Japanese attack, these forward posts are intended to delay the enemy advance as long as possible while reserves are brought from the rear to block in force the oncoming enemy troops. A blitz attack is impossible because mechanized units cannot travel over the narrow mountain trails. However, the Japanese have planes here and the Chinese have not.

There have been thirty encounters on this front in fourteen months, and two major Japanese offensives. The Chinese line, that is to say its scattered mountain strong points, remains where it was after the fall of Canton. Actually in mountains when you see the front what you see is one mountain, large and green and silent against the sky. The Japanese are there. Across a narrow valley is another mountain. The Chinese hold it. Unless you are in an engagement, a mountain front is a calm place. Or unless you happen to be in a village when the Japanese come over and bomb. The Japanese are not being wasteful these days; bombs and gasoline cost them money too.

Generalissimo Chiang Kai-shek's armies are divided into nine war zones. The Seventh War Zone is about the size of Belgium, with a population of thirty million people. Two army groups, or about 150,000 men, hold this area. Communication at the front between Army, divisional and regimental commanders is maintained by military telephone. Often more than a day's ride separates their headquarters. There is no leave in the Chinese Army, as it would be practically impossible to return soldiers to their homes in a country which has one remaining railroad, five hundred miles long, and where neither trucks, gasoline nor roads are plentiful. So an army stays where it is, sometimes for as long as two years, and it builds up its own life.

Each regiment has its training ground, athletic field, classrooms, reading rooms and barracks. The Chinese Army does a surprising and thorough job of practical military education. After each engagement, noncommissioned and junior officers are taken out of active service and sent for one month or three months to school at their divisional training camp. Returning to their regiments, they teach the common soldiers. The Army is constantly studying from experience and making profit out of mistakes. This sounds as if the countryside were dotted with white stone buildings where uniformed, spruce young men learn the art of war. Actually all the headquarters and school buildings are made of bamboo or mud brick and plaster. They are Spartan-simple and were built by the soldiers themselves. The buildings and grounds of the Army are the cleanest and best cared for we have seen in China. What this Army lacks in equipment, it tries to make up in training and organization. The discipline is Prussian in its sternness and efficiency and the result is an Army of five million men which has no shoes but has a sound knowledge of how to fight.

The Army is the least well paid of the government services; in fact it is the least well paid of anything in China. A colonel (who may have had fourteen years' active service, first against the War Lords, then in the long Civil War, and finally against the Japanese), a graduate of Whampoa Military Academy, Chiang Kai-shek's own school, earns 150 Chinese dollars a month. In American money this is seven dollars and twenty-five cents, but there is an inflation in China so such comparisons do not mean much. However, a pair of leather shoes costs 200 national dollars in Chungking. Rice has gone up seven times its prewar price. A common soldier earns 4.50 Chinese dollars a month (or twenty-three U.S. cents) and he has a rice allowance. With his rice allowance of eighty U.S. cents a month the soldier—who sees plenty of food all around him—cannot buy enough to eat. A carrying coolie earns twice as much per month as an Army colonel. This strange system of military under-pay, and the tragic lack of provision for the wounded, are the two greatest misfortunes of the Chinese Army. Always excepting war, which is a misfortune for everyone.

When we dismounted at the first divisional headquarters, we were greeted by posters in English, their red letters streaked and running in the rain, tacked up on a bamboo guardhouse and barracks and on the mud wall of the General's headquarters. The posters said, "Welcome to the Representatives of Righteousness and Peace," "Consolidate All Democracy Nations We Will Resist until Final Victory." There was one sign which baffled us, saying, "Democracy Only Survives Civilization." (These slogans had been invented and printed by workers in the Political Department. Once a little man rushed in from a neighboring village to find out where we were going next, so that they could hurry and nail up the posters.) We shook the rain from our faces and bowed and smiled our thanks for this reception, and the General, wearing white cotton gloves in honor of the event, saluted back. The wind beat against the house and blew through the glassless windows. We sat around a pot of glowing charcoal, trying furtively to dry our shoes and our pants legs, and the General talked.

What he said, boiled down, was that if America would send planes, arms and money, China could defeat Japan alone. By a persistent campaign of frightfulness in captured villages and cities, the Japanese have roused this almost too long-suffering, reasonable, pacific race to fierce hate. There is no talk of compromise or peace among the Chinese fighting forces. A Chinese soldier gets one thousand national dollars for any Japanese prisoner captured alive. Despite this huge sum of money, the soldiers shoot any Japanese troops they can lay hands on, as an immediate personal vengeance for the misery of people like themselves in villages like their own homes.

The wind blew wildly all night, and it was too cold to sleep, but in the morning the sky was swept clean and we could see ahead the curving mountains, blurring in the distance. We were riding over a high ridge. Mr. Ma, our interpreter, rode just behind me. Mr. Ma is a little man with enormous horn-rimmed spectacles, an enormous appetite, a heart of gold, two American university degrees and no military experience whatever, and now he works in the Political Department of the Seventh Army Zone at Shaokwan and is a major, by politeness.

"Mr. Ma," I said, "Why have they burned off that mountain over there?"—pointing ahead to a charred hill.

"They do that to get rid of the tigers," Mr. Ma said brightly. "You see, the tigers eat some kind of tender little roots and grasses, and when it is all burned off they get hungry and go away." There will always now be a special breed of cats, Mr. Ma's vegetarian tigers.

After five hours in the saddle, we stopped to rest under a tree. Its roots grew like heavy ropes over the grass and the leaves were small and fine as petals.

"What kind of tree is this, Mr. Ma?"

He considered it thoughtfully. "Ordinary tree," he said.

Two men carrying a new wooden coffin passed on the trail, followed by a man carrying a load of toothpicks in cardboard boxes. Then an emaciated, filthy man wearing a rain cape made of dried grass, like a hula skirt, paused to look at us. In a country were no one looks well off, this man really looked as if things had gone hard with him. The Colonel knew this man in the rain cape; they had seemed to nod to each other. He was one of their secret agents, who worked behind the Japanese lines and in Canton. Seeing him, and seeing the country, you realized how easily the Chinese can filter in and out of Japanese-occupied territory, and what a hopeless job it is for the Japanese to try to block this constant stream of information.

After nine hours' riding, and no food or water, I was fairly tired, but not so the Chinese. They accept calmly anything that happens: hunger, fatigue, cold, thirst, pain or danger. They are the toughest people imaginable, as no doubt the Japanese realize. We dismounted in a village which was also a regimental headquarters. It was made of sunburned brick, it had been often bombed, its streets were mud paths sprinkled with garbage and mangy chickens, and its sewage system (as everywhere in China) was nonexistent. From the horse to the parade ground, without pause, we followed the General to inspect a battalion of nine hundred men. These soldiers were all peasants and coolies, people who have never handled anything as complicated as a flashlight before joining the Army. Seen alone, or straggling in small bands on the trails, they look as sad as orphanage children and as tattered as beggars. But here in rigid formation, with their mortars and machine guns, automatic rifles and hand grenades, they looked a solid, self-confident body of experienced troops. Now they drilled, to the screamed orders of a little fighting cock of a sergeant major. The village elders watched silently, but with evident pride, from the side of the field. The same peasants, when fighting starts, carry the wounded, joggling them on bamboo stretchers, over these bumpy endless trails to a hospital in the rear. There is no water to drink on the way, no dressing station, and if the peasants were unwilling to carry there would be no wounded, only the dead.

"Tonight we will go to a play," the General said. The Japanese were just over the nearest hills.

They lighted bonfires along the side of the parade ground and twelve hundred soldiers sat in the flaring dark on the cold hard-packed clay, waiting for the play to begin. On the bamboo stage, behind the blue cotton curtains, they struggled for half an hour with an acetylene lamp. Suddenly it blazed up, went dim, and then settled into a fixed glare. The curtains were pulled open by two shy soldiers. The play, called *A Group of Devils,* was on.

The play dealt with a loyal Chinese woman and her husband in Japanese-occupied Canton. The husband masqueraded as her servant, while the woman lured Japanese officers. It was not clear what she was luring them to or for, but they were constantly trying to pull her through the bedroom door. The audience roared with laughter when the husband-servant spilled tea on the Japanese officers or burned their noses lighting their cigarettes. They shouted with joy when the Japanese officers, using noisy Italian gestures, quarreled over the woman. The Japanese officers wore paper hats resembling the regulation Japanese Army headgear, and mustaches made of lamp-black. You could tell they were villains by the mustaches. They acted like conceited fools and brutes and the audience loved it. Finally, with a terrific noise off stage, the woman shot the two Japanese officers, the curtain was pulled together and the twelve hundred soldiers applauded more than any audience at a successful first night in New York. Each week the Political Department puts on a play for the troops. It is their only and adored fun, and actors never had a better public.

In the morning Mr. Ma came into my section of the bamboo hut, where I was washing with two cups of water, and remarked, "Some planes will be coming over. Would you prefer to go out into the fields?" Exactly as he might have said, "Will you take tea or coffee with your breakfast?"

"What would you like to do?" I asked.

There were no shelters in the village, of course, and a thatched roof is not much use, but wading through the mud of the rice fields would not be too jolly either. As we discussed the problem from every angle, we heard the buzz, rounding into a roar, of the planes. We stood looking up into a blank gray sky, waiting during that moment of tight cold listening, waiting for the first bomb. The planes passed. The air-raid alarm in this village is a gong made from the nosecap and cylinder of an unexploded Japanese bomb.

80

"Maybe they are going to bomb Shaokwan," Mr. Ma said unhappily. His wife and child live in Shaokwan.

They climbed us up to a fortified position. On the Japanese side there was no sign of life, no sound. The front was the most restful place in China.

The General could not very well wake these sleeping mountains and put on a battle for our benefit, but he wanted to show off his troops. So we withdrew one range beyond the Japanese, and there they staged a maneuver duplicating this war in the mountains. From the Hill of the Heroes, we observed the enemy—artillery, machine-gun positions, infantry all represented by white flags—opposite us on the Hill of the Unknowns. Behind us, suddenly, a huge coughing-chug widened into a roar and became a whistling sword-sharp invisible drive through the air. Seconds later, a mile and a quarter away on the Hill of the Unknowns, dirt spouted up, a black cloud rose slowly and the mountains echoed with the mortar explosion. Now the machine guns opened up, below us to the left and right. Through field glasses, we could see the bullets slashing into the marked enemy positions. The mountains doubled and trebled the roar of the mortars and the metal hammering of the machine guns and rocked the sound back and forth. Down in the gully, small khaki figures camouflaged with leafy twigs raced across the dikes of the rice fields, flung themselves flat against the protecting hill, started to climb, dropped when the ground offered less cover, and we could scarcely see them wriggling forward, upward, toward the enemy positions. They were not only demonstrating the minor tactics of war, they had got also the deadly feeling, the tenseness, the effort, the curious silence that lies under the raw, pounding, shrieking noise of high explosives.

These soldiers moved with the sureness and purpose of much experience and good training. The 81-mm. Brandt mortars, the Hotchkiss and the Czech machine guns fired with accuracy and provided excellent cover for the troops, who knew how to use it. As in war, every tiny figure crawling its way forward seemed terribly alone on that hill, yet all followed the orders and the plan, all understood the technique of killing men. For one hour, this lost and silent corner of China shook with sound. (I thought, perhaps the Japanese advance posts will report to headquarters that there is mutiny in the Chinese Army.)

A Véry pistol fired up a red slow-sinking rocket. The maneuver was over.

"You see," General Wong said. He looked like a Walt Disney drawing of a little Chinese boy, with his round face and round bright eyes and tiny pursed-up pink mouth. He was pleased with his troops. "That is how we work. We can always hold them in the mountains."

For two days we rode back toward the river. After you have seen three rice paddies you do not need to look any more. The comic horse plodded on, and I thought about this amazing army. Here was a front that had one piece of mechanized transport, an antique twenty-four-foot motorboat. And ten days' travel to the north, near Tibet at Chengtu, they were building by hand an airfield where Flying Fortresses could land.

The Japanese can never conquer China by force. People who can move their capital three times, carry factory machinery and university equipment over the mountains to safety, supply a front by sampan and coolie carrier, burrow into rock and survive endless bombing, build a 1,000-acre airfield in a hundred days without machinery will endure to the end.

And time does not matter in China. Four years of war is a long time. But perhaps if your history goes back four thousand years it does not seem so long. The Chinese are born patient, and they learn endurance when they start to breathe.

No, time does not matter in China. It took thirty-six hours in the motorboat to get back upstream to the town where we had left our truck. The road was now impassable with rain, and trucks were stuck in the mud like flies in flypaper. We would have to make the rest of the journey to Shaokwan by boat. Only seven hours, Mr. Ma said optimistically. We chugged on for half an hour and the sampan towrope caught around the propeller of the Chris-Craft. The pilot reversed the engine, thus tying up the propeller for good. At night we piled into the sampan and slept on the floor, all of us snugly together. In the morning they hitched the sampan onto a river paddle-wheel steamer that carries produce, people and cattle to Shaokwan. Eighteen hours later we saw the long bridge that the Japanese have not been able to destroy in a year's bombing. At the hotel we hoped to get a bath in a tin washtub. Shaokwan seemed the center of civilization.

We stood in the bow of the sampan and Mr. Ma said, "What do you think of our Army? Not so bad, eh?"

"No, Mr. Ma, not bad at all. Very, very good, Mr. Ma."

He beamed with pleasure. "And what," he said, "do you think of China?"

"Well, Mr. Ma," I said, "in the long run, I'd hate to be Japanese."

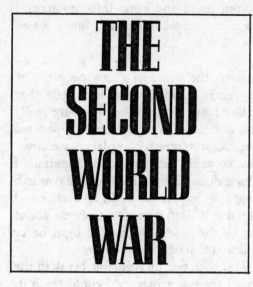

THE SECOND WORLD WAR

We were drinking daiquiris in a mingy little bar on the Mexican border and talking about cattle-raising in Arizona. A tattered Indian child came in, with some clutched newspapers, and said *"Con la guerra, la guerra"* mildly. No one noticed him the first time round. Then the word caught, we called to the boy, he sold us a Mexican paper, damp with his own sweat. Smeary type announced Pearl Harbor and America's declaration of war. It seemed a dreadful way for a great nation to get into a war—blown in, with its fleet down.

Between that time and November 1943, when I finally reached England (filled with joy to be there, to be home in the world again), I was paralyzed by conflicting emotions: private duty, public disgust and a longing to forget both and join those who were suffering the war. It is too hard to sit on the outside and watch what you can neither help nor change; it is far easier

85

to close your eyes and your mind and jump into the general misery, where you have almost no choices left, but a lot of splendid company.

England was a new country, the home of a new people. The English are an amazing nation and I think it is true that nothing becomes them like catastrophe. When they are really up against it, their negative qualities turn positive, in a glorious somersault. Slowness, understatement, complacency change into endurance, a refusal to panic, and pride, the begetter of self-discipline. What is "not done" is to be a crook or a coward; and they are able to laugh, no matter what. In an earlier and more innocent age, Edmund Wilson invented a phrase about Russia: "The moral top of the world, where the light never quite goes out." England was that, during the war.

From November 1943, with one unavoidable break in the spring of 1944, I followed the war wherever I could reach it. The U.S. Army public relations officers, the bosses of the American press, were a doctrinaire bunch who objected to a woman being a correspondent with combat troops. I felt like a veteran of the Crimean War by then, and I had been sent to Europe to do my job, which was not to report the rear areas or the woman's angle. The P.R.O.s in London became definitely hostile when I stowed away on a hospital ship in order to see something of the invasion of Normandy. After that, I could only report the war on secondary fronts, in the company of admirable foreigners who were not fussy about official travel orders and accreditation. By stealth and chicanery I managed to sneak to Holland and watch the superb U.S. 82nd Airborne Division at work. But it was only during the Battle of the Bulge, and from then on, that I dared attach myself to American fighting units. The war may have softened the P.R.O.s, or they no longer cared what anyone did, with the end so near.

These articles are in no way adequate descriptions of the indescribable misery of war. War was always worse than I knew how to say—always. And probably from an instinct of self-preservation, one tried to write most often of what was brave and decent. Perhaps now my articles on Germany and on the behavior of the Gestapo, the S.S. and other sections of the German Army will seem untimely paeans of hate. I reported

86

what I saw, and hate was the only reaction such sights could produce.

Nazi doctrine extolled "frightfulness" as a weapon, as a means to the end of victory. The human race is still sickened by the poison of that doctrine, by crimes committed everywhere and answered with other crimes. We have before us the memory and the lesson: let us not imagine that anyone can use frightfulness in a good cause.

The Bomber Boys

November 1943

They were very quiet. There was enough noise going on around them, but they had no part in it. A truck clanked past with a string of bomb trolleys behind it. The ground crew was still loading the thousand-pound high-explosive bombs that look like huge rust-colored sausages. A WAAF's clear high English voice, relaying orders, mixed with the metal noises. A light on the open bomb bay made the darkness around the plane even darker. The moon was skimmed over with cloud, and around the field the great black Lancasters waited, and men finished the final job of getting them ready. But the crews who were going to fly seemed to have nothing to do with this action and haste. Enormous and top-heavy in their Mae Wests or their electrically heated flying suits, these men seemed over-life-size statues. They stood together near their planes.

The Group Captain had been driving fast around the perimeter track of the field in a beetle of a car, checking up. He appeared the way people seem to, suddenly out of the flat black emptiness of the airdrome, and said, "Come and meet the boys." The pilot of this crew was twenty-one and tall and thin, with a face far too sensitive for this business. He said, "I was in Texas for nine months. Smashing place." This would mean that Texas was wonderful. The others said how do you do. They were polite and kind and far away. Talk was nonsense now. Every man went tight and concentrated into himself, waiting and ready for the job ahead, and the seven of them who were going together made a solid unit, and anyone who had not done what they did and would never go where they were going could not understand and had no right to intrude. One could only stand in the cold darkness and feel how hard we were all waiting.

We drove to the control station, which looks like a trailer painted in yellow and black checks, and though there was no wind the cold ate into you. The motors were warming up, humming and heavy. Now the big black planes wheeled out and one by one rolled around the perimeter and got into position on the runway. A green light blinked and there was a roar of four motors that beat back in an echo from the sky. Then the first plane was gone into the blackness, not seeming to move very fast, and we saw the tail-light lifting, and presently the thirteen planes that were taking off from this field floated against the sky as if the sky were water. Then they changed into distant, slow-moving stars. That was that. The chaps were off. They would be gone all this night. They were going to fly over France, over known and loved cities, cities they would not see and that did not now concern them. They were going south to bomb marshaling yards, to destroy if possible and however briefly one of the two rail connections between France and Italy. If they succeeded, the infantry in southern Italy would have an easier job for a little while.

Several hundreds of planes, thousands of bomber boys, were taking off into the wavering moon from different fields all over this part of England. They were out for the night with the defended coast of France ahead, and the mountain ranges where the peaks go up to ten thousand feet and the winter weather is never a gift; and then of course there would be the target. This trip, however, came under the heading of "a piece of cake," which means in the wonderful RAF language a pushover. If you were taking a pessimistic view of this raid you might have called it "a long stooge," which means simply a dreary, unsatisfactory bore. No one would have given the mission more importance than that. Still they were very quiet and the airdrome felt bleak when they were gone and the waiting had simply changed its shape. First you wait for them to go and then you wait for them to get back.

Perhaps this is a typical bomber station; I do not know. Perhaps every station is different as every man is different. This was an RAF station and the crews flying tonight were English and Canadian, except for one South African and two Australians and an

American pilot from Chicago. The youngest pilot was twenty-one and the oldest thirty-two and before the war they had been various things: a commercial artist, a schoolteacher, a detective, a civil servant, a contractor. None of this tells you anything about them. They look tired, and they look older than they are. They fly by night and sleep somewhat during the day and when they are not flying there is work to do and probably it is exhausting to wait to fly, knowing what the flying is. So they look tired and do not speak of this and if you mention it they say they get plenty of rest and everyone feels very well.

The land where they live is as flat as Kansas and cold now and dun-colored. The land seems unused and almost not lived in, but the air is always busy. At sunset you see a squadron of Spitfires flying back to their station against a tan evening sky, looking like little rowboats and flying home, neat and close. In the thin morning, the day bombers roar over toward the Channel. The air is loud and occupied and the airdrome is noisy too. But the home life of the men is quiet.

They say that if you find all the chaps in the mess reading at teatime, you know there are operations scheduled for that night. This afternoon they sat in the big living room of the country house that has become their mess, and they looked like good tidy children doing their homework. If you read hard enough you can get away from yourself and everyone else and from thinking about the night ahead. That morning they would have made a night flying test, taking the planes up to see that everything was okay. Between the test and the afternoon briefing is the rumor period, during which someone finds out how much gasoline is being loaded on the planes and everyone starts guessing about the target, basing guesses on miles per gallon. The briefing (the instructions about the trip and the target) would normally be finished by late afternoon and then there is an operational meal and then the few bad hours to kill before take-off time. It is a routine they all know and have learned to handle; they have taken on this orderly unshaken quietness as a way of living.

Of course there is relaxation in the nearest village on free nights—the village dance hall and the local girls to dance with, the pubs where you can drink weak war beer, and the movies where you can see the old films. At eleven o'clock all such gaieties stop and the village shuts firmly. No one could say this is a flashing romantic existence; it is somewhere between a boarding school and a monastery. They have their job to do and they take this sort of life as it comes and do not think too much about it or about anything. There is only one clear universal thought and that is: finish it. Win the war and get it over with. There's been enough; there's been too much. The thing to do is win now soon, as fast as possible.

The old life that perhaps seemed flat when they had it becomes beautiful and rare when they remember it. No one who flies could make any detailed plans; there is no sense in counting your bridges as well and safely crossed when you know how many tough bridges are ahead. But vaguely each man thinks of that not-so-distant almost incredible past, when no one did anything much, nothing spectacular, nothing fatal, when a day was quite long and there was an amazing number of agreeable ways to spend it. They want that again, though they want a life that has grown lovelier in their memories. They want a future that is as good as they now imagine the past to have been.

It is a long night when you are waiting for the planes from Europe to come back, and it is cold, but it has to end. At four o'clock or around then, the duty officers go to the control tower. The operations officers walk about a certain amount and smoke pipes and say casual things to each other and the waiting gets to be a thing you can touch. Then the first plane calls in to the control tower switchboard. Two WAAFs, who have been up all night and are still looking wide-awake, wonderfully pink-cheeked, perfectly collected and not frozen stiff, begin to direct the planes in. The girls' voices that sound so remarkable to us (it is hard to decide why, perhaps because they seem so poised, so neat) begin: "Hello George pancake over." In the glassed-in room you hear the pilots answer. Then the girl again: "Hello Queen airdrome one thousand over." The night suddenly becomes weird, with the moon still up and the bright stars and the great searchlights like leaning trees over the runway and the wing lights of the plane far off and then nearer, the noise of the motors circling the field, the ambulances rolling out, and the girls' voices going on and on, cool, efficient, unchanging. "Hello Uncle airdrome twelve fifty over." This means that a plane, U for Uncle, is to circle the field at twelve hundred and fifty feet until told to "pancake" or land. The planes come in slowly at first and then there will be four of them circling and landing. The more planes that come in and are marked up on the blackboard, the

92

worse the waiting gets. None of this shows. No voice changes, no one makes a movement that is in any way unusual, the routine proceeds as normally as if people were waiting in line to buy theater tickets. Nothing shows and nothing is said and it is all there.

Finally all the planes were in except P for Peter and J for Jig. They were late. The job was a piece of cake. They should be in. They would of course be in. Obviously. Any minute now. No one mentioned the delay. We started to go down to the interrogation room and the Group Captain remarked without emphasis that he would stay up here for a bit until the chaps got in.

The crews of the eleven planes that had returned were coming into the basement operations room for questioning. They all had mugs of tea, white china shaving mugs filled with a sweetish ghastly lukewarm drink that seems to mean something to them. They looked tireder around their eyelids and mouths, and slanting lines under their eyes were deeply marked. The interrogation again gives the curious impression of being in school. The crews sit on a wooden bench in front of a wooden table, and the intelligence officer, behind the table, asks questions. Both questions and answers are made in such low ordinary voices that the group seems to be discussing something dull and insignificant. No one liked this trip much. It was very long and the weather was terrible; the target was small; there was a lot of smoke; they couldn't see the results well.

The Group Captain in command sat on a table and spoke to the crew members by name, saying, "Have a good trip?" "Fairly good, sir." "Have a good trip?" "Not bad, sir." "Have a good trip?" "Quite good, sir." That was all there was to that. Then he said, "Anyone get angry with you?" "No sir," they said, smiling, "didn't see a thing." This is the way they talk and behave and this is the way it is. When it was known that all the planes were back, and all undamaged and no one hurt, there was a visible added jovialness. But everyone was tired, anxious to get through the questioning and back to the mess, back to the famous operational fried egg, and fried potatoes, the margarine and the marmalade and the bread that seems to be partially made of sand, and then to sleep.

The bomber crews were standing at the mess bar, which is a closet in the wall, drinking beer and waiting for breakfast. They were talking a little now, making private jokes and laughing easily at them. It was after seven in the morning, a dark cold unfriendly hour. Some of the men had saved their raid rations, a can of American orange juice and a chocolate bar, to eat now. They value them highly. The orange juice is fine, the chocolate bar is a treat. There are those who drink the orange juice and eat the chocolate early on, not wanting to be done out of them at least, no matter what happens.

The Lancasters looked like enormous deadly black birds going off into the night; somehow they looked different when they came back. The planes carried from this field 117,000 pounds of high explosive and the crews flew all night to drop the load as ordered. Now the trains would not run between France and Italy for a while, not on those bombed tracks anyhow. Here are the men who did it, with mussed hair and weary faces, dirty sweaters under their flying suits, sleep-bright eyes, making humble comradely little jokes, and eating their saved-up chocolate bars.

Three Poles

March 1944

"In my village," the man said, "the people stood in front of the church and cried, 'Is there a God? If there is, He would not allow these things to be.'" That was when the Germans came for the men and boys to send them away as slave labor. They took also what women they wanted; it was known that from these they would pick the girls to use in brothels on the Eastern Front. The other women would become work animals. In a nearby village, when the Germans made the Jews dig their own graves, and afterward shot them, the peasants ran away because they were too frightened to watch. Then the Germans confiscated all farms and gave them to German colonists; some Poles were allowed to remain as servants in their own houses, as serfs on their own land. The man went on speaking of these things slowly, in an ordinary voice.

The man had a good face, with a wide sensible mouth and gray eyes that, before, must have been laughing and kind. He could have been thirty-eight or forty-eight or more or less; his hair was brownish gray and he wore a new badly fitting suit. He had just come to London and he was ill, with his skin very yellow about the eyes. He had been four months en route from Poland, which is a quick journey these days. In life, that is before the German occupation, he was a farmer who owned some few acres in Silesia and he had stayed to slave for the Germans in his own fields. He became the chief of the underground in his district and now after four years, he had been sent from Poland as a representative to the Polish National Committee in London.

The Germans are very kind to animals, the man went on. They sent commissions to Poland to verify that the dogs and horses were living under good conditions. These same committees then arranged to send our old people to concentration camps, since the old are useless. The old die in these camps, the man said, as no one thinks it worthwhile to look after them. The Germans of course took all the young. There were 300,000 people deported from this part of Silesia. The land is not especially good, he said, though the coal mines are very valuable. The Germans sent their own colonists because they intended this part of Poland to remain German.

It is very interesting, the man said in his quiet unchanging voice, to see that the exploitation of our coal mines, under German rule, is greater than before the war; in the same way the forests are four times more productive. This is because the Germans conserve nothing; they cut down all the trees, mine all the veins. It is not their own property they are destroying. Then it is so easy with labor, he added, if workers are slaves and all you have to do is give them barely enough food to keep them alive. If a farm laborer is late for work, if a miner is sick a few days, his German boss can always report him to the Gestapo as a saboteur and the penalty for sabotage is death. The Germans do not tolerate labor problems, the man said, and looked up to make sure that he was understood.

In the morning we began work on the farms at four o'clock in the frozen dark and we finished when the Germans decided we had worked enough. They gave us whatever food we had; each Pole depended entirely on the German colonist who owned him. There was not much food. For breakfast we had potatoes and salt, for lunch vegetable soup, potatoes and vegetables, for supper potatoes. The Germans gave us three slices of bread a day and sometimes currant jam. We had no fats of course and no meat. It is not very much and always the same. The tuberculosis is bad now and especially among the children.

If you were lucky enough to live near forests or coal mines you could steal a little wood or coal, but if not then you would live in a house without heat. The Germans gave us some work clothes. We wore ersatz non-wool suits, wooden shoes, and had no underwear or socks. But people sill owned some clothing of their own from the time of peace, and on Sundays these clothes were shared in each family. If the father went out, the son stayed home: there was usually one jacket and one pair of trousers to a family. I don't know how the women dressed, he said thoughtfully. They tried to keep warm.

But we did not complain, the man said, we were happy to stay and work as serfs on our own farms. We would be there then, when the Day came, and we would catch the necessary Germans. We would also prevent the Germans from destroying our mines or burning our villages before they left. We have seen everything, the man said simply, the cattle trains where they kill the Jews, the executions of Jews in the village squares. The Germans never hid any of this; they wanted to terrorize us with their murders. They have killed millions of Jews, he said, and thousands of Polish families have been shot for trying to help Jews. If a man shelters a Jew, the Germans shoot him and his whole family; they published an order that any Pole who gave a piece of bread to a Jew would be killed. We used to leave bread or whatever we had in the forests, where the Jews were hiding. We could do nothing for our own people because they were gone into Germany, and we never knew where the girls were taken nor where they had our old people. One's parents, you understand, he said, one's daughters.

Just before I left, the man said, the Germans were changing. In the beginning they were so sure of winning the war that they did not even bother to work; the colonists were lazy and incompetent. But lately they tried to bribe us with food and to make friends. The German colonists began to cry on us saying, look at our side of it, if we lose the war we will have no farms to go back to. We said nothing, and we smiled to ourselves, and we are all waiting and ready and the Germans know it and they are afraid.

For an instant his face looked less stony and tired. The fear of the Germans, who had done nothing but torment others with fear, was a patiently waited-for reward. There had been unimaginable suffering and it would not go unrevenged. Now the man did not wish to talk anymore, having said all he wanted to say. He was not going to talk of himself since clearly he did not care about himself. In a way too it made him uneasy to speak so freely of these things which had been spoken of only in secret for years. London must have seemed very strange to him, with people speaking so much and without danger.

The younger man had been in London longer and he was used to talking by now. He was tall and dark, twenty-eight probably, good-looking, too thin and he spoke English with a soft almost

97

singing accent. Before the war he had been a student and he was writing his thesis in Paris when the war started. Like the Silesian farmer, nothing about his own life seemed to surprise the student, nothing of his own life seemed important. He spoke of the Germans in Poland as if he were describing a deadly disease which must be controlled and eradicated. Obviously it was hard dangerous work. The Poles had not invented the disease; they simply fought it.

It did not seem amazing to him that 85- to 100,000 children in the Warsaw district alone were going to secret schools. The Polish underground State paid the teachers and printed the text books, and carried education through from primary training to the final examinations and awarding of high school diplomas. If the Germans caught them, the teachers were shot; the parents of the students were sent to concentration camps, and the children who studied were deported for forced labor. But naturally the schools continued; the Germans could not be allowed to destroy all education in Poland. There were also technical schools in the country where young boys and girls learned to make grenades, derail trains, ruin motor transport, and—as a sort of academic side-line—studied the organization of the Gestapo so that they could combat it. Yes, there was a corps of specialists whose only job was to teach destruction. The schools were small and could easily change their location: their work was very valuable.

The young man spoke of the organization of the underground state saying that there were four branches of the government: the civil administration, the Army, the Parliament, the Judiciary. He himself acted as liaison officer between the Army and the other three branches of the government. It sounded so orderly and normal that you could make no picture of it, and then he said of course the officials of the government must always seem to be something else: a shop owner, an advertiser, a bank clerk, a milkman, working for a few hours at these ordinary jobs and equipped with the necessary German identity cards and ration books. We often had meetings inside the German factories, he said as if this were the most usual idea in the world.

He himself had jumped from a train, when the Germans deported him for forced labor to East Prussia. He returned to Warsaw, changed his appearance, his name and his papers and the man who jumped from the train was officially dead. He was a book-keeper in a German barrel factory during these years. The underground government sent him on missions around Poland, to make reports on the German New Order for Poles.

He knows nothing about book-keeping or barrel-making but he knows a great deal about the Germans as rulers because he studied them, as that was his job. Not many civil servants are called upon to report the functioning of German breeding farms where selected Polish girls are kept so as to augment the great Aryan race. Not many civil servants, in their normal course of duty, make eye-witness reports on the German policy of extermination for the Jews. This was perhaps the worst, the young man said, he had nightmares for weeks after that. There were Jewish women and children and old people, as well as men: they were packed 130 to a cattle car, there were 46 carloads of them, and the train was run 12 kilometers outside a town, and it took the Jews seven or eight hours to die. "The whole train was moving with their cries," he said.

Then it was necessary also to perform courier service from Poland to the outside world; it was another part of his job. The Germans caught him on his second trip out of Poland. "The young S.S. officer who questioned me was very nice," the Pole said, "He told me we only want to be friends with you; we wish to know who the leaders of your movement are so that we can co-operate with them." The S.S. man asked questions and as each question remained unanswered another German, who stood behind his chair, beat him scientifically with a rubber truncheon on the exposed skull bones behind the ear. One cannot imagine what this pain would be, but after four days the young Pole feared the damage to his brain, so he opened the veins in his wrists. The Germans found him too soon and, scientific always, gave him blood transfusions as they still wanted him alive. Later he escaped from a German prison hospital and went on with his duties as a civil servant.

In his own eyes there is no more to the story than that. He had spoken of himself reluctantly and with the greatest indifference: he spoke of what the Germans were doing to his country very calmly, relating facts, and he spoke without hate. It is possible that disgust can be greater than hate; that disgust can be the strongest emotion of all. The Germans were a disease that had spread over Europe; if one was healthy in spirit one could only feel disgust for this sickness.

In their quiet factual voices, the two Poles had been telling of horrors which to them were the very climate of life. But when the Jew, speaking in the same way, began to talk of the Ghetto in Warsaw even the Poles were appalled. This man wore British battle dress and is now a private in the army here. Before the war, he was an official of the League of Nations, a lawyer, a traveled cultivated man who had lived the life he wished to lead. He left all this freely and went back to the Ghetto in Warsaw and he lived there until the magnificent desperate battle at the end. The Poles helped him to escape to France because his knowledge could serve those of his people who were still alive in Europe. He worked in France as long as he could and then came to England to join the army. He was thirty-six years old and he had seen too much and it showed in his eyes.

The Jews fled from other parts of Poland to Warsaw; the Germans rounded up all the Jews in Warsaw and drove them into the Ghetto: then they built a wall ten feet high and sealed off this corner of the city. Inside the wall 350,000 people were herded together. They were denied the right to go outside the wall and work. As no one can grow food from cobblestones they were kept alive by the rations the Germans allowed them. So there was hunger, tightening around them every day. Hunger is a slow torment and can be used to destroy the dignity of man. You can throw bread into a street and watch starved people scrambling for it, and it is a funny sight and young uniformed Germans always had that to laugh about. If there is hunger and people living crowded into unheated houses and no way to maintain the sanitation system of a city, there comes disease. Typhus spread through the Ghetto. The Germans did not allow doctors or medicines to be given the Jews. In the mornings, the Jew said, people went out and covered the corpses in the street with newspapers. It was all they could do for the dead. Later the German trucks would drive through the streets and collect the bodies.

The Germans also organized shooting parties, the Jew said. He spoke of this wryly as if he were ashamed to repeat it. Young German soldiers would prowl through the Ghetto shooting at anyone they saw and the Jews fled from them like hunted animals.

They never killed many that way, the Jew said, but it amused them. All the time, the Jews waited in the Ghetto, never knowing what was going to happen to them. All the time they hoped. They could not believe they had been isolated so that it would be easier, more efficient to destroy them. They could not accept with their minds that every Jew in Warsaw was meant to die.

But they did know this finally, having watched hunger and disease and the execution of hostages and murder in the streets. They looked at the wall around them and they realized exactly what it meant. They then decided to fight, with what few smuggled arms they could get. It was obvious from the beginning that the battle of the Ghetto was a mass suicide: but it was a beautiful gesture and the last one the Jews could make. The people in the Ghetto never doubted that the Allies would win the war, the Jew said, but they knew it would be too late for them. It is a hard thing to die knowing that help is coming.

He spoke now for the dead, for two and a half million Jews who were killed in Poland alone. He had watched the greatest organized destruction the world has known, and he refused to believe in it. His people could not be destroyed. The Jews are a nation, he said, they must have a country. They must never be driven over the earth again. They must have a home. This colossal suffering could not be wasted. He was thinking of the future; he was thinking of the world that would be safe and honorable and free. It was amazing that he never commented on the Germans at all.

Poland seemed dreadfully far away, dark and silent, and the Germans had tried to make it into a cemetery. But here were these men, and in Poland there are tens of thousands of others like them and in four and a half years of organized repression, the Germans have never been able to stop them. It is almost impossible for us to imagine life in Poland but these men without names can testify to that life, and speak for the silenced millions of their own people. It is not impossible to imagine that the Germans who have ruled Poland and never conquered it must now be afraid.

Visit Italy

February 1944

The French soldier driving the jeep had large dark sad eyes. He was small, thin and dirty and he looked ill. The windshield and the top of the jeep were down and the snow had changed to hail. The road circling up the mountains was narrow and slippery. Wind blew across the gray stone sides of the mountains and over the snow peaks and drove the hail into our faces.

The little jeep driver was having a bad time, as was everyone else on the road. From time to time we would pass a completely unnecessary sign: a skull-and-bones painted on a board, with underneath the phrase in French: "The enemy sees you." No one needed to be warned. There you were, on a roller-coaster road freezing to death, and if the enemy couldn't see you, he was blind; he was sitting right across there, on that other snow mountain.

The jeep driver spoke with sudden bitter mockery. *"Visitez l'Italie!"* he said.

There used to be tourist posters in France, in all the railroad stations, showing a sunstruck and enchanting glimpse of country with a dark-haired girl eating grapes or maybe just laughing, and the posters urged, "Visit Italy."

Now we were visiting Italy. It was a small, peculiar and unhealthy piece of Italy—the French front. It was a bulge of mountains; the French held these mountains, and opposite them, on higher mountains, were the Germans. The mountains to the right were occupied by the Poles, and to the left, around Cassino, were the Americans. The Italian front is very curious anyhow. One day we figured there were twenty races and nationalities stretched across Italy from the Mediterranean to the Adriatic, all fighting the Germans. The French held the highest mountains of all: this front. It was colder here than anywhere else—though it was cold enough everywhere—and no one believed this wind would ever blow at less than gale force, and just when you began to hope that spring might come it would snow again.

Before he came to this naked road, the jeep driver had been a barman in Casablanca. Now he said, through stiff, cold lips: "Have you ever had an Alexander cocktail, Mademoiselle?"

We passed a burned American tank, rounded a curve and saw two trucks which had plunged down a ravine and were hanging almost perpendicularly against the side of the mountain. An Alexander is a horrible, sweet drink made with *crème de cacao.*

"Yes, indeed," I said, holding a tin hat in front of my face as a shield against the hail.

"I do not mean to brag," the Frenchman said, "but I made the best Alexanders in Casablanca."

Then we were silent because it was too hard to talk. Perhaps he was thinking of his bar, or the small café he hoped to have in France after the war. I was thinking about that wonderful phrase, "Visit Italy."

Coming north from Naples, you drive in a steady stream of khaki-colored traffic: trucks and jeeps, command cars and ambulances, wrecking cars and trucks and tank destroyers and munitions carriers. There is no end to the traffic, and if you are unlucky you will find yourself behind a convoy which rumbles along like marching elephants, and, since the roads are narrow and the traffic is thick both ways, you are forced to learn patience.

Along the sides of the road are endless tent camps pitched in the mud lakes that form under olive trees or in the deep gluey mud of open fields. One soldier is always shaving under the forbidding sky, with care and a comic solemnity and quite alone. Naked to the waist in the cold, he wages the losing battle to keep clean. Acres of cars are parked, with men working on broken motors in a misery of mud. There never was so much wheeled transport, you think; all Italy seems to be moving.

When you first pass through the villages they are incredible; it is not possible that once these places stood up foursquare and people lived in them. No cyclone could have done as thorough a job as high explosive has. After a while you do not even notice the sliced houses, the landslides of rubble, the torn roofs.

The roads are bordered with telephone wires, looking like thick, twisted vines in the jungle; dozens of wires, draped and hung over what trees remain, or simply trailing on the ground. Then there are the neatly placed tent hospitals, and suddenly out of a side road tanks appear, loud, blind and waiting for nothing.

As you get nearer the front, Italy becomes an even stranger country to visit. Three Italian children take turns swinging on a piece of old telephone wire hung from a tree in an ammunition dump. Blown bridges rest like boxcars in the river beds. Jeeps pass, with their names painted on them: Calamity II, Death Dodger, Betty Ann.

In a hollow below the climbing road, Italian women are washing clothes at an old stone trough, and six-wheeled trucks plow somehow up the hill through mud that looks like churned brown cement. The echo of shell explosions bangs crazily against the mountains. You pass through a mud flat, where nothing grows except guns, and two French batteries of 155s open up against the Germans, who are on a mountain you cannot see, and everyone on the road is briefly deafened. If you are right under the guns, you open your mouth and breathe hard.

The road keeps climbing and now there are soldiers' camps on the upright sides of the mountain. They are French native troops wearing American uniforms. Suddenly the road turns and before you there is a wilderness of mountains, crushed against one another, rolling higher and higher to the north, with the snow very clean on them. It is the most beautiful view of all—so beautiful that everyone notices it, though everyone dislikes it, for the Germans are there.

At the turning, a French colonial soldier wearing a long, striped robe and a turban is standing on the roof of a pillbox, inspecting the German mountain range. He stands like a statue, as if he had just found this nice place to rest when he had some free time to himself. From now on, you circle down to the Rapido, and the war gets smaller and you see fewer people and less transport. You begin to hear and see with fierce concentration, holding your body tight together.

Visit Italy, indeed! It is all this and so much more. It would take a rare kind of guidebook to tell you the sights of Italy alone. And how about the new tourists, the soldiery? How will you ever know about the twenty races and nationalities who fight as allies in Italy? How will you ever know all they have done and seen and felt and survived? Some of them will write about this campaign after the war, and that will be the good writing. But perhaps it is impossible to understand anything unless it happened to you yourself.

The jeep driver and I were going to San Elia, which used to be a town and is now a mass of blown-up masonry. Two French first-aid posts operate here. They are stationed in dirty basements that have beautiful thick walls. Otherwise there is no use for the town; it is only a place that troops and transport pass through, a place to be shelled whenever the Germans think it profitable.

Across the Rapido from the town is the Belvedere, a bleak gray stone mountain that the French took. What the French take they stay on, and it is quiet on the mountains now. A sizable unit went into the attack and hardly more than twenty percent were able to walk off the mountain, but the French hold it, and that is what they want. Because each mountain they take, at whatever cost, is a mountain nearer home.

The French are earning their way home and they do not complain. They know exactly what they are doing and they are doing it superbly. They are fighting for the honor of France, which is not just a phrase, as you might think, but the personal, undying pride of every one of them. And they are fighting to get home to a country cleansed of Germans. Home means a street, a house, a face that has not been seen for too many years. Home means the lovely sky and the lovely land of France.

The mountains of Italy are horrible; to attack always against heights held by well-entrenched and well-trained enemy troops is surely the worst sort of war. Nothing can help the infantry much in mountains: Germans dug into the stone sides of these cliffs can survive the heaviest shelling. Tanks cannot operate. So at last it is the courage and determination of a Frenchman against the courage and determination of a German. The French have been taking their objectives.

The jeep driver belonged to a *compagnie de ramassage*, which means literally a pick-up company. His outfit has to collect the wounded from the sides of these mountains, carry them down on stretchers and drive them back to base hospitals over roads which would be dangerous even if no one shelled them. In these mountains it is not unusual for a wounded man to be carried for ten hours before he reaches a road and a waiting ambulance. The present headquarters of his company was one of the basements in San Elia. We drove rapidly past the two known evil points at the entry of the town—there are always the places that are certain to be shelled, and then there are the surprise places.

An ambulance was parked inside the front door of the first-aid station. The stretcher-bearers slept on straw on the floor next to the ambulances. Down a dark, stony passageway was the room where the doctor worked. A fine-faced, cocoa-colored soldier from Martinique lay on the improvised operating table. He had very bright eyes and he was quite silent but there was this odd, birdlike curiosity in his eyes. Across the room a white soldier sat on a chair, not moving, but looking at his friend. Under the blanket you could see that the Martiniquan had only one leg. They had just been brought in.

These two were repairing a telephone line beside the Rapido when a shell landed near them. A sliver of the shell pierced the left eye of the Frenchman, another fragment almost severed the leg of the Martiniquan. The blinded man made a tourniquet of telephone wire to stop his friend's hemorrhage, and then, because the torn leg was hanging by skin and tendons only, he cut the leg off with his clasp knife. After this he carried his comrade to the road and went for help.

The Martiniquan kept saying in his soft, old-fashioned French, "I love my friend very much but he should not have cut off my leg."

The soldier who had only one eye refused treatment until he was sure his comrade was well cared for, then he accepted a shot of morphine. Nothing could be done for his eye; it would have to be taken out at the base hospital.

There were no more wounded, so the doctor, the transport officer and I went down to their living quarters, a very cold room in another cellar. Half the dirt floor had been covered with old doors to keep the damp from the mattresses they slept on. There was a table with a marble top, an iron stove that barely worked, two kerosene lamps, four uncertain chairs, an upright piano with planks for legs, a radio, some mice, a pervading odor of damp and good thick walls.

We sat with a bottle of Italian cognac, which tastes like perfume and gasoline, and waited for dinner. An American AMG (Allied Military Government) major was in town with his aide. They had evacuated the entire civil population and were leaving for another village in the morning, but tonight they were coming to dine. They would presumably arrive before the evening shelling started.

We got Switzerland on the radio in order to learn what was happening in Cassino, seven kilometers away. We also tuned in on Berlin to hear what they were giving out, and they announced that they would now play the music of a grenadier regiment fighting on the Italian front. These were the German troops two kilometers away from our cellar. "It is not bad music," the transport officer said, "except for all that boom-boom they always have."

The two Americans arrived and were warmly greeted. The evening shelling started while we ate our C rations. The French doctor told the American major that there were three civilian corpses in the church, and the American said, "My God! Are they still there? It's too awful the way the Italians won't take the trouble to bury one another." The twenty-year-old soldier who was the major's aide said he was going to write a book entitled *My Life on a Bull's-eye*. This reminded the French of a wonderful American book they had once read, called *Gentlemen Prefer Blondes,* and they rocked with laughter as they retold each other all the jokes.

Then a soldier came in and said someone was wounded by a mine in a field near the Rapido, so the transport officer went out to get the wounded man. The Americans went home after a while. They lived in a house that always seemed to get shells in the garden but never in the building, and they were counting on this.

The doctor said it was terrible about the mine fields; they no longer allowed anyone to walk into a field to pull out wounded men, because one day seven men were killed trying to get one man out. The mines were perhaps the worst of all. Now one just threw a rope to the wounded man and dragged him back to the swept, safe ground.

"Think of it," he said, "for years after this war, people will be killed all over Europe in such fields; men will be killed sowing their wheat and children will be killed playing. It is horrible. Everything about war is too horrible to consider."

The transport officer came back after a while and said the man was dead.

That night I lay in my cot and listened to the mice and the shells, and thought about the French in Italy. It is impossible to describe the hardships of their life; it would take too long, and the words wouldn't mean anything. They eat the same food all the time, the universally loathed C and K rations; they are never warm; they are never sure to be dry; they have no possible relaxation. They watch their comrades die and know how entirely expendable they are, and that they have no replacements.

I remember the dead girl ambulance driver, lying on a bed in a tent hospital, with her hands crossed on a sad bunch of flowers, and her hair very neat and blond, and her face simply asleep. She had been killed on the road below San Elia, and her friends, the other French girls who drove ambulances, were coming to pay their last respects. They were tired and awkward in their bulky, muddy clothes. They passed slowly before the dead girl and looked with pity and great quietness at her face, and went back to their ambulances.

I remember the troops on the roads, tough and hard, watching the Italian refugees pass by with their usual bundles, the usual blank eyes and the usual slow, weary walk. There was no kindness in the French soldiers. One man said to himself but speaking for everyone, "There were refugees on all the roads in France. Each one in his turn."

I remembered the snow-topped mountain called La Mainarde, and the deep, beautifully placed German machine-gun posts, and I thought of the Frenchmen who had taken this mountain. They are dying very fast, but they always go on to the higher and higher mountains.

You hear a lot of rot, traveling around the world. You hear people say France is finished, the French are no good, look at their politics, look at the collapse of France, they will never be a great people again. So I lay in my cot and thought that anyone who speaks or thinks like that is a fool, and if he wants to know how foolish he is, he'd better visit Italy.

The First Hospital Ship*

June 1944

There were four hundred and twenty-two bunks covered with new blankets, and a bright, clean, well-equipped operating room, never before used. Great cans marked "Whole Blood" stood on the decks. Plasma bottles and supplies of drugs and bales of bandages were stored in handy places. Everything was ready and any moment the big empty hospital ship would be leaving for France.

The ship itself was painfully white. The endless varied ships clotted in this English invasion port were gray or camouflaged and they seemed to have the right idea. We, on the other hand, were all fixed up like a sitting pigeon. Our ship was snowy white with a green line running along the sides below the deck rail, and with many bright new red crosses painted on the hull and painted flat on the boat deck. We were to travel alone, and there was not so much as a pistol on board in the way of armament, and neither the English crew and ship's officers nor the American medical personnel had any notion of what happened to large conspicuous white ships when they appeared at a war, though everyone knew the Geneva agreement concerning such ships and everyone wistfully hoped that the Germans would take the said agreement seriously.

There were six nurses aboard. They came from Texas and Michigan and California and Wisconsin, and three weeks ago they

*D-Day was June 4, 1944. This report concerns the three following days, then known as D+1, D+2, D+3.

109

were in the U.S. completing their training for this overseas assignment. They had been prepared to work on a hospital train, which would mean caring for wounded in sensible, steady railway carriages that move slowly through the green English countryside. Instead of which they found themselves on a ship, and they were about to move across the dark, cold green water of the Channel. This sudden switch in plans was simply part of the day's work and each one, in her own way, got through the grim business of waiting for the unknown to start, as elegantly as she could. It was very elegant indeed, especially if you remembered that no one aboard had ever been on a hospital ship before, so the helpful voice of experience was lacking.

We had pulled out of the harbor in the night, but we crossed by daylight and the morning seemed longer than other mornings. The captain never left the bridge and, all alone and beautifully white, we made our way through a mine-swept lane in the Channel. The only piece of news we had, so far, was that the two hospital ships which preceded us struck mines on their way over, fortunately before they were loaded with wounded soldiers and without serious damage to the personnel aboard. Everyone silently hoped that three would be a lucky number; and we waited very hard; and there was nothing much to see except occasional ships passing at a distance.

Then we saw the coast of France and suddenly we were in the midst of the armada of the invasion. People will be writing about this sight for a hundred years and whoever saw it will never forget it. First it seemed incredible; there could not be so many ships in the world. Then it seemed incredible as a feat of planning; if there were so many ships, what genius it required to get them here, what amazing and unimaginable genius. After the first shock of wonder and admiration, one began to look around and see separate details. There were destroyers and battleships and transports, a floating city of huge vessels anchored before the green cliffs of Normandy. Occasionally you would see a gun flash or perhaps only hear a distant roar, as naval guns fired far over those hills. Small craft beetled around in a curiously jolly way. It looked like a lot of fun to race from shore to ships in snub-nosed boats beating up the spray. It was no fun at all, considering the mines and obstacles that remained in the water, the sunken tanks with only their radio antennae showing above water, the drowned bodies that still

110

floated past. On an LCT near us washing was hung up on a line, and between the loud explosions of mines being detonated on the beach dance music could be heard coming from its radio. Barrage balloons, always looking like comic toy elephants, bounced in the high wind above the massed ships, and invisible planes droned behind the gray ceiling of cloud. Troops were unloading from big ships to heavy cement barges or to light craft, and on the shore, moving up four brown roads that scarred the hillside, our tanks clanked slowly and steadily forward.

Then we stopped noticing the invasion, the ships, the ominous beach, because the first wounded had arrived. An LCT drew alongside our ship, pitching in the waves; a soldier in a steel helmet shouted up to the crew at the aft rail, and a wooden box looking like a lidless coffin was lowered on a pulley, and with the greatest difficulty, bracing themselves against the movement of their boat, the men on the LCT laid a stretcher inside the box. The box was raised to our deck and out of it was lifted a man who was closer to being a boy than a man, dead white and seemingly dying. The first wounded man to be brought to that ship for safety and care was a German prisoner.

Everything happened at once. We had six water ambulances, light motor launches, which swung down from the ship's side and could be raised the same way when full of wounded. They carried six litter cases apiece or as many walking wounded as could be crowded into them. Now they were being lowered, with shouted orders: "That beach over there were they've got two red streamers up." "Just this side of Easy Red." We lay at anchor halfway between those now famous and unhealthy beaches, Easy Red and Dog Red. "Take her in slow." "Those double round things that look like flat spools are mines." "You won't clear any submerged tanks, so look sharp." "Ready?" "Lower her!"

The captain came down from the bridge to watch this. He was feeling cheerful, and he now remarked, "I got us in all right but God knows how we'll ever get out." He gestured toward the ships that were as thick around us as cars in a parking lot. "Worry about that some other time."

The stretcher-bearers, who were part of the American medical personnel, started on their long back-breaking job. By the end of that trip their hands were padded with blisters and they were practically hospital cases themselves. For the wounded had to be carried from the shore into our own water ambulances or into other craft, raised over the side, and then transported down the winding stairs of this converted pleasure ship to the wards. The ship's crew became volunteer stretcher-bearers instantly. Wounded were pouring in now, hauled up in the lidless coffin or swung aboard in the motor ambulances; and finally an LST tied alongside and made itself into a sort of landing jetty, higher than the light craft that ran the wounded to us, but not as high as our deck. So the wounded were lifted by men standing on the LST, who raised the stretchers high above their heads and handed them up to men on our deck, who caught hold of the stretcher handles. It was a fast, terrifying bucket-brigade system, but it worked.

Belowstairs all partitions had been torn out and for three decks the inside of the ship was a vast ward with double tiers of bunks. The routine inside the ship ran marvelously, though four doctors, six nurses and about fourteen medical orderlies were very few people to care for four hundred wounded men. From two o'clock one afternoon until the ship docked in England again the next evening at seven, none of the medical personnel stopped work. And besides plasma and blood transfusions, re-dressing of wounds, examinations, administering of sedatives or opiates or oxygen and all the rest, operations were performed all night long. Only one soldier died on that ship and he had come aboard as a hopeless case.

It will be hard to tell you of the wounded, there were so many of them. There was no time to talk; there was too much else to do. They had to be fed, as most of them had not eaten for two days; shoes and clothing had to be cut off; they wanted water; the nurses and orderlies, working like demons, had to be found and called quickly to a bunk where a man suddenly and desperately needed attention; plasma bottles must be watched; cigarettes had to be lighted and held for those who could not use their hands; it seemed to take hours to pour hot coffee, via the spout of a teapot, into a mouth that just showed through bandages.

But the wounded talked among themselves and as time went on we got to know them, by their faces and their wounds, not their names. They were a magnificent enduring bunch of men. Men smiled who were in such pain that all they really can have wanted to do was turn their heads away and cry, and men made jokes when they needed their strength just to survive. And all of them looked after each other, saying, "Give that boy a drink of water," or "Miss, see that Ranger over there, he's in bad shape, could you go to him?" All through the ship men were asking after other men by name, anxiously, wondering if they were on board and how they were doing.

On A deck in a bunk by the wall lay a very young lieutenant. He had a bad chest wound and his face was white and he lay too still. Suddenly he raised himself on his elbow and looked straight ahead of him, as if he did not know where he was. His eyes were full of horror and he did not speak. Later he spoke. He had been wounded the first day, had lain out in a field and then crawled back to our lines, sniped at by the Germans. He realized now that a German, badly wounded also in the chest, shoulder and legs, lay in the bunk behind him. The gentle-faced boy said very softly, because it was hard to speak, "I'd kill him if I could move." After that he did not speak for a long time; he was given oxygen and later operated on, so that he could breathe.

The man behind him was a nineteen-year-old Austrian. He had fought for a year in Russia and half a year in France; he had been home for six days during this time. I thought he would die when he first came on board, but he got better. In the early morning hours he asked whether wounded prisoners were exchanged, would he ever get home again? I told him that I did not know about these arrangements but that he had nothing to fear, as he could see. The Austrian said, "Yes, yes." Then he said, "So many wounded men, all wounded, all want to get home. Why have we ever fought each other?" Perhaps because he came from a gentler race his eyes were full of tears. He was the only wounded German prisoner on board who showed any normal human reaction to this disaster.

An American soldier on that same deck had a head wound so horrible that he was not moved. Nothing could be done for him and anything, any touch, would have made him worse. The next morning he was drinking coffee. His eyes looked very dark and strange, as if he had been a long way away, so far away that he almost could not get back. His face was set in lines of weariness and pain, but when asked how he felt, he said he was okay. He was never known to say anything more; he asked for nothing and made no complaint, and perhaps he will live too.

On the next deck there were many odd and wonderful men who were less badly wounded and talked more. It was all professional talk; where they had landed, at what time, what opposition they had met, how they had got out, when they were wounded, how that happened. They spoke of the snipers, and there was endless talk about the women snipers, none of the talk very clear but everyone believing it. There were no French officers with these men, who could have interpreted, and the Americans never knew what the villagers were saying. Two men who thought they were being volubly invited into an old woman's house to eat dinner were actually being warned of snipers in the attic; they somehow caught on to this fact in time. They were all baffled by the French and surprised by how much food there was in Normandy, forgetting that Normandy is one of the great food-producing areas of France. They thought the girls in the villages were amazingly well dressed. Everything was confused and astounding: first there were the deadly bleak beaches and then the villages where they were greeted with flowers and cookies and often snipers and boobytraps.

A French boy of seventeen lay in one of the bunks; he had been wounded in the back by a shell fragment. He lived and worked on his father's land, but he said the Germans had burned their house as they left. Two of the American boys in bunks alongside were worried about him. They were afraid he'd be scared, a civilian kid all alone and in pain and not knowing any English and going to a strange country. They ignored their respective smashed knee and smashed shoulder and worried about the French kid. The French boy was very much a man and very tight-lipped, and he made no complaints and kept his anxiety inside himself though it showed in his eyes. His family was still there in the battle zone and he did not know what had happened to them or how he would ever get back. The American soldiers said, "You tell that kid he's a better soldier than that Heinie in the bunk next to him."

We did not like this Heinie who was eighteen years old and the most demanding Master Race aboard. Finally there was a crisp little scene when he told the orderly to move him as he was uncomfortable and the orderly said no, he would bleed if moved, and when I explained the German said angrily, "How long, then, am I to lie here in pain in this miserable position?" I asked the orderly what to say and the orderly answered, "Tell him there are a lot of fine boys on this ship in worse pain in worse positions." The American soldiers in the bunks around said, "What a Heinie,"

114

wearily, and then they began wondering how they'd find their old units again and how soon they'd get mail.

When night came, the water ambulances were still churning in to the beach looking for wounded. Someone on an LCT had shouted out that there were maybe a hundred scattered along there somewhere. It was essential to try to get them aboard before the nightly air raid and before the dangerous dark cold could eat into their hurt bodies. Going in to shore, unable to see, and not knowing this tricky strip of water, was slow work. Two of the launch crew, armed with boat hooks, hung over the side of the boat and stared at the black water, looking for obstacles, sunken vehicles, mines, and kept the hooks ready to push us off the sand as we came closer in. For the tides were a nasty business too, and part of the time wounded had to be ferried out to the water ambulances on men's shoulders, and part of the time the water ambulances simply grounded and stuck on the beach together with other craft, stranded by the fast-moving sea.

We finally got onto a cement troop barge near the beach called Easy Red. The water ambulance could not come inshore near enough to be of any use at this point, so it left us to look for a likelier anchorage farther down. We waded ashore in water to our waists, having agreed that we would assemble the wounded from this area on board a beached LST and wait until the tide allowed the water ambulance to come back and call for us. It was almost dark by now and there was a terrible feeling of working against time.

Everyone was violently busy on that crowded dangerous shore. The pebbles were the size of melons and we stumbled up a road that a huge road shovel was scooping out. We walked with the utmost care between the narrowly placed white tape lines that marked the mine-cleared path, and headed for a tent marked with a Red Cross just behind the beach. Ducks* and tanks and trucks were moving down this narrow rocky road and one stepped just a little out of their way, but not beyond the tapes. The dust that rose in the gray night light seemed like the fog of war itself. Then we got off on the grass and it was perhaps the most surprising of all the day's surprises to smell the sweet smell of summer grass, a smell

*Amphibious Jeeps.

of cattle and peace and sun that had warmed the earth some other time when summer was real.

Inside the Red Cross tent two tired unshaven dirty polite young men said that the trucks were coming in here with the wounded and where did we want to have them unloaded? We explained the problem of the tides and said the best thing was to run the trucks down to that LST there and carry the wounded aboard, under the canvas roof covering, and we would get them off as soon as anything floated. At this point a truck jolted up and the driver shouted out a question and was told to back and turn. He did not need to be told to do this carefully and not get off the mine-cleared area. The Red Cross men said they didn't know whether wounded would be coming in all night or not—it was pretty tough to transport them by road in the dark; anyway they'd send everything down to our agreed meeting place and everyone said, well good luck fella, and we left. No one wasted time talking around there. You had a feeling of fierce and driven activity, with the night only being harder to work in than the day.

We returned to our small unattractive stretch of the beach and directed the unloading of this truck. The tide was coming in and there was a narrow strip of water between the landing ramp of the LST and the shore. The wounded were carried carefully and laid on the deck inside the great whale's-mouth cavern of the LST. After that there was a pause, with nothing to do. Some American soldiers came up and began to talk. This had been an ugly piece of beach from the beginning and they were still here, living in foxholes and supervising the unloading of supplies. They spoke of snipers in the hills a hundred yards or so behind the beach, and no one lighted a cigarette. They spoke of not having slept at all, but they seemed pleased by the discovery that you could go without sleep and food and still function all right. Everyone agreed that the beach was a stinker and it would be a great pleasure to get the hell out of here sometime. Then there was the usual inevitable comic American conversation: "Where're you from?" This always fascinates me; there is no moment when an American does not have time to look for someone who knows his hometown. We talked about Pittsburgh and Rosemont Pa. and Chicago and Cheyenne, not saying much except that they were sure swell places and a damn sight better than this beach. One of the soldiers remarked that they had a nice little foxhole about fifty yards inland and we were very welcome there when the air raid started if we didn't mind eating sand, which was unavoidable in their nice little foxhole.

A stretcher-bearer from the hospital ship thanked them for their kind invitation and said that on the other hand we had guests aboard the LST and we would have to stay home this evening. I wish I had ever known his name because I would like to write it down here. He was one of the best and jolliest boys I've met any place, any time. He joked no matter what happened, and toward the end of that night we really began to enjoy ourselves. There is a point where you feel yourself so small and helpless in such an enormous insane nightmare of a world, that you cease to give a hoot about anything and you renounce care and start laughing.

He went off to search for the water ambulances and returned to say there wasn't a sign of them, which meant they couldn't get inshore yet and we'd just have to wait and hope they could find this spot when it was black night. If they never found this place the LST would float later, and the British captain said he would run our wounded out to the hospital ship, though it would not be for hours. Suddenly our flak started going up at the far end of the beach and it was beautiful, twinkling as it burst in the sky, and the tracers were as lovely as they always are—and no one took pleasure from the beauty of the scene. "We've had it now," said the stretcher-bearer. "There isn't any place we can put those wounded." I asked one of the soldiers, just for interest's sake, what they did in case of air raids and he said, well, you could go to a foxhole if you had time, but on the other hand there wasn't really much to do. So we stood and watched and there was altogether too much flak for comfort. We could not hear the planes nor hear any bomb explosions but as everyone knows flak is a bad thing to have fall on your head.

The soldiers now drifted off on their own business and we boarded the LST to keep the wounded company. It seemed a specially grim note to be wounded in action and then have to lie helpless under a strip of canvas while any amount of steel fragments, to say nothing of bombs, could drop on you and complete the job. The stretcher-bearer and I said to each other gloomily that as an air-raid shelter far better things than the hold of an LST had been devised, and we went inside, not liking any of it and feeling miserably worried about our wounded.

The wounded looked pretty bad and lay very still; and in the light of one bare bulb, which hung from a girder, we could not see them well. Then one of them began to moan and he said something. He was evidently conscious enough to notice this ghastly racket that was going on above us. The Oerlikons of our LST now opened fire and the noise inside the steel hold was as if your own eardrums were being drilled with a rivet. The wounded man called out again and I realized that he was speaking German. We checked up then and found that we had an LST full of wounded Germans and the stretcher-bearer said, "Well, that is just dandy, by golly, if that isn't the payoff." Then he said, "If anything hits this ship, dammit, they deserve it."

The ack-ack lifted a bit and the stretcher-bearer climbed to the upper deck, like Sister Anne on the tower, to see where in God's name those water ambulances were. I clambered like a very awkward monkey up a ladder to the galley to get some coffee and so missed the spectacle of two German planes falling like fiery comets from the sky. They hit the beach to the right and left of us and burned in huge bonfires which lighted up the shore. The beach, in this light, looked empty of human life, cluttered with dark square shapes of tanks and trucks and jeeps and ammunition boxes and all the motley equipment of war. It looked like a vast uncanny black-and-red flaring salvage dump, whereas once upon a time people actually went swimming here for pleasure.

Our LST crew was delighted because they believed they had brought down one of the German planes and everyone felt cheerful about the success of the ack-ack. A soldier shouted from shore that we had shot down four planes in all and it was nice work, by God. The wounded were silent and those few who had their eyes open had very frightened eyes. They seemed to be listening with their eyes, and fearing what they would hear.

The night, like the morning, went on longer than other nights. Our water ambulances found us, and there was a lot of good incomprehensible Cockney talk among the boatmen while the wounded were loaded from the now floating LST to the small, bucking launch. We set out, happy because we were off the beach and because the wounded would be taken where they belonged. The trip across that obstacle-studded piece of water was a chatty affair, due to the boat crew. "Crikey, mate, wot yer trying ter do, ram a destroyer?" And "By God, man, keep an eye in yer head for God's sake that's a tank radio pole." To which another answered,

"Expect me to see a bloody piece of grass in this dark?" So, full of conversation, we zig-zagged back to the hospital ship and were at last swung aboard.

The raid had been hard on the wounded in the wards of the ship, because of the terrible helplessness of being unable to move. The ship seemed to lie directly under a cone of ack-ack fire, and perhaps it would have been easier if the wounded had heard the German planes, so that, at least through their ears, they would know what was happening. The American medical personnel, most of whom had never been in an air raid, tranquilly continued their work, asked no questions, showed no sign even of interest in this uproar, and handed out confidence as if it were a solid thing like bread.

If anyone had come fresh to that ship in the night, someone unwounded, not attached to the ship, he would have been appalled. It began to look entirely Black-Hole-of-Calcutta, because it was airless and ill lit. Piles of bloody clothing had been cut off and dumped out of the way in corners; coffee cups and cigarette stubs littered the decks; plasma bottles hung from cords, and all the fearful surgical apparatus for holding broken bones made shadows on the walls. There were wounded who groaned in their sleep or called out and there was the soft steady hum of conversation among the wounded who could not sleep. That is the way it would have looked to anyone seeing it fresh—a ship carrying a load of pain, with everyone waiting for daylight, everyone hoping for the anchor to be raised, everyone longing for England. It was that but it was something else too; it was a safe ship no matter what happened to it. We were together and we counted on each other. We knew that from the British captain to the pink-cheeked little London mess boy every one of the ship's company did his job tirelessly and well. The wounded knew that the doctors and nurses and orderlies belonged to them utterly and would not fail them. And all of us knew that our own wounded were good men and that with their amazing help, their selflessness and self-control, we would get through all right.

The wounded looked much better in the morning. The human machine is the most delicate and rare of all, and it is obviously built to survive, if given half a chance. The ship moved steadily across the Channel and we could feel England coming nearer. Then the coast came into sight and the green of England looked quite different from the way it had looked only two days ago; it looked cooler and clearer and wonderfully safe. The beaches along this coast were only lovely yellow sand. The air of England flowed down through the wards and the wounded seemed to feel it. The sound of their voices brightened and sharpened, and they began making dates with each other for when they would be on convalescent leave in London.

We saw again the great armada of the invasion, waiting or moving out toward France. This vast directed strength seemed more like an act of nature than a thing men alone could manage. The captain shouted down from the bridge, "Look at it! By God, just look at it!"

American ambulance companies were waiting on the pier, the same efficient swift colored troops I had seen working on the piers and landing ramps before we left. On the quay there were conferences of important shore personages and our captain and the chief medical officer; and a few of us, old-timers by now, leaned over the rail and joked about being back in the paper-work department again. Everyone felt happy and you could see it in all their faces. The head nurse, smiling though gray with weariness, said, "We'll do it better next time."

As the first wounded were carried from the ship the chief medical officer, watching them, said, "Made it." That was the great thing. Now they would restock their supplies, clean the ship, cover the beds with fresh blankets, sleep whatever hours they could, and then they would go back to France. But this first trip was done; this much was to the good; they had made it.

The Carpathian Lancers*

July 1944

This field grew huge dead cattle. They lay with their legs pointing up, and their open eyes were milky and enormous, and the air stank of their swollen bodies. We could not tell what had killed them because we were driving too fast through a long tunnel of dust which was the road. Aside from the hideous dead animals everything looked lovely, with the Adriatic a flat turquoise blue and the sky a flat china blue and the neat green hilly country of the Marche ahead. The Major drove as usual like mad. There was plenty of dust in Italy all the time, but when he drove a roaring surf of dust beat out behind us.

We were going up to have a look at the front before lunch.

We came to a village where the armored cars of the Third Squadron were stationed. They stood in the narrow side streets and were covered with leafy branches, had a pair of German steel helmets over each set of headlights, and flew the small red-and-blue pennant of the Carpathian Lancers from their radio antennae. Poppi, who commanded this squadron, leaned out the window of a house by the road and invited us in. The infantry was moving forward very slowly in trucks. All the infantry had dusty white faces, as if they had decided on some new sort of masquerade, using flour for make-up. They looked hot and unenthusiastic.

*This article was not published by *Collier's*. At the time, it must have seemed too critical of our popular allies, the Russians.

Poppi is more than six feet tall, exaggeratedly blond, about twenty-five years old, with bright-blue eyes and a funny husky voice. I wouldn't have thought that he was a Pole but I have now given up thinking that people look like Poles or don't look like Poles. The Poles cannot be classified, which is one of their chief charms.

Poppi was living in a bedroom on the second floor of this peasant house. The furniture was shiny, brown and modern and seemed but recently imported from Grand Rapids. We sat on the large bed and tried hopelessly to beat off the torrent of flies that flows over you the moment you sit still. We looked at maps as usual. The Major wanted to know where the Germans were. That was the main job of this armored regiment at the moment; their armored cars and scout cars were engaged in keeping contact with the Germans, who were withdrawing in their own time and style.

The Germans were beyond a ruined medieval tower which was our farthest advance position. They held somewhere on the hills and in whatever farmhouses they thought useful. The tower was being shelled. The Germans had anti-tank guns placed in farmhouses where they dominated the roads. The Lancers' armored cars were intended for war in the Western Desert; they could not operate across country, so they had to stick to the roads. The Germans waited and shot at them point-blank. It was like roulette; you either won or you got burned inside your car or maybe you crawled out in time. This went on during the daytime, and the infantry pushed ahead a little, and our artillery shelled the German positions, and at night usually the Germans retired a few kilometers farther north. It was a tiny war at the moment, though people get killed in tiny wars also.

The Major said he thought he would go on and have a look at the tower. Poppi said he couldn't drive there in his jeep—the dust attracted the Germans and then they shelled the place and this made the infantry, which was dug in all around, cross. We could walk if we wanted to. There wasn't anything to see, though. It was too hot to walk, so we gave it up. For three weeks the Carpathian Lancers had been the spearhead of the Polish Corps in a spectacular advance of two hundred miles up the Adriatic coast; and nobody was feeling violently energetic now, a few days after the capture of the port of Ancona. It was too soon for another big Polish drive, and the Lancers and the Germans were only prodding each other, while the Polish Corps reorganized for the next push.

We roared away in our private dust storm. The Major was disappointed in this tour. "Nossing," he said. *"Très ennuyeux pour vous. Sie haben nichts gesehen."* The use of three scrambled languages was our regular communication system. Everyone understood everyone else perfectly.

Since the war had so delightfully stopped, and since it was beautiful weather, and since Second Squadron was in reserve near us and doing nothing in particular, we decided to go swimming. There was a slight snag because no one had had time to investigate the beach and the approaches to the beach for mines; but as the Poles said, if you spent your life always considering mines it would be quite impossible. So we climbed over a German-destroyed railway bridge, climbing as delicately as if we were Balinese dancers, stepped softly on the torn-up wooden ties and jumped prudently down the embankment and then walked very very lightly along a dusty road to the shore. Andrew, who is a second lieutenant and commands a platoon of armored cars, and I did this noble work of reconnaissance. We decided to walk side by side or closely following each other, on the grounds that it would not be fair for just one of us to explode. There were no mines, at least we did not step on any, and there was the warm pale sea and a beach of smooth white pebbles.

We swam about, observing with interest that our artillery was shelling the Germans to the right, and that the British engineers were probably detonating mines in Ancona to our left, since there were bangs and great black clouds of smoke rising from that port. Then we began to plan what we would do in case the Germans broke through and we were in swimming during this operation. We decided it would be wisest just to go on swimming.

Second Squadron was camped in a hayfield a kilometer from the Regimental HQ village, and we had a party that night. We sat at a table between two haystacks; the tablecloth and the crockery were a loan from the nearby Italian farmhouse and we ate fried duck which had been bought from the farm and tomatoes which had probably been pinched, and bully beef and pickles, and drank raw new wine. In the middle of our meal we heard a great deal of artillery fire and Joe, one of the platoon commanders, hurried to the squadron communications car and came back with the news that poor old Poppi was being shelled like anything. There was a thin new moon and the sky was crimson and pink and the air had turned cool. Then we heard ack-ack fire and a light thumping of bombs, and presently our own artillery opened up, making a close and deafening racket. We went on eating and talking about Russia.

All the Poles talk about Russia all the time. The soldiers gather several times a day around the car which houses the radio and listen to the news; they listen to all the news in Polish wherever it comes from. They follow the Russian advance across Poland with agonized interest. It seemed to me that up here, on the Polish sector of the Italian front, people knew either what was happening ten kilometers away or what was happening in Poland, and nothing else. We never found out what the Eighth Army was doing in front of Florence or how the French were getting on above Siena or whether the Americans had raced ahead to take Pisa. And Normandy was another world. But what went on in Poland could be seen in every man's face, in every man's eyes.

They had come a long way from Poland. They call themselves the Carpathian Lancers because most of them escaped from Poland over the Carpathian mountains. They had been gone from their country for almost five years. For three and a half years this cavalry regiment, which was formed in Syria, fought in the Middle East and the Western Desert. They changed from horses to armored cars in Egypt and they fought wonderfully at Tobruk and El Alamein. They had sweltered in Iraq, defending the petrol fields, for almost a year. Last January they returned to their own continent of Europe, via Italy, and it was the Polish Corps, with this armored regiment fighting in it as infantry, that finally took Cassino in May. In June they started their great drive up the Adriatic, and the prize, Ancona—which this regiment had entered first—lay behind us.

It is a long road home to Poland, to the Great Carpathian mountains, and every mile of the road has been bought most bravely. But now they do not know what they are going home to. They fight an enemy in front of them and fight him superbly. And with their whole hearts they fear an ally, who is already in their homeland. For they do not believe that Russia will relinquish their country after the war; they fear that they are to be sacrificed in this peace, as Czechoslovakia was in 1938. It must be remembered that almost every one of these men, irrespective of rank, class or economic condition, has spent time in either a German or a Russian prison during this war. It must be remembered that for five years they have had no news from their families, many of whom are still prisoners in Russia or Germany. It must be remembered that these Poles have only twenty-one years of national freedom behind them, and a long aching memory of foreign rule.

So we talked of Russia and I tried to tell them that their fears must be wrong or there would be no peace in the world. That Russia must be as great in peace as she has been in war, and that the world must honor the valor and suffering of the Poles by giving them freedom to rebuild and better their homeland. I tried to say I could not believe that this war which is fought to maintain the rights of man will end by ignoring the rights of Poles. But I am not a Pole; I belong to a large free country and I speak with the optimism of those who are forever safe. And I remembered the tall gentle twenty-two-year-old soldier who drove me in a jeep one day, and how quietly he explained that his father died of hunger in a German prison camp, and his mother and sister had been silent for four years in a labor camp in Russia, and his brother was missing, and he had no profession because he had entered the Army when he was seventeen so he had had no time to learn anything. Remembering this boy, and all the others I knew, with their appalling stories of hardship and homelessness, it seemed to me that no American had the right to talk to the Poles, since we had never even brushed such suffering ourselves.

But as they were all young, and as a man cannot worry all the time even for his country and his family and his very hope of life, we stopped talking about Russia and the future and went over to the repair truck, where two soldiers were playing a violin and an accordion. We made ourselves comfortable on bundles of hay around the truck and soldiers drifted together, and the singing started. It is most lovely music, mournful and gay at once, and always full of memories. The soldiers have invented songs to commemorate every place they have lived and fought these last years. There are the songs of Alamein and Tobruk, and the song of the regiment, and soldier songs that make marching easier. The desert songs are sadder than the others. They played their own tangos, and *tzigane* music and Brahms and then a sweet, sad love song.

Someone translated the words: "The roses are fading, Johnny, oh come back from the war, come back from the war and kiss me as you did so long ago. Come back from the war, Johnny, and I will give you the loveliest rose of all."

The moon was clear and new and the music spread over us, interrupted only by the noise of our own artillery. Suddenly war was the way you remember it, not the way it is while it is happening. Just for a moment the present had the strange quality of already being the past, and one saw this night as it would look five years from now, and it was beautiful and perfect without needing five years to gild the memory. Nothing mattered except that these men should be always young, always brave and gay and fine to look at, always alive. The violinist and the accordion player grew tired at last and we walked home through the deep white powder of road dust. All that night our artillery hammered against the sky so that it seemed the walls of our village would have to crack and give under this ceaseless pounding in the air.

We moved the next day and every day after that. It was great fun, like being gypsies or a small-town circus. We were a long convoy on the roads, with the sirens of the armored cars screaming at every turning and the dust like a tent to cover us. We camped in fields and the moment we had anchored, the scrounging parties got busy. The object was to rush off and buy the local geese, ducks or rabbits before other soldiers had copped them. Wine too, of course. An Italian peasant offered to sell us five geese if we would come and get them—only four kilometers away, he said. On closer questioning it proved that his village four kilometers away was in German hands, and the project was renounced. We had a lovely and extravagant dinner that night, sitting on a haystack, to counteract the usual dinners that were sent up in containers from Section B. But everyone was so distressed by the news from Poland that the dinner was not a success. They were all thinking of their families, who had survived or not survived almost five years of German tyranny, and were wondering desperately what they would have to endure from the Russians.

In the very early morning we went on reconnaissance. Emile, who commanded the Second Squadron, led this outing of five scout cars. Emile briefed us, standing in his car, and though I did not understand what he said I understood the enchanting laughing sound of his voice and the courteous bow with which he finished.

We sat on top of the scout cars to get the sun and the air and a view of the countryside. The object of this jaunt was to find a way for the armored cars to proceed across country without using the roads. We passed the courtyards of small farms where the peasants were ambling sleepily around in mussed silk pajamas and dressing gowns. It seemed odder than one could believe, and we stared at them as hard as they stared at us. We bought some ducks and some wine and when we returned we learned that Poppi's squadron and George's squadron were attacking. Suddenly the fog of war descended.

No one could find the Major. The Major, who is as inquisitive as he is brave, had preceded the attack—both the armored cars and the infantry—and driven his jeep into the outskirts of the town we were supposedly going to take. He was quite alone, but some accurate German mortar fire convinced him he had better abandon his solitary war. He returned to headquarters at about one o'clock, full of information and good humor.

After lunch we went back up to the front, to find everybody stalemated. The infantry was lying low, the German anti-tank guns were operating, the sun was disgustingly hot, and the battle had not advanced. There were a great number of newly dug-up mines, the antitank mines which look like badly made carpenters' tool chests and the antipersonnel mines which look like a badly made small cigar boxes. Men were moving around George's squadron with pointed alpenstocks, prodding the fields, to locate more mines, and George was sitting at the head of a long line of armored cars, waiting. Poppi's squadron was getting shelled. We had been lightly shelled the night before, in our encampment, and all in all it looked as if everyone would settle down for a while and let the artillery work.

It had been a hectic day, though it did not prove anything. Casualties were light and only a few cars were damaged by shellfire. Then the regiment was ordered to retire and hand over to the infantry. War in an armored regiment seemed to consist of one day of big goings-on, one day of sitting in a haystack, and the third of getting yanked out of the line. As this was the first rest in over three weeks, everyone was pleased, and we returned to an earlier camping ground and the whole regiment tried to get clean in canvas washbowls, or by dousing itself under the Italian irrigation pipes.

They appeared the next morning in church, looking spotless.

An armored car becomes a sort of tourist trailer for five men after they have lived in it and near it long enough. It is a bar and an icebox, a trunk and a dressing table, as well as a swift steel-encased machine which sprouts machine guns. Johnny, the chaplain, who is about thirty and loves being a soldier, celebrated the Mass rather shyly, as if he were taking someone else's place. The villagers came too, old women and young women, with lace scarves on their heads and rosaries in their hands. The church had a charming painting over the altar: the Wise Men seeing the Star of Bethlehem, and a dog, who was with them, raising his head and seeing the Star as well as they did.

The clean brown lined faces of the Poles were quiet and respectful and rather sad. There was the Major, who had been reprieved from a German death sentence in order to act first as a servant to German NCOs and then as a slave laborer on a German prison farm. He escaped from that farm, and a Jewish underground organization smuggled him out of Poland via Czechoslovakia and Hungary. He did not know where his wife was and had not heard for five years. There was Mike, the second in command, very young and blond and alone now that his brother had been killed in Italy this summer. He and his brother, posing as students with a mythical rich aunt in Tokyo, escaped via Russia and the Trans-Siberian Railroad to Japan and managed to get back to Egypt and to their regiment a week before Tobruk. There was Chrostek the boxer, square and as strong as a tree, whose job was to locate and disarm the mines, to clear the way for the advance of the armored cars. He had had two days' leave to marry a Polish nurse, who had joined the Polish Corps after four years in a Russian labor camp. His first fiancée was killed by the Gestapo, after being tortured to tell what she knew of the underground in Poland. There they all stood, the officers and the men, friends and partners, each one with his long journey behind him and each one with the long uncertain journey ahead.

At the end of the service, they sang their national prayer. The music is fine and slow and their voices carried out through the open door of the church into the sunny fly-ridden village.

"Thou God who through many centuries cared for our country and kept it splendid; Thou who now defends our motherland with the shield of Thy love from the misfor-

128

tunes which have befallen our home; we bring our prayers to Thy altar and beg Thee to bless our country and to make it free."

The rich, sad voices were quiet now and there was silence in the church. The soldiers filed out into the hot sunshine to rest, to spend the Sabbath in peace, in order that they could start fighting again, mile by mile on the long road home.

The Gothic Line

September 1944

The Gothic Line, from where we stood, was a smashed village, an asphalt road and a pinkish-brown hill. On a dusty mined lane leading up to the village, the road and the hill, the Canadian infantry was waiting to attack. They stood single file, spaced well apart, and did not speak and their faces said nothing either. The noise of our artillery firing from the hills behind us never stopped. No one listened to it. Everyone listened to sudden woodpecker beats of German machine-gun fire ahead, and everyone looked to the sky on the left, where German airbursts made dark loose small clouds.

In front of us a bulldozer was working as bulldozers do, according to their own laws and in a world of their own. This machine was trying to fill in a portion of the deep antitank ditch which the Germans had dug along the entire face of the Gothic Line. The bulldozer now scraped up two mines in its wide steel shovel; the mines exploded, the bulldozer shook a little, and the driver removed his tropical helmet and cursed the situation. An infantry officer shouted something to him and he swerved his big machine, leaving two feet cleared between the side of his shovel and the mined side of the lane. Through this gap the infantry now passed. Each man seemed very alone, walking slowly and steadily toward the hills he could not see, and to whatever peril those hills would offer.

The great Gothic Line, which the Germans have used as a

130

threat ever since the Hitler Line was broken, would under normal circumstances be a lovely range of the Apennines. In this clear and dreaming weather that is the end of summer, the hills curve up into a water-blue sky; in the hot windless night you see the hills only as a soft rounded darkness under the moon. Along the Via Emilia, the road that borders the base of these hills, the Germans dynamited every village into shapeless brick rubble so that they could have a clear line of fire. In front of the flattened villages they dug their long canal to trap tanks. In front of the tank trap they cut all the trees. Among the felled trees and in the gravel bed and low water of the Foglia River, they laid down barbed wire and they sowed their never-ending mines: the crude little wooden boxes, the small rusty tin cans, the flat metal pancakes which are the simplest and deadliest weapons in Italy.

On the range of hills that is the actual Gothic Line the Germans built concealed concrete machine-gun pillboxes which encircle the hills and dominate all approaches. They sank the turrets of tanks, with their long thin snout-ended 88-mm. guns, in camouflaged pits, so that nothing on wheels or tracks could pass their way. They mined some more. Using as a basis the handiwork of nature, they turned the beautiful hills into a mountain trap four miles deep, where every foot of our advance could be met with concentrated fire.

And it is awful to die at the end of summer when you are young and have fought a long time and when you remember with all your heart your home and whom you love, and when you know that the war is won anyhow. It is awful and one would have to be a liar or a fool not to see this and not to feel it like a misery, so that these days every man dead is a greater sorrow because the end of all this tragic dying seems so near.

The Canadians broke the Gothic Line by finding a soft place and going through. It makes me ashamed to write that sentence because there is no soft place where there are mines and no soft place where there are Spandaus and no soft place where there are long 88-mm. guns, and if you have seen one tank burn with its crew shut inside it you will never believe that anything is soft again. But relatively speaking, this spot was soft or at any rate the Canadians made it soft, and they got across the mined river and past the dynamited villages and over the asphalt road and up into the hills, and from then on they poured men and tanks into the gap and they

131

gouged the German positions with artillery fire and they called in the Desert Air Force to bomb, and in two days they had come out on the other side of the Gothic Line at the coast of the Adriatic. Before that, many things had happened.

First of all, the main body of the Eighth Army moved from the center of Italy to the Adriatic coast in three days' time, and the Germans did not know it. That sounds easy too, when written in one sentence. What it meant was that for three days and three nights the weaving lateral roads across the Apennines, and the great highways that make a deep V, south from Florence and back up to Ancona, were crowded with such traffic as most of us have never seen before. Trucks and armored cars and tanks and weapons carriers and guns and jeeps and motorcycles and ambulances packed the roads, and it was not at all unusual to spend four hours going twenty miles. The roads were ground to powder by this traffic and the dust lay in drifts a foot thick, and whenever you could get up a little speed the dust boiled like water under the wheels. Everyone's face was greenish white with dust, and it rose in a blinding fog around the moving army and lay high over the land in a brown solid haze.

The road signs were fantastic too because more than one hundred thousand men, who could not speak Italian, were moving through complicated unknown country trying to find places which would never have been simple to find, even with empty roads and complete control of the language. The routes themselves, renamed for this operation, were marked with the symbols of their names: a painted animal or a painted object. There were the code numbers of every outfit, road warnings (bridge blown, crater, mines, bad bends) indications of first-aid posts, gasoline dumps, repair stations, prisoner-of-war cages and a marvelous Polish sign urging the troops to notice that this was a malarial area; this sign was a large green death's-head with a mosquito sitting on it. Along the coast, road signs were in Polish and English and at one crossroads a mine warning was printed in Polish, English and Hindu. And everywhere you saw the dirty white tapes that limit the safe ground from the treacherous ground where mines are still buried. On the main highways, there were signs saying "Verges cleared," which means the sides of this road have been de-mined, or "Verges checked," which means the sides of this road have been rapidly swept, and you can suit yourself if you want to take a chance.

So this enormous army ground its way across Italy and took up positions on a front thirteen miles long. The Eighth Army, which was now ready to attack the last German fortified line outside the Siegfried Line, had fought its way to these mountains from the Egyptian border. In two years, since Alamein, the Eighth Army had advanced across Africa through Sicily and up the peninsula of Italy. All these men, of how many races and nationalities, felt that this was the last push and after this they would go home. They will one day go home to Poland and Canada and South Africa and India and New Zealand and England and Scotland and Ireland, for there are all these nationalities in this army and you would have to speak several Indian dialects and French Canadian and Polish and whatever is spoken by the Negroes of Basutoland, as well as every available accent in English, to be perfectly understood in the Eighth Army. What is so comic and amazing and wonderful is how this huge hodgepodge of humanity gets on. The long trek they have done together and the sandstorms of the desert and the mud of the Italian winter and the danger and the dying and the lonely years have made them very neighborly men.

We watched the battle for the Gothic Line from a hill opposite, sitting in a batch of thistles and staring through binoculars. Our tanks looked like brown beetles; they scurried up a hill, streamed across the horizon and dipped out of sight. Suddenly a tank flamed four times in great flames, and other tanks rolled down from the skyline, seeking cover in the folds of the hill. The Desert Air Force cab rank, the six planes which cavort around the sky like a school of minnows, was signaled to bomb a loaf-shaped hill, called Monte Lura. Monte Lura went up in towering waves of brownish smoke and dirt. Our artillery dug into the Gothic Line, so that everywhere cotton balls of smoke flowered on the slopes. Our own airbursts now rained steel fragments over the German positions on Monte Lura. The young British major who was directing this artillery through a radiophone said, "I must say, I do think our airbursts are doing very nicely." The battle, looking absolutely unreal, tiny, crystal-clear, spread out before us. But there were men in the tanks, and men under those trees where the shells landed, and men under those bombs. The noise was so exaggerated that nothing like it had been heard since the movies.

All that day and the next the noise of our own guns was physically painful. The Canadian brigadier commanding the brigade which was attacking this sector of the line amused us by outlining a postwar garden party he hoped to give. Supper would be served on a long wooden table covered with a soiled white cloth; the guests would sit on benches which had a tendency to tip over backward. In one corner of the garden a flat voice would start saying, "I am now giving you a short tuning call, roger over, victory, victory, victory," and would go on saying this uninterruptedly for the rest of the evening. In another corner of the garden, tractors would be organized to act like tanks and they would first race their motors, which is a sound like the end of the world, and then they would roll back and forth on screaming treads. In another corner of the garden, some sort of radio apparatus would imitate the sound effect of six-inch guns firing, and it is almost impossible to believe how appalling they sound. In another corner of the garden a dust machine, imported from Hollywood, would spray dust imported from the roads of Italy onto the guests. A waiter would then walk in and release a thousand flies at a time. The dinner would consist of a slab of cold bully beef as appetizer, followed by not very heated-up meat and beans, the staple canned ration of the British forces, and hardtack. For dessert there would be hardtack with jam. The tea would have been brewed that morning and would be coal-black and lukewarm, with drowned flies in it. If the guests behaved nicely and did not complain too much, they would be given, as a prize, a finger of issue rum, a drink guaranteed to burn out anyone's palate. This was a perfect picture of our own meal except that issue rum was lacking, and we laughed contentedly at the brigadier's mythical guests.

Later, but I don't remember when, because time became more and more confused, we crossed the Foglia River and drove up the road our tanks had taken, and there we saw the remnants of a tank battle. An American Sherman, once manned by an English crew, lay near a farmhouse; across the road a German Tiger tank was burned and its entire rear end had been blown off. The Sherman had received an 88 shell through its turret. Inside the turret were plastered pieces of flesh and much blood. Outside the Tiger the body of a German lay, with straw covering everything except the two black clawlike hands, the swollen blood-caked head and the twisted feet. He did not smell too much yet. Some Canadian soldiers, who were sightseeing, stood around the dead German. It is remarkable how quickly soldiers start sightseeing where they have fought, perhaps trying now to discover what really happened. "Not much fresh meat on that guy," one of them said.

You cannot note everything that happens during a battle, you cannot even see what happens, and often you cannot understand it. Suddenly you will see antlike figures of infantry outlined against the sky; probably they are going in to attack that cluster of farmhouses. Then they disappear, and you do not know what became of them. Tanks roll serenely across the crest of a hill, then the formation breaks, you lose most of them from sight, and then in what was a quiet valley you unexpectedly see other tanks firing from behind trees. On a road that was quite empty and therefore dangerous, because nothing is more suspect at the front than the silent places, you see a jeep racing in the direction of a town which may or may not be in our hands. And when you imagine you have found a nice restful place to camp in for a few minutes, German mortar shells start landing.

A battle is a jigsaw puzzle of fighting men, bewildered terrified civilians, noise, smells, jokes, pain, fear, unfinished conversations and high explosives. A medical captain in a ruined first-aid farmhouse speaks with regret of a Canadian padre who volunteered as a stretcher-bearer to carry wounded men out of the mine fields in the riverbed. The padre lost both his legs, and though they rushed him out, he died at the first hospital. Bloody stretchers are stacked all around, and now a jeep arrives with fresh wounded. "Come back and see us any time," the medical captain says. "Get some more wire splints, Joe." A group of English tankists, drinking tea outside a smashed house on Monte Lura, invite you into their mansion, which is mainly fallen beams and the rubble of masonry. The place stinks because of two dead oxen at the side of the road. One of the soldiers, who had his tank shot from under him that morning, is waiting for another job. He hopes the war will be over in time for him to celebrate his twenty-first birthday in England. A Canadian soldier lies dead on another roadside, with a coat spread lovingly over him. There are two captured 88-mm. guns with a welter of German paper around them, for apparently the Germans also are the slaves of paper. Amongst this paper is a postcard with a baby's picture on it, addressed presumably to one of the gunners from his wife. And no one feels the slightest pity. A young Italian woman, wrapped in a blanket, sits on the doorstep of a poor little hovel that one of our shells had hit during the night; this was in a town the Germans held until a few hours ago. She wakes up and starts to laugh, charming, gay and absolutely mad.

Twelve parachutist prisoners, the crack troops of the Germans, stand in a courtyard guarded by the Canadians who captured them. They are all young and they wear the campaign medals of the Crimea, as well as the medal of Italy. These were the men who held Cassino all winter. You talk to them without any special feeling, and suddenly like a shock it occurs to you that they really look evil; the sadism which their General Kesselring ordered them to practice in Italy as they retreat shows now in their mouths and their eyes.

A fat old Italian in Cattolica, who had worked for twelve years on the Pennsylvania Railroad, was trundling his pitiful possessions home in a handcart. The Germans had occupied Cattolica for three months and had evacuated the citizens one month ago, and during this month they looted with horrid thoroughness, like woodworms eating down a house. What they did not wish to steal, they destroyed; the pathetic homes of the poor with smashed sewing machines and broken crockery and the coarse linen sheets and towels torn to shreds bear witness to their pointless cruelty. This old man was going home to a gutted house, but he was a healthy happy old man, and he was overjoyed to see us and he invited me to visit him and his wife the next day. The next day his wife was dead, as the Germans came over that night and plastered the little town with anti-personnel bombs.

The Canadian troops which I had seen two days ago, going in to attack the Gothic Line, were now swimming in the Adriatic. The beaches were laced with barbed wire but holes had been cut through it and engineers appeared with the curious vacuum-cleaner-like mine detectors, to sweep the beach. The infantry, sunburned the color of expensive leather, beautifully strong, beautifully alive, were bouncing around the flat warm sea and racing over the sand as if there were nothing terrible behind them and nothing terrible to come. Meantime you could sit on the sand with a book and a drink of sweet Italian rum and watch two British destroyers shelling Rimini, just up the coast; see German shells landing on the front three kilometers away; follow a pilot in a slowly sinking parachute, after his plane had been shot down; hear a few German shells whistle overhead to land two hundred yards farther down; and you were getting a fine sunburn and life seemed an excellent invention.

Historians will think about this campaign far better than we can who have seen it. Historians will note that in the first year of the Italian campaign, in 365 days of steady fighting, the Allied armies advanced 315 miles. It is the first time in history that any armies have invaded Italy from the south and fought up the endless mountain ranges toward the Alps. The historians will be able to explain with authority what it meant to break three fortified lines, attacking up mountains, and the historians will also describe how Italy became a giant mine field and that no weapon is uglier, for it waits in silence, small and secret, and it can kill any day, not only on the day of battle.

But all we know, we who are here, is that the Gothic Line is broken and that it is the last line. Soon our armored divisions will move on to the Lombardy plain and then at last the end of this long Italian campaign will become a fact, not a dream. The weather is lovely and no one wants to think of those who must still die and those who must still be wounded in the fighting before peace comes.

A Little Dutch Town*

October 1944

This is a story about a little Dutch town called Nijmegen and pronounced any way you choose. The moral to the story is: it would be a good thing if the Germans did not make a war every twenty years or so and then there would be no story about little towns called Nijmegen.

I have no idea what Nijmegen used to look like; there was probably quite a sweet old part to the city, judging from some of the ruins, some remnants of roofs and a carved doorway here and there. Also I imagine the curve of houses on the bluff by the Waal River was charming, but as the houses are all burned out it is hard to tell. And through the center of the town, where the university stood, it was also very likely pleasant and clean and untroubled; but due to uninterrupted shelling for a month or more the place looks now as if it had been abandoned years ago, following an earthquake and a flood.

Today Nijmegen is a town where people sleep in cellars and walk with care on the streets, listening hard for incoming shells. The Dutch sweep up broken glass every morning, in a desparingly tidy way, but there is no transport to cart glass away, so under the dripping autumn trees and along the shell-marked streets there are neat mounds of rubble and glass. The center of the town can be

*Opposite Arnhem, on the side of the river where the bridge was secured, while The Battle of Arnhem disastrously failed.

138

ignored, since it is not livable, having no windows left and too many houses burned hollow; but on the fringes of the town, ugly unimaginative comfortable modern red-brick homes, which were cheap to rent or own, remain intact. Nijmegen shows no signs of great wealth, but the poorest parts of the city, which are also the oldest and most attractive, are not as bad as slums in an equivalent-size English or American town. The people who lived in Nijmegen were obviously people accustomed to safety; they are a God-fearing folk, devoutly Cahtolic, who led a quiet provincial life and worked hard and neither wasted nor wanted and could count on a measure of security in their old age.

A great road bridge at Nijmegen crosses the Waal River, and this part of Holland bears a strategic relationship to Germany and the constructions of the Siegfried Line and the course of the Rhine. For these reasons (to put it very simply) Nijmegen found itself in the path of the opposing armies. So Nijmegen, in modern times, becomes a besieged citadel, which means that the Germans are a few kilometers away to the east, a few more kilometers away to the west, even more kilometers away to the north. The Allies hold the town and a long narrow corridor which stretches back to Belgium. Any town within range of artillery is an unlucky town.

There is no heat in Nijmegen, and the small and dwindling supply of coal is used for electricity. At night, behind all the blackout curtains, people can at least look at each other while they listen for the shells. The food ration tickets are the same as those issued by the Germans, only now the tickets are honored and people can actually buy the basic foodstuffs allowed them. This is not to say that stores are open; it is impossible to have a system of shops, working on fixed hours, when half the shops are blown open by artillery and at given times, quite unpredictably, not even a cat would want to slink through the shopping district. But some stores are open occasionally and the housewives tell each other of these, and here one can buy a very little food. What the careful Dutch are really living on is the reserves each housewife somehow managed to scrape together during these years. The communal kitchens, which feed the great bulk of the people who have no homes left and therefore no reserves, offer a regulation day's diet of ersatz coffee or watery tea and two black-bread sandwiches in the morning, a plate of potatoes at lunch, and the same tea or coffee and sandwiches at night.

Life is not exactly dull in Nijmegen, though I do not imagine life was ever really gay here. It is not a town that has a café or a bar or a dance hall, and I never saw a sign of a movie house. However, nowadays while riding one's bicycle (which is the usual civilian means of transport in Europe at present) one can watch a dogfight over the city, between one Messerschmitt and three Spitfires. It is also easy enough to sightsee gun batteries and machine-gun emplacements and foxholes. And at night there are always the fires, huge roaring fires that eat out the center of a house. After dark the streets are empty and there is no sound except the artillery, our artillery and the German artillery. Shells exploding in the confinement of four walls often set houses afire, and on one street there will be three sets of double houses burning wildly, and the small dark figures of the firemen spraying a weak thin stream of water onto a blaze that obviously nothing will stop.

As most of the town buildings have been opened by high explosive, there are large signs all over Nijmegen saying, "Do not loot. Penalty death." But I do not feel these signs are necessary. The British and American soldiers like the Dutch and respect them, and because Nijmegen is what it is, a small, not very rich town, the soldiers recognize it and find it understandable and like home, and they know what it means to these people to watch their city and their safety being destroyed. In the most literal sense, the people of Nijmegen have no choice but to take freedom or death. They have been freed and freedom has not been cheap.

The civilian side of this war is in many ways the most pitiful. The Dutch folk of Nijmegen, to whom this now routine appalling life of war comes as a grim surprise, do not complain. They are ignorant of all the techniques that soldiers learn; it takes a while to gauge shell bursts and to know what is dangerous and what is not. The old people and the children have been fairly stationary in cellars for the last month, either in the small cellars of their own beaten-up houses or in the communal cellars under the hospitals or the town hall. No one likes to live in fear, and it is more bewilderment than cowardice which so numbs the people now.

The members of the underground organizations, the police, the Red Cross, the doctors, the Boy Scouts and Girl Scouts, the civilian volunteers, have no time for cellars and no mind for safety. Among other activities, the police and the underground have been busy rounding up collaborators and tracking down German agents in the town. They put the collaborators in a big schoolhouse, which is pockmarked with shell holes, and they feed them as they feed themselves, and they await the return of the Dutch government so that proper trials may be held. The schoolhouse-jail has the awful familiar smell of dirty bodies, and the rooms full of arrested people look like the sad rooms I once saw in Prague where the refugees from the Sudetenland gathered to live and wait for nothing.

The Dutch are not brutal to these people and the prisons are lightly guarded. One is always surprised to see what kind of people are arrested, and most surprised by their apparent poverty. Some rooms are filled with dreary-looking young women, ill, lying in bed with very small babies; these are the women who lived with German soldiers and are now the mothers of Germans. Other rooms are jails for old people who trafficked with Germans, or worked for the Dutch Nazi government, or denounced or in some way harmed the true Dutch and the country. There is a nun in one room, by herself, looking frozen and unforgiving, and alongside her two stupid homely girls who worked in the Germans' kitchens and were soldiers' delights as a sideline. The only well-dressed collaborators I have seen were in the prison camp at Drancy near Paris, where I actually saw a woman in a chinchilla coat, and a few men who had bought their clothes at expensive tailors. But at this stage of the war and the liberation it is to be noted that little people (or should one say little crooks?) have been caught; the real evil ones, the big enemies, are either safely away with the Germans or well hidden. Arresting collaborators is as much a part of cleaning up a town as is the maintenance of the sewage system and the street sweeping.

Due to the fact that most of Holland is still occupied, it is impossible to write now about the Dutch underground. But it is possible to say that the Dutch people, individually and in their underground organizations, tried to help Jews, who in Holland as elsewhere were doomed. The penalty for sheltering Jews was death, and nevertheless Jews are reappearing in the light of day who have been forced to live like escaping criminals for four years. We gave a lift to a thin dark worried-looking woman who worked in the Dutch Red Cross. She did not seem a particularly inspiring woman and she seemed unusually nervous (which, in perilous places, is always unpleasant, because the proper manner under such circumstances is a real or assumed calm). She was going to the

141

civilian hospital to see her little girl. Her child, aged twelve, was badly wounded by shell fragments; her husband had been shot; her possessions had long since been confiscated by the Germans; and now her house had been destroyed by shellfire. She worked twelve hours a day in the Red Cross and during lunchtime—unless she got a chance lift—she walked four miles to the hospital to visit her child. She was a Jewess. She had been back in the daylight for a month. Tragedy in Europe is now so general, so usual, so common, that one does not even specially notice a case like this, which in a normal world would fill one with fury and pity.

There were twelve hundred Jews kept in a concentration camp near Nijmegen. The Germans took them in freight cars to Poland. One of the S.S. guards returning from this journey told a Dutchman what had happened. These twelve hundred Jews, old and young, men, women and children, were taken to a rather nice-looking building and told they could have showers. As they had lived in misery and filth for months, they were very happy. They were ordered to undress and leave their clothes outside; notably they were to leave their shoes. From vents, which looked like air vents, the Germans pumped what they call "blue gas" into the clean white-tiled bathroom. It appears that this gas works faster on slightly humid naked bodies. In some few minutes, twelve hundred people were dead, but not before the S.S. guard had heard them scream and had watched them die in what agony we cannot know. Then the shoes were all carefully sorted and sent back to Germany for use, and before the mass cremations all gold fillings and gold teeth were removed from the corpses.

We know now of many places where Jews have been gassed to death, we have written of it for a long time. People in Europe could not believe this evil and now they do; and to have lived close to such evil and to have seen, heard, and understood it does something to people which will never be wiped out.

For the Dutch Jews, the Germans meant death in agony; for the rest of the Dutch (apart from the underground, who risked the usual hazards of imprisonment, torture and death) the Germans meant slow hunger and the destruction of their families. The Germans deported half a million Dutchmen between the ages of nineteen and thirty-five to work as forced labor in Germany, and for a year now none of these men has been seen or heard from. In a small country half a million men leave a great sad gap in the life of every community. The Dutch did very well at saving their young men from deportation, but they could not save all. Aside from these physical facts, hunger and loss, the Dutch suffered as everyone has suffered under the Germans, from the outrage and humiliation of the Nazi regime. Free people cannot learn to live without disgust under that domination, and these were terrible years in which each man alone found each day that this tyranny, this stupidity, this corruption were unendurable; and yet there would always be tomorrow and tomorrow, and the tyranny had to be accepted since there was nothing to do but wait.

The Germans are fiends for paper. You had to have a pass for every move, a paper for rations, identity cards, paper and paper to burst a wallet; and they liked to check their papers frequently. The Dutch forged paper themselves, in quantity, and everyone who was doing underground work or simply escaping deportation had wads of false documents. Finally the Germans began to drown in their own paper; they could trust nothing. They admitted defeat, refused to recognize any documents, even their own, and solved the problem by simply arresting anyone they chose to, for any reason whatsoever. The Germans were also very shrewd in Holland in the taking of hostages, and they used this filthy weapon as a way to destroy the intellectual life and the leadership of the country. But that too they had done before; there has been little variety in the German technique of terror.

A story with a moral should be short. Even the moral should be short. What best points the moral of this story is short; it would take you only ten minutes to see and a paragraph to describe. In the basement of the civilian hospital (for Nijmegen has many hospitals, but now they are full of wounded American soldiers) there are corridors where the heating and water pipes run. These corridors have become wards because they are safe from shellfire. In one long corridor the wounded children lie in small white iron beds. The children are often too young to speak, but in all cases they are amazingly silent. There is not much for the children to eat, no special little things to please them and make their pain easier. The light is not good either, and sometimes the child is so small that you think the white crib is empty. One thin little girl of four had both her arms broken by shell fragments, and a shell fragment had been cut out of her side and another from her head. All you could see was a tiny soft face, with enormous dark eyes looking at you, and the arms like flower stalks strapped to splints and the bandage around her head which was almost as big as she was. She would never be able to understand what had happened or what sort of world it was that could so wound a little girl of four who had been playing in the garden of her house, as surely little girls ought to be able to play in all the gardens on earth.

So the moral of this story is really short: it would be a good thing if the Germans were never allowed to make war again.

The Battle of the Bulge

January 1945

They all said it was wonderful Kraut-killing country. What it looked like was scenery for a Christmas card: smooth white snow hills and bands of dark forest and villages that actually nestled. The snow made everything serene, from a distance. At sunrise and sunset the snow was pink and the forests grew smoky and soft. During the day the sky was covered with ski tracks, the vapor trails of planes, and the roads were dangerous iced strips, crowded with all the usual vehicles of war, and the artillery made a great deal of noise, as did the bombs from the Thunderbolts. The nestling villages, upon closer view, were mainly rubble and there were indeed plenty of dead Krauts. This was during the German counteroffensive which drove through Luxembourg and Belgium and is now driven back. At this time the Germans were being "contained," as the communiqué said. The situation was "fluid"—again the communiqué. For the sake of the record, here is a little of what containing a fluid situation in Kraut-killing country looks like.

The road to Bastogne had been worked over by the Ninth Air Force Thunderbolts before the Third Army tanks finally cleared the way. A narrow alley was free now, and two or three secondary roads leading from Bastogne back to our lines. "Lines" is a most inaccurate word and one should really say "leading back through where the Germans weren't to where the Americans were scattered

145

about the snowscape." The Germans remained on both sides of this alley and from time to time attempted to push inward and again cut off Bastogne.

A colleague and I drove up to Bastogne on a secondary road through breath-taking scenery. The Thunderbolts had created this scenery. You can say the words "death and destruction" and they don't mean anything. But they are awful words when you are looking at what they mean. There were some German staff cars along the side of the road: they had not merely been hit by machine-gun bullets, they had been mashed into the ground. There were half-tracks and tanks literally wrenched apart, and a gun position directly hit by bombs. All around these lacerated or flattened objects of steel there was the usual riffraff: papers, tin cans, cartridge belts, helmets, an odd shoe, clothing. There were also, ignored and completely inhuman, the hard-frozen corpses of Germans. Then there was a clump of houses, burned and gutted, with only a few walls standing, and around them the enormous bloated bodies of cattle.

The road passed through a curtain of pine forest and came out on a flat, rolling snow field. In this field the sprawled or bunched bodies of Germans lay thick, like some dark shapeless vegetable.

We had watched the Thunderbolts working for several days. They flew in small packs and streaked in to the attack in single file. They passed quickly through the sky and when they dived you held your breath and waited; it seemed impossible that the plane would be able to pull itself up to safety. They were diving to within sixty feet of the ground. The snub-nosed Thunderbolt is more feared by the German troops than any other plane.

You have seen Bastogne and a thousand other Bastognes in the newsreels. These dead towns are villages spread over Europe and one forgets the human misery and fear and despair that the cracked and caved-in buildings represent. Bastogne was a German job of death and destruction and it was beautifully thorough. The 101st Airborne Division, which held Bastogne, was still there, though the day before the wounded had been taken out as soon as the first road was open. The survivors of the 101st Airborne Division, after being entirely surrounded, uninterruptedly shelled and bombed, after having fought off four times their strength in Germans, look—for some unknown reason—cheerful and lively. A young lieutenant remarked, "The tactical situation was always good." He was very surprised when we shouted with laughter. The front, north of Bastogne, was just up the road and the peril was far from past.

At Warnach, on the other side of the main Bastogne road, some soldiers who had taken, lost and retaken this miserable village were now sightseeing the battlefield. They were also inspecting the blown-out equipment of two German tanks and a German self-propelled gun which had been destroyed here. Warnach smelled of the dead; in subzero weather the smell of death has an acrid burning odor. The soldiers poked through the German equipment to see if there was anything useful or desirable. They unearthed a pair of good bedroom slippers alongside the tank, but as no one in the infantry has any chance to wear bedroom slippers these were left. There was a German Bible but no one could read German. Someone had found a German machine pistol in working order and rapidly salted it away; they hoped to find other equally valuable loot.

The American dead had been moved inside the smashed houses and covered over; the dead horses and cows lay where they were, as did a few dead Germans. An old civilian was hopelessly shoveling grain from some burned and burst sacks into a wheelbarrow; and farther down the ruined street a woman was talking French in a high angry voice to the chaplain, who was trying to pacify her. We moved down this way to watch the goings-on. Her house was in fairly good shape; that is to say, it had no windows or door and there was a shell hole through the second-floor wall, but it was standing and the roof looked rainproof. Outside her parlor window were some German mines, marked with a white tape. She stood in her front hall and said bitterly that it was a terrible thing, she had left her house for a few moments that morning, and upon returning she found her sheets had been stolen.

"What's she saying?" asked an enormous soldier with red-rimmed blue eyes and a stubble of red beard. Everyone seems about the same age, as if weariness and strain and the unceasing cold leveled all life. I translated the woman's complaint.

Another soldier said, "What does a sheet look like?"

The huge red-bearded man drawled out, "My goodness," a delicious expression coming from that face in that street. "If she'd of been here when the fighting was going on, she'd act different."

Farther down the street a command car dragged a trailer; the bodies of Germans were piled on the trailer like so much ghastly firewood.

We had come up this main road two days before. First there had been a quick tempestuous scene in a battalion headquarters when two planes strafed us, roaring in to attack three times and putting machine-gun bullets neatly through the second-story windows of the house. The official attitude has always been that no Germans were flying reclaimed Thunderbolts, so that is that. No one was wounded or killed during this brief muck-up. One of the battalion machine-gunners, who had been firing at the Thunderbolts, said, "For God's sake, which side are those guys fighting on?" We jumped into our jeep and drove up nearer the front, feeling that the front was probably safer.

A solitary tank was parked close to a bombed house near the main road. The crew sat on top of the tank, watching a village just over the hill which was being shelled, as well as bombed by the Thunderbolts. The village was burning and the smoke made a close package of fog around it, but the flames shot up and reddened the snow in the foreground. The armed forces on this piece of front consisted, at the moment, of this tank, and out ahead a few more tanks, and somewhere invisibly to the left a squadron of tanks. We did not know where our infantry was. (This is what a fluid situation means.) The attacked village would soon be entered by the tanks, including the solitary watchdog now guarding this road.

We inquired of the tank crew how everything went. "The war's over," said one of the soldiers, sitting on the turret. "Don't you know that? I heard it on the radio, a week ago. The Germans haven't any gasoline. They haven't any planes. Their tanks are no good. They haven't any shells for their guns. Hell, it's all over. I ask myself what I'm doing here," the tankist went on. "I say to myself, boy, you're crazy, sitting out here in the snow. Those ain't Germans, I say to myself, didn't they tell you on the radio the Germans are finished?"

As for the situation, someone else on the tank said that they would gratefully appreciate it if we could tell them what was going on.

"That wood's full of dead Krauts," said another, pointing across the road. "We came up here and sprayed it just in case there was any around and seems the place was full of them, so it's a good thing we sprayed it all right. But where they are right now, I wouldn't know."

"How's your hen?" asked the Captain, who had come from Battalion HQ to show us the way. "He's got a hen," the Captain explained. "He's been sweating that hen out for three days, running around after it with his helmet."

"My hen's worthless," said a soldier. "Finished, no good, got no fight in her.'

"Just like the Germans," said the one who listened to the radio.

Now two days later the road was open much farther and there was even a rumor that it was open all the way to Bastogne. That would mean avoiding the secondary roads, a quicker journey, but it seemed a good idea to inquire at a blasted German gun position. At this spot there were ten Americans, two sergeants and eight enlisted men; also two smashed German bodies, two dead cows and a gutted house.

"I wouldn't go up that road if I was you," one of the sergeants said. "It's cut with small-arms fire about a quarter of a mile farther on. We took about seventeen Heinies out of there just a while back, but some others must of got in."

That seemed to settle the road.

"Anyhow," the sergeant went on. "They're making a counter-attack. They got about thirty tanks, we heard, coming this way."

The situation was getting very fluid again.

"What are you going to do?" I said.

"Stay here," said one of the soldiers.

"We got a gun," said another.

War is lonely and individual work; it is hard to realize how small it can get. Finally it can boil down to ten unshaven gaunt-looking young men, from anywhere in America, stationed on a vital road with German tanks coming in.

"You better take that side road if you're going to Bastogne," the second sergeant said.

It seemed shameful to leave them. "Good luck," I said, not knowing what to say.

"Sure, sure," they said soothingly. And later on they got a tank and the road was never cut and now if they are still alive they are somewhere in Germany doing the same work, as undramatically and casually—just any ten young men from anywhere in America.

About a mile from this place, and therefore about a mile and a half from the oncoming German tanks, the General in command of this tank outfit had his headquarters in a farmhouse. You could not easily enter his office through the front door, because a dead horse with spattered entrails blocked the way. A shell had landed in the farmyard a few minutes before and killed one cow and wounded a second, which was making sad sounds in a passageway between the house and the barn.

The air-ground-support officer was here with his van, checking up on the Thunderbolts who were attacking the oncoming German tanks. "Argue Leader," he said, calling on the radiophone to the flight leader. "Beagle here. Did you do any good on that one?"

"Can't say yet," answered the voice from the air.

Then over the loud-speaker a new voice came from the air, talking clearly and loudly and calmly. "Three Tigers down there with people around them."

Also from the air the voice of Argue Leader replied rather peevishly, "Go in and get them. Don't stand there talking about it." They were both moving at an approximate speed of three hundred miles an hour.

From the radio in another van came the voice of the Colonel commanding the forward tank unit, which was stopping this counterattack on the ground. "We got ten and two more coming," said the Colonel's voice. "Just wanted to keep you posted on the German tanks burning up here. It's a beautiful sight, a beautiful sight, over."

"What a lovely headquarters," said a soldier who was making himself a toasted cheese sandwich over a small fire that served everyone for warmth and cookstove. He had opened the cheese can in his K ration and was doing an excellent job, using a German bayonet as a kitchen utensil.

"Furthermore," said a lieutenant, "they're attacking on the other side. They got about thirty tanks coming in from the west too."

"See if I care," remarked the soldier, turning his bread carefully so as to toast it both ways. A shell landed, but it was farther up the road. There had been a vaguely sketched general ducking, a quick reflex action, but no one of course remarked it.

150

Then Argue Leader's voice came exultantly from the air. "Got those three. Going home now. Over."

"Good boys," said the ground officer. "Best there is. My squadron."

"Listen to him," said an artillery officer who had come over to report. "You'd think the Thunderbolts did everything. Well, I got to get back to work."

The cow went on moaning softly in the passageway. Our driver, who had made no previous comment during the day, said bitterly, "What I hate to see is a bunch of livestock all beat up this way. Goddammit, what they got to do with it? It's not their fault."

Christmas had passed almost unnoticed. All those who could, and that would mean no farther forward than Battalion Headquarters, had shaved and eaten turkey. The others did not shave and ate cold K rations. That was Christmas. There was little celebration on New Year's Eve, because everyone was occupied, and there was nothing to drink. Now on New Year's Day we were going up to visit the front, east of Luxembourg City. The front was quiet in the early afternoon, except for artillery, and a beautiful fat-flaked snowstorm had started. We decided, like millions of other people, that we were most heartily sick of war; what we really wanted to do was borrow a sled and go coasting. We borrowed a homemade wooden sled from an obliging little boy and found a steep slick hill near an abandoned stone quarry. It was evidently a well-known hill, because a dozen Luxembourg children were already there, with unsteerable sleds like ours. The sky had cleared and the ever present Thunderbolts returned and were working over the front less than four kilometers away. They made a lot of noise, and the artillery was pounding away too. The children paid no attention to this; they did not watch the Thunderbolts, or listen to the artillery. Screaming with joy, fear, and good spirits, they continued to slide down the hill.

Our soldier driver stood with me at the top of the hill and watched the children. "Children aren't so dumb," he said. I said nothing. "Children are pretty smart," he said. I said nothing again. "What I mean is, children got the right idea. What people ought to do is go coasting."

When he dropped us that night he said, "I sure got to thank you folks. I haven't had so much fun since I left home."

On the night of New Year's Day, I thought of a wonderful

151

Martha Gellhorn

New Year's resolution for the men who run the world: get to know the people who only live in it.

There were many dead and many wounded, but the survivors contained the fluid situation and slowly turned it into a retreat, and finally, as the communiqué said, the bulge was ironed out. This was not done fast or easily; and it was not done by those anonymous things, armies, divisions, regiments. It was done by men, one by one—your men.

The Black Widow

January 1945

In the daytime the Thunderbolts, snarling bulldog planes, roared on and off this field, and the pilots poured into the briefing shack and announced their kills to the interrogating officer, or stood huddled around a big map getting last-minute instructions before the next mission. Across the field, a fleet of C-47s was lined up and ambulances moved slowly and carefully over the deep frozen ruts, and orderlies lifted the blanketed wounded into the planes. When the cargo was completed, tier after tier of pain, the heavy freight planes moved down the runway en route to England. Nothing broke the wind and it swept in waves over the iron mud of the field and swirled the snow in dusty clouds. The field was as ugly as all forward airfields are, with the claptrap buildings of the squadrons and a tent hospital outlining its edges. The air hammered with the noise of planes and everyone looked small, eaten with cold, and intently busy.

When darkness came, the field was silent and nothing moved and this place then seemed a wasteland in Siberia, a plateau on the moon, the very end of the world. When darkness came, the Black Widows took over.

Now the Major in command of these Black Widow night-fighters, a man of twenty-six but with the ageless hard tired look one is used to seeing on the faces of all the young, was making a speech. His squadron headquarters had been pieced together from the wood of a German barracks and it was very cold, with one iron stove to heat the room, and badly lighted by a few unshaded bulbs. "Everybody shoots at us," he said. "Friendly bombers and friendly flak and enemy flak and enemy fighters. Just anybody at all; they all got a right to shoot at us. I wouldn't advise it."

Last night one of their planes had been shot down, and the squadron doctor, who drove over to the place where the plane crashed, returned to report that nothing remained of the pilot and radio operator except four feet and two hands. There is never any time for pity or sorrow, at least there is no time to show these feelings; death only seems to make the survivors angrier and more aware of what is after all a constant danger. Death reminds you that it can happen to you too, and everyone fears and resents this reminder.

"Well," said the Major, "if you're going, you better come with me. I'm on the first mission."

We ate supper at five, and it was already night. Americans call any sizable building a château and they had their mess in a château, which was nothing but a large untidy dark icy house. The pilots and radio operators ate in a big room, wearing their flying clothes, and they passed heavy dishes of lukewarm unpalatable food around the long tables and laughed and shouted to each other, eating in haste. A Captain beside me began to list again the horrors of night flying, until the Major said, "She's coming with us now, so leave her alone. Tell her something good."

The Captain said at once, "It will be beautiful anyhow. It's certainly beautiful up there, and it's going to be a fine night."

I handed a bowl of congealed mashed potatoes to the Major and thought that the myth of the glamorous lives of pilots is the silliest myth of all. Probably we got it from the movies about pilots in the last war, who always seemed to live in authentic châteaux and eat at fine tables loaded with cut glass and china and ornamented with occasional champagne buckets. Pilots, according to myth, return from their hazardous work and have a hot bath and step into perfectly tailored uniforms and while away their spare time in a frolic of stout-hearted laughter and singing. Actually they live like hell at these forward fields. It is only one step better than the foxhole. Mostly they sleep in tents and there is no escaping the cold and there is nothing to do but fly, sleep, eat and wait in black discomfort to fly again. They always speak with pity of the infantry, who have a really "rugged" life.

After supper, during which everyone except myself ate heartily, we went back to Squadron Headquarters. I was zipped into flying pants, flying boots, and a flying jacket, feeling more and more like a breathless package. The Major appeared with an oxygen mask and there was some difficulty in fitting the thing on. "They didn't make these for ladies," he said. "Can you breathe?" Someone was stuffing gloves into my hand, and someone else was attempting to fasten a parachute on me. I found myself choking inside the mask and shook my head and the Major said, "Okay, that'll do." He put an escape kit in my pocket and led me to the map, which was enormous and incomprehensible, and picked up a piece of string that was attached to the map; where the string was attached was our base. He described a rough semicircle to the east with the string and said, "We'll be patrolling this area. If anything happens, walk southwest."

We now piled into a jeep, the Major, the radio operator, the driver and I. It was difficult to hoist one's body around and there was a marked tendency to sit down when one meant to stand up, due to the weight of the parachute. It was so cold that one shrank into one's clothes and felt oneself shriveling in the wind. Now we could see the sleek sharp outlines of the black plane ahead. It is a beautiful plane, with two upcurling tails and long narrow wings, and it looked in the night like a delicate deadly dragonfly. The name of these P-61s, the Black Widow, seemed all wrong for such beauty of line. No one spoke in the jeep. Then the radio operator said thoughtfully, "This is the worst part of any mission." After that we were too busy to think about better or worse.

The Major climbed into the cockpit and began getting the plane ready. The radio operator was delegated to give me the necessary information. This was all so hopelessly mad that it could only be taken as a joke. He said in the dark, "If anything happens you turn this handle." What handle? Where? "That will open the trap. Then turn this other handle on the right—it's wired, but you won't have any trouble. That will drop the ladder out and then all you have to do is fall out backwards. You know where your rip cord is, don't you?"

"Yes," I said sadly.

"If anything goes wrong with those two, you turn this handle on the cowling and that whole piece of glass will fall out and you can climb out through that. It's a little narrow with all those clothes

155

on, but it will be all right, I guess. Well, that's about all," said he. "Have you got a cushion for her?" he asked the crew chief, and from nowhere a flat little sofa cushion appeared and was put on top of the wooden crate which was to be my seat. They had found it impractical to carry a gunner here in the glass bulb between the twin tails and there was no seat or safety belt.

"Oh, and your oxygen mask," said the radio operator, "It plugs in here, and this is your earphone plug-in."

I had given up hope by now; it was all too complicated and I thought gloomily that every one of these damned wires would come undone, I would fall out without meaning to or get hurled off my crate and mashed against the confused steel sides of my little glass cage, and I was already cold and so I decided to try hard to think of something else. Meanwhile a brisk businesslike conversation was going on in the cockpit; voices came through the earphones so deafeningly that I could scarcely distinguish words, but from the tone it sounded as calm and sensible as if you were talking about whether there was enough gas in the car to get to the country club.

We hurtled into the night and soared for the stars. I have never been part of such a take-off; the actual feeling of flying became so intense that one felt free of the plane, and as if one were moving nakedly and with no hindrance through a sky that was bigger than any sky ever seen before. It was beautiful too, with a glowing moon and the stars very close. I knew that the beauty was not going to soothe my spirit or hold my attention. The beauty was a vast emptiness in which we roared alone, and the beauty was a good deal too scary for my taste.

A conversation began on the radio; or rather it had been going on all along, only it seemed clearer now. Somewhere on the distant dark snow-covered earth, men would be sitting in a hidden caravan crouched over instruments of black magic—the radar—and a voice came from wherever they were, speaking a most technical code, and this plane obeyed that voice. At 265 miles an hour we fled blindly through the night, and our eyes were some place behind us in Luxembourg on the ground. A night fighter pilot is directed by radar to his quarry, which he cannot see, and he must not fire until he has a visual target (that is, until he actually sees and identifies the other plane) and he can be as close as two hundred yards from the enemy plane before he is certain of it. Until that time, the Black

156

Widow swerves and swoops, climbs and falls alone like a strange mad bird, obeying the voice of the ground controller.

The conversation between ground and sky was weird beyond believing. Since it was all code, it cannot be repeated; but these odd and mystical sentences filtered through the air in rather loud matter-of-fact voices, and when the ground spoke the plane responded. We were over Germany, and a blacker, less inviting piece of land I never saw. It was covered with snow, there were mountains, there was no light and no sign of human life, but the land itself looked actively hostile. Then the voice from the ground said something; the pilot said "Roger," and the plane vaulted up the sky. This ranked easily as one of the nastiest sensations I have ever felt. We climbed, in a matter of seconds, from 11,000 to 22,000 feet. One's body turned to iron and was crushed down, feeling as if an enormous weight were pressing on something that would not yield. My oxygen mask was too large and had to be held on, and as I held it with my right hand, and held onto some kind of steel shelf with my left hand (so as not to fall backwards off my darling little crate) I thought that (a) my stomach was going to be flattened against my backbone and (b) that I was going to strangle. This loathsome set of feelings went on and meanwhile the radio conversation sharpened and went faster and louder, and I knew, though the words were muddled, that we were being led to our quarry.

I had reached a stage of dull resignation and only prayed that we would stop doing whatever we were doing and do something else. The plane stopped climbing and now it was just hard to breathe. An added charm is that one's nose, a reasonably earthy instrument, flows steadily in this cold and of course is unwipable; presently, since the temperature inside the plane was thirty below zero, one finds oneself with a small frozen river on one's face. This is mentioned only in passing, because it is a very minor matter, but there it is. One is anyhow so cold that one more misery doesn't count. The plane, driven on by the loud ground voice, was roaring high and straight through the sky. Then, for no reason I could discover, we turned over on a wing and dropped sideways a few miles toward the ground. That too was an undesirable sensation; one's insides seemed to drain away, leaving one empty and weak and not at all certain which side was upright. The pilot said something to me, in a nice cozy voice, but I did not understand. He

157

repeated it. I gathered that we had just dropped through the sky that way in order to avoid flak at Cologne. It appeared that we had been following a friendly plane which must have been a bomber and was copping the Cologne flak. It seemed restful to be flying level at 11,000 feet again. The radio voices chatted to each other, apparently saying what a pity the whole thing had been, and better luck next time.

Everything was calm now, except for the fact that we were still over Germany. Then the pilot called to me on the intercom, and, looking where he told me, I saw the trail of a V-2. It came from somewhere deeper inside Germany and was at this distance a red ball of fire, and it rose perpendicularly from the ground and passed out of sight over the top of the sky in a few seconds. Then there were gun flashes to the west, where the front seemed to be waking up. One huge gun opened like a blast furnace, but I could not tell whether it was theirs or ours. On the ground I saw fixed flares, and again I did not know what they were; then there would be the sudden quaking soundless fire of the guns. There was also a frightening star, which I believed to be following us. I was considering how to call it to the pilot's attention when finally I decided it was a star, once and for all, and could be classed as harmless.

The ground was not saying anything much and the pilot seemed to have more time, for he started an amiable conversation over the intercom, practically none of which I understood, but his voice and manner of speaking filled me with admiration. It was as if he were making friendly talk with someone he had just met in a bar. The intercom worked only one way; I could not have answered even if I had known what he was saying. The ground voice spoke again, giving brisk orders, and the plane flicked neatly over on a wing and glided steeply downward. The pilot was asking questions, and more orders came from the ground. I could tell that we were hunting and getting close. By now this journey seemed to have gone on forever; one had sat since the beginning of time on a wobbly crate in the middle of heaven, and there obviously was no end to it. The plane slowed terrifyingly; it felt as if it were standing still in the air, and at the same time the pilot's voice cracked angrily on the radio. Nothing happened. There was some reply from the ground and the pilot said very angrily, "For God's sake." The snow-covered land was nearer now and so were the gun flashes.

The pilot spoke again on the intercom. We had been on the

trail of an authentic enemy plane, but due to some miscalculation we were brought down on top of the enemy plane instead of under it. We were therefore briefly in the unfortunate position of getting shot at, rather than doing the shooting, but luckily the German did not wish to fight and had streaked off west and lost himself. The pilot was furious.

Now we were going home, as the time limit was nearly up. Suddenly the pilot said, "See the flak?" I has seen it to the left; I thought it was low and far away and I was sad for the unlucky men who were getting it. This justifies completely the ignorance-is-bliss school of thought. The flak was shooting at us, the distance was too close for comfort, and I imagined that the shells went no higher than the tracers. We did another quick aerial pirouette and roared for home.

We landed as we had taken off, which is to say like a bolt of lightning. We had been out a little over two and a half hours, and the Major was almost blue with cold. He had not been heavily dressed because he could not fly the plane if his body was hampered by all that clothing. So for two and a half hours now and for two and a half hours later that night, and every other night, he would sit in a plane in a temperature of thirty below zero and simply take it. He did say, in passing, "Gosh, it's cold."

The Major was depressed about the evening, it had been a boring patrol, nothing happened, there was one good chance of a fight and it had been mucked up, and all in all he felt browned off. So we climbed stiffly into the jeep and went back to the squadron shack. The other planes of this mission were coming in, landing at that soul-shaking speed, and a new mission would be leaving within a few minutes. The radio operator came back to headquarters to report to the interrogating officer and left again immediately, as he was flying with another pilot on the second mission. He had no time for a cup of coffee, or any chance to get warm; I do not think there was a cup of coffee available, for that matter.

But there was much excitement in the headquarters shack; a tall towheaded boy with a shining face was passing a box of cigars around and getting heavily beaten on the back. His smile was enormous and he couldn't give out cigars fast enough. A cable had just come, announcing the birth of a baby daughter.

"Thank God," said the Major, "I've been sweating out that baby for ten days."

The towheaded pilot showed his cable and a picture of his wife and offered his cigar box.

"How long is a baby?" he said. He held his hands about three feet apart. "That long?"

"Hell, no," said an elderly father of twenty-four. "About so long." And he held his hands a foot apart.

There followed a heated argument about the length of babies. No one spoke of the mission completed or of the missions to come; it was after all just another night's work. But people didn't become fathers every night; becoming a father was really something.

The Thunderbolt pilots had invited us to have a drink in their club. They had fixed up a shack as a mess and built a fireplace out of armor plate from a German tank and rigged up a bar, and they had whiskey and scrambled-egg sandwiches. We drove along the bad road beside the field and the Major said, "Let's not talk about Black Widows down there, see? What I mean is, we think those Thunderbolt pilots do a lot tougher job than we do, so let's just not talk about our stuff." None of the Thunderbolt boys will ride in the Black Widows for anything, on the grounds that the whole performance is unsound.

The Thunderbolt pilots were all very young and were trying to be gay tonight, because they had lost their squadron leader the day before, and they loved him, and one dare not mourn. He was last seen headed straight down, with his machine guns still firing ten feet above the ground. His last heard remark was "give 'em hell." So now everyone was drinking and talking shop. One boy said that he never got used to shooting people, because they rolled so much when they were hit. He just didn't like it, that was all. It was different for the Airborne boys, and such as them, they were real killers; but he just didn't like the way people rolled. The phrase that recurred most was "We sure clobbered the Herman." This means we definitely shot up the Germans. It can mean that they shot up trucks, tanks, command cars, or troops; anything German is Herman and "clobbered" means liquidated. The Major was rather silent and was mainly occupied trying to get warm in front of the curious fireplace. I have never felt better in my life, due to my pleasure in being around at all, and I ate scrambled-egg sandwiches like a starving Armenian. Then the Major had to get back to his headquarters, as he was flying again, so we left with many expressions of mutual esteem and gratitude.

In the jeep, the Major said thoughtfully, "Those P-47s. I don't hack their talk."

"Why?" I asked.

"Clobber the Herman," he said, with a very faint air of contempt. "What talk is that?"

"What do you say?"

"We say 'hose the Hun,' of course."

We dropped him at the door and for a moment we stood there, shivering and shrunken with cold. "Well, so long, he said. "Come and see us again. Give you a ride anytime." In the light from the headquarters shack, he looked tired and cold. You were sure he would not think about being tired or cold or think in any way about himself. They all did their job, that was all. Some men fly by day and others by night, some men work in tanks, others drop out of planes in parachutes, and there is always the infantry. All jobs and all appalling jobs. They do not think of them; they do them; there is nothing else to do.

As we drove away, another sleek sharp plane tore up into the night sky, climbed and headed east toward Germany.

Das Deutsches Volk

April 1945

No one is a Nazi. No one ever was. There may have been some Nazis in the next village, and as a matter of fact, that town about twenty kilometers away was a veritable hotbed of Nazidom. To tell you the truth, confidentially there were a lot of Communists here. We were always known as very Red. Oh, the Jews? Well, there weren't really many Jews in this neighborhood. Two maybe, maybe six. They were taken away. I hid a Jew for six weeks. I hid a Jew for eight weeks. (I hid a Jew, he hid a Jew, all God's chillun hid Jews.) We have nothing against the Jews; we always got on well with them. We have waited for the Americans a long time. You came and liberated us. You came to befriend us. The Nazis are *Schweinhunde*. The Wehrmacht wants to give up but they do not know how. No, I have no relatives in the Army. Nor I. No, I was never in the Army. I worked on the land. I worked in a factory. That boy wasn't in the Army either; he was sick. We have had enough of this government. Ah, how we have suffered. The bombs. We lived in the cellars for weeks. We refused to be driven across the Rhine when the S.S. came to evacuate us. Why should we go? We welcome the Americans. We do not fear them; we have no reason to fear. We have done nothing wrong; we are not Nazis.

It should, we feel, be set to music. Then the Germans could sing this refrain and that would make it even better. They all talk like this. One asks oneself how the detested Nazi government, to which no one paid allegiance, managed to carry on this war for five

162

and a half years. Obviously not a man, woman or child in Germany ever approved of the war for a minute, according to them. We stand around looking blank and contemptuous and listen to this story without friendliness and certainly without respect. To see a whole nation passing the buck is not an enlightening spectacle. It is clear that all you have to do in Germany, in order to lead the country, is to be successful; if you stop being successful, no one will admit they ever heard of you.

At night the Germans take pot shots at Americans, or string wires across roads, which is apt to be fatal to men driving jeeps, or they burn the houses of Germans who accept posts in our Military Government, or they booby-trap ammunition dumps or motorcycles or anything that is likely to be touched. But that is at night. In the daytime we are the answer to the German prayer, according to them.

At the moment we are sitting on the west bank of the Rhine, facing the Ruhr pocket. The Germans here are peeved about the Ruhr pocket and wish us to push it back ten miles so that they will no longer be troubled by their own artillery, which fires into their villages whenever it can spare some shells. The 504th Regiment of the 82nd Airborne Division sent a company across the Rhine in landing craft one night and took and held a town for thirty-six hours. These landing craft are built like enlarged shoe boxes and are propelled forward by dint of paddles, and the current is swift, and the river is wide, and on the other side was the Wehrmacht, which was not giving up by any manner of means. The company of paratroopers drew onto themselves a great deal of armed attention—two German divisions, it was estimated. This small Airborne action relieved pressure at another part of the front, and the company lost many men.

In the afternoon of the day they got back, two officers and four sergeants were decorated with the Silver Star by General Gavin, who commands the division. This ceremony took place in a nondescript street, amidst brick rubble and fallen telephone wires. Some German civilians stuck their heads cautiously out of windows and watched with interest. It was very simple: one officer read the citations and General Gavin pinned on the medals. The six who received the medals were not dressed for the occasion; they had come directly from their work. Their faces were like gray stone and their eyes were not like eyes you will see every day and no one was

163

talking about what had just been lived through across the river. If you had friends in the company who did not come back, that made it worse; if you knew no one personally it was bad enough.

The German civilians looked with wonder at this row of dirty silent men standing in the street. It makes little or no difference to anyone around here whether the Germans are Nazis or not; they can talk their heads off; they can sing "The Star-Spangled Banner"; they are still Germans and they are not liked. None of these soldiers has forgotten yet that our dead stretch back all the way to Africa.

The villages along the Rhine here are in pretty good shape. In the middle, of course, is Cologne, and Cologne is one of the great ruins of the world; but by and large these adjacent villages have nothing to complain of. The houses are well built and each one of them has a small cellar where large quantities of Germans sleep at night. As the soldiers say, they are not hurting for anything. There is food and clothing, coal, bedding, all household equipment, livestock. The Germans are nice and fat too, and quite clean and orderly and industrious. They carry on their normal lives within seven hundred yards of their Army, which is now their enemy.

The *Bürgermeister,* whom we appoint, rule the people by decrees which we publish and slap up on the walls. The Germans seem to love decrees, and they stand in line busily to read anything new that appears. We went to call on one *Bürgermeister* of a front-line village; he was, he said, a Communist and a half-Jew and he may be for all I know, but it is amazing how many Communists and half-Jews there are in Germany. He was a working man before and he says that plenty of people in the village are furious about his being *Bürgermeister;* he has got above himself, they think, because of the Americans. If the Americans fired him he would be killed, he said. He stated this in a matter-of-fact way, as if it were only to be expected.

We said, "Then that means the people here are Nazis."

"No, no," he said. "It is that they think I have too good a position."

We then told him we thought his fellow villagers must be lovely people; it was not regulation, we felt, to murder a man just because he had a good job.

He spoke with some despair about the future of Germany and finished by saying that America must help Germany to recover. We listened to this remark with surprise and asked him why; why did he imagine America was going to help Germany do anything? He admitted that perhaps we had a reason to hate Germany but they were relying on our well-known humanitarianism.

"Nuts," said the sergeant, who spoke German.

"Translate nuts," said the Lieutenant. "Where does he get these fancy ideas?"

The *Bürgermeister* went on to say that if the Americans did not occupy Germany for fifty years, there would be war again. Some man with a bigger mouth than Hitler, he said, will come along and promise them everything and they will follow and there will be war again.

"I believe him," said the Lieutenant.

After the tidy villages, Cologne is a startling sight. We are not shocked by it, which only goes to prove that if you see enough of anything you stop noticing it. In Germany, when you see absolute devastation you do not grieve. We have grieved for many places in many countries but this is not one of the countries. Our soldiers say, "They asked for it." Between two mountains of broken brick, and backed by a single jagged wall, a German had set up a push-cart and was selling tulips, narcissuses and daffodils. The flowers looked a little mad in this *décor*, and considering there are no houses to put flowers in, the whole set-up seemed odd. Two young men on bicycles rode up and one of them bought a bunch of tulips. We asked him what he wanted tulips for and he said he was Dutch. So of course he needed the tulips. He had been a slave laborer in this city for three years; his friend had been here only five months. They came from Rotterdam. Anything that happened to Cologne was all right with them.

The flower vendor came over to talk. Yes, this was his regular business; he walked eighteen kilometers a day to get the flowers. Now I think of it, he was allowed to travel only six kilometers from his dwelling place, so I wonder how he did it. He made very little money, but before we came he sold his flowers to the hospitals as well as to some old customers. He was alone in the world and he would go on with the flowers as long as there were any flowers and then he would probably sell vegetables. His family was dead. His whole family, forty-two of them, including his grandparents and parents, his wife and children, his sisters and their children and husbands. They had all been buried in one cellar during one air raid. He brought pictures out of his wallet. "Of this sister," he said, "we found only her torso. During the bombings, we prayed a great deal." The two soldiers and I sat in the jeep and wondered why he talked to us; if forty-two members of our families had been killed by German bombs we would not talk pleasantly to Germans.

A crowd gathered around us; since no one speaks to Germans, except on official business, you can collect a crowd anywhere simply by saying *"Guten Tag."* This desire to be chummy baffles us as much as anything. The crowd was varied and everyone talked at once. I asked them when things had started to go bad in Germany, because my editor wanted me to ask that. I had a private bet with myself on the answer, and I won. Things have been bad in Germany since 1933, they all said loudly. I said, No, I am talking about since the war. Since 1941 it has been bad. Why? Because of the bombs. *"Danke schön,"* I said. Then I asked what form of government they hoped for after the war. I had another bet with myself, and I won. Democracy, they cried. But one day in another village it came out much better than that, and much more truthfully. The women said that if they had enough to eat and could live quietly they did not care who ruled them. Note: *who.* The men said they had not talked politics for eleven years and no longer knew anything about government. However, democracy is a fine word and in frequent use in Germany. Then I asked them (for my editor) whether they had traveled during the war, had anyone made a side trip to Paris? No one had traveled anywhere at all; they were assigned their work and they stayed to do it, good and bad, twelve hours a day. After that the talk degenerated into the usual condemnation of the Nazis.

We decided to go and see friends for a change, so we went down to the riverfront to call on some Airborne pals. It is a stone jungle, through which the American soldiers roam on foot or bicycle. The Company CP was in a candy factory and we were taken to see the vast stocks of sugar, chocolate, cocoa, butter, almonds and finished candies that remained. Then we were led to a huge wine cellar, only one of three they had located. Next we visited a flour warehouse which had more flour in it than any of us had seen at one time. After this (and by now we were all in a temper, thinking how well off the Germans had been) we went through a jumble of factory buildings used as a general food depot, and we looked with anger on rooms full of Dutch and French cheese, Portuguese sardines, Norwegian canned fish, all kinds of jams and canned vegetables, barrels of syrup. We had seen the individual food supplies throughout Germany, and this small portion of wholesale food stock only convinced us further that the Germans had not given up butter for guns but had done very nicely producing or stealing both. We figured that the Germans could afford to starve for the next five years, just to catch up with the rest of Europe.

A row of German women sat outside the white tape which marked off the military zone. They were watching their houses. No roof or window remains and often there is not a wall left either and almost everything in those houses has been blown about thoroughly by high explosives, but there they sat and kept mournful guard on their possessions. When asked why they did this, they started to weep. We have all seen such beastly and fantastic suffering accepted in silence that we do not react very well to weeping. And we certainly do not react well to people weeping over furniture. I remember Oradour in France, where the Germans locked every man, woman and child of the village into the church and set the church afire, and after the people were burned, they burned the village. This is an extremely drastic way to destroy property, and it is only one of many such instances. The Germans themselves have taught all the people of Europe not to waste time weeping over anything easy like furniture.

Farther down the river, U.S. Military Government was registering German civilians in the villages. The Germans queued up in a line four deep and filed into a little house and made a thumbprint on a piece of paper and got the great pleasure of owning another bit of official printing matter, which said they lived in this village. "It goes okay," said the young paratroop lieutenant who was in command here. "If they start shoving I just say something in a loud voice and boy, they snap right back into line."

During the war this village had lost ten civilian dead; during the last week German shells had killed seven more civilians. We talked with some German women about the horrors of war. The bombs, they said, oh God the bombs. Two thousand eight hundred bombs fell on this village alone, they said. Do not be crazy, we told them, there would be no sign of a village if that were true. We are very near Cologne, they said (it was about ten miles away). That is not the same thing, we said. Ah, the bombs, they said, firmly convinced that their village was flat and they were all dead.

167

The bombs continue, though not now in this vicinity, but every day the bombers go over and while there is still that steady smooth roaring in the sky the Germans remember the war. However, it is only on this side of the river that the Germans are happy in defeat, and just across the river the German ack-ack continues to operate. Yesterday it operated effectively and a B-26 was shot down and a column of black smoke rose straight and mountain-high. It looked like a funeral pyre to all of us. Tanks of the Thirteenth Armored Division were moving up across the river, behind the burning plane, but the crew was there in a belt of Germans, and no one could reach them. From a 505th Regimental observation post, some paratroopers had seen four men get out of the plane. That was at about one o'clock on a soft clear day. At six o'clock began one of the strangest episodes anyone had yet seen in this war—and there were a few men present who had survived all four 82nd Airborne missions and the Battle of the Bulge and could be expected to have seen everything.

Across the Rhine on the green bank someone started waving a white flag. This was ignored, because it does not necessarily mean anything. Then a procession came down to a landing pier. They carried a Red Cross flag. Through binoculars, we could see a medic, a priest, and two German soldiers carrying a stretcher. A landing craft put out from our bank, well covered by our machine guns in case this was all a sinister joke. Presently on both banks of the Rhine there was an audience; normally no one would move in this area in daylight, and even at night you would be careful. Now we stood in the sun and gaped. Slowly three more stretchers were carried down to our boat. We could see civilians over there, children, German soldiers; everyone was out staring at everyone else. We could not quite believe it and were still prepared to dive for cover quickly. Then the little boat was launched into the current, but it drifted farther downstream and we followed it on our side, like people streaming along a racecourse to watch the horses come in. The boat landed and our medic, who had gone over to get these four wounded men, the survivors of the B-26 crew, shouted to clear the banks because the Krauts said they'd give the ambulance time to load and then they would open up. The war had stopped for approximately an hour on a hundred-yard front.

"I never saw the Krauts act so nice," one soldier said, as we wandered back to the buildings where we would not make such tasty targets.

"They know our tanks are coming up," another soldier said. "Krauts don't act nice for nothing."

The DPs (displaced persons, if you have forgotten) tell us that Krauts never act nice. There are tens of thousands of Russian and Polish and Czech and French and Yugoslav and Belgian slave laborers around here, and they pour in every day in truckloads to the camps which the 82nd Airborne now run. There is apparently an inexhaustible supply of human beings who were seized from their families and who lived in misery for years, with no medical care and on starvation rations, while working twelve hours a day for their German masters. They do not feel kindly toward the Germans. The only time I have seen a Russian cry was when a Russian nurse, a girl of twenty-five, wept with rage telling of the way her people were treated. They had all seen their dead thrown into huge lime-filled pits, which were the communal graves. "Everywhere the graves became as high as a mountain," she said. The anger of these people is so great that you feel it must work like fire in the earth.

British prisoners of war are starting to come through now, still joking, still talking in understatement, but with bitterness behind the jokes and the quiet words. The ones we saw had walked for fifty-two days from the Polish frontier to Hanover, where their tank columns freed them, and on that fearful march those who fell out, from hunger and exhaustion, died. Their Red Cross parcels kept them alive during five years but since last November no parcels had arrived. In one small group, nine men had died of starvation after the long march and their bodies lay for six days in the crowded barracks because, for some unknown reason, the Germans did not feel like burying them or allowing them to be buried.

"They're not human at all," a New Zealander said.

"I wish they'd let us take charge of the German prisoners," a boy from Wales said.

A man who was lying on the grass near him now spoke up thoughtfully. "You can't really learn to like those people," he said, "unless they're dead."

Meanwhile the Germans, untroubled by regret—because after

all they did nothing wrong, they only did what they were told to do—keep on saying with energy; we are not Nazis. It is their idea of the password to forgiveness, probably followed by a sizable loan.

We are not Nazis; we are friends. Hundreds of thousands of people in khaki around here, and equal numbers of foreigners in rags, cannot see it that way.

The Russians

April 1945

One Russian guard stood at the pontoon bridge on our side of the Elbe. He was small and shaggy and bright-eyed. He waved to us to stop and came over to the jeep and spoke Russian very fast, smiling all the time. Then he shook hands and said, *"Amerikanski?"* He shook hands again and we saluted each other. A silence followed, during which we all smiled. I tried German, French, Spanish and English, in that order. We wanted to cross the Elbe to the Russian side and pay a visit to our allies. None of these languages worked. The Russians speak Russian. The GI driver then made a few remarks in Russian, which I found dazzling. "You got to talk a little bit of everything to get around these days," he said. The Russian guard had listened and digested our request and he now answered. The operative word in his answer was: *nyet.* It is the only word in Russian I know, but you hear it a lot, and afterwards there is no use arguing.

So we drove back to the CP of a Russian officer, who perhaps controlled that bridge. Here we had another brilliant and enjoyable conversation, filled with handshakes, laughter and good will; the operative word again was *nyet.* It was suggested that I go to a building in Torgau, a little way farther back from the river, where I would find more of my compatriots who were waiting for one thing or another. This was a square gray German house, outside of which were parked various jeeps and staff cars belonging to various American and English officers who were waiting to cross the Elbe on business. The situation seemed to be permanently snafu. The atmosphere was one of baffled but cordial resignation. Officers stood in the street and speculated on Russian time, which was either one or two hours earlier or later than ours. They asked themselves whether the Russian General who was due today (they thought), but who had actually arrived and departed yesterday, would possibly come tomorrow and if so at whose hour, ours or theirs. They said that it was pointless to try to telephone across the river because the telephone, which was located in the first Russian office I had visited, was in a purely experimental stage and anyhow you never got an answer to anything by telephone, if in the first place the telephone worked and you happened to reach anyone at the other end. They said, this is the way it is, chum, and you may as well get used to waiting because wait is what you do. You could cross the Elbe to the Russian side only if accompanied by a Russian officer who had come to get you to take you to a specific place for a specific purpose. There was no nonsense about walking across a few hundred yards of pontoon bridge and fraternizing with our allies.

It was quite agreeable in the sun, and the street was interesting. Two Russian girl soldiers passed, and a Russian nurse wearing a pistol competently on her hip. A Russian soldier in a blue overall, with blue eyes to match, wandered up and said *"Amerikanski?"* and shook everyone's hand and was treated to a flood of GI jokes, to all of which he responded with smiles and the word *"Russki."* Then he said, *"Na,"* with a little sigh, and shook hands all around again and went about his business. The morning wore on and obviously nothing was going to happen, so we drove through the Russian part of Torgau and across a bridge guarded by MPs, and went to the American Battalion Headquarters for lunch. There we found a very large jolly soiled Russian colonel and his interpreter, doing their best to cope with a plate of K rations. They were no more enthusiastic about K rations than we are, which proves them to be men of taste, but they did like the coffee. No one was looking very spick-and-span in Battalion Headquarters, since combat troops are too hurried and occupied to look spick-and-span and also there is usually no water in newly liberated towns. However, the Russians all looked as if they hadn't had time for a bath since Stalingrad.

The colonel was delightful and had a handshake like the death squeeze of a grizzly bear, and through his interpreter he said he

172

would take me across the Elbe tonight, as he was going back to his Division Headquarters, and he would call for me at five-thirty. After a certain amount of discussion we agreed on whose five-thirty that would be, his or ours, and everyone was happy. At five-thirty he had not come and runners went out to search for him. At six-thirty I went back to the Russian part of Torgau and tracked him down.

He insisted that I come and eat with them; they were having a little snack. The little snack was a dream, consisting of hard-boiled eggs and three kinds of sausage and pickles and butter and honey and various wines, and I decided that the Russians had a more sensible approach to rationing than we have. It is old-fashioned but effective and saves a lot of trouble; you live off the land and any land can beat K rations. We began to talk about crossing the Elbe. It appeared that the Colonel had not understood my request; no, it would be impossible to go unless the General gave his permission. Then could he telephone to the General? What, now? Yes, now.

"Time is money," said the interpreter.

"You are in such a hurry," said the Colonel. "We will talk this all over later."

"You do not understand," I said, "I am a wage slave. I work for a bunch of capitalist ogres in New York who drive me night and day and give me no rest. I will be severely punished if I hang around here eating with you citizens, when it is my duty to my country to cross the Elbe and salute our gallant allies."

They thought this was fine, but still nothing happened.

"Go on and call the General," I said, trying the wheedle angle. "What difference will it make to the General if one insignificant female correspondent pays him a visit?"

"Hokay," said the Colonel, that being the one American word he knew. He went out to telephone the General, and more time passed.

There was another colonel and the interpreter, and between mouthfuls of hard-boiled eggs we had a splendid talk. We discussed the Germans and were in perfect agreement all along the line. We discussed the American Army and were in perfect agreement all along the line. I was told of the wonders of Russia, which I have never seen, and I was urged to visit the Crimea in the summer, since it is of surpassing beauty. I said I would. I was asked what I thought about the Russian Army. I said I would give anything to see it but in the meantime I thought it was wonderful, the whole world thought it was wonderful. We had a few toasts. We toasted "Treemann" for quite a while before I realized we were toasting the President; the way they said it, I imagined it was some crisp Russian term meaning bottoms up. The the Colonel came back. The operative word again was *nyet*. I do not think he had telephoned the General, but it was *nyet* anyhow.

The conversation had been purely gay and they are very gay, but all of a sudden it got serious. We were talking about their medals. They do not wear ribbons, they wear the entire medal, officers and men alike, and the medals are worn on both sides of the chest and look terrific. There are handsome enamel decorations for killing Germans—I believe each decoration equals fifty dead Germans but I am not sure of this—and there are medals for individual heroism and for battles.

Out of the blue, the interpreter said, "I am a Polish Jew. My father was shot by the Germans. Three months later my mother was put to death in a gas chamber. They came for my wife and she was still bandaged from an operation, she could not even stand up straight. They took her away to work and there was the child, four months old, left behind. They killed the child by striking it across the head with a pistol, but my wife did not know this. She got a little letter to me, that was more than four years ago, and said, 'Do not wait for me, I will never come back, take the child and find him a mother and make a new life.' She did not know the child was dead." He brought from his pocket a Russian newspaper with pictures in it, such as you have all seen by now. These were taken at Lemberg and showed the horribly familiar but never endurable piles of dead and the mass hangings and the mutilated bodies of those who had been tortured. "Lemberg was my home," said the interpreter. "When the Germans come crying to me, asking for this or asking for that, I show them these pictures and I say to them, 'Look first and then cry!'"

"Let us go out and walk," said the Colonel. "We must not be sad. We hate war and we would like to go home, for it is many years since we have been home, but we will kill Germans as long as they ask for it. Meanwhile it is a nice night, so we will go walking."

Torgau in the evening was a picturesque place. From one building came the lovely sad sound of Russian singing, low and slow and mourning; from another building, a young man leaned out of a window and played a very fast bright tune on a harmonica. Rare-looking types wandered around the street; there is the greatest possible variety in the faces and uniforms of the Russian soldiery. There were blonds and Mongols and fierce-looking characters with nineteenth-century mustaches and children of about sixteen, and it felt like a vast encampment of a nomad people, where everyone is eating around campfires, singing, playing cards and getting ready to roll into blankets and sleep. We heard a few stray shots and met a few stray drunks and no one paid the slightest attention. We passed a couple of burning houses which looked very pretty and a yard where a wealth of Torgau bicycles had been collected and stacked—and tomorrow no doubt more of the Russian Army would be mobile.

I said it was all charming, but how about getting across the Elbe? In two weeks, the Colonel said, I am sure it will be arranged. If there was anything I was sure of, it was that I wouldn't be waiting around Torgau for two weeks. It is a political question, said the interpreter, you are capitalists and we are Communists. I told them heatedly that I did not consider it any of my business whether they were Mormons, cannibals or balletomanes, the point being that we were allies and naturally we were interested in each other and each other's armies. No one, said I crossly, minded where they went; their correspondents moved freely with our Army and everyone was delighted to see them. If, on the other hand, they behaved in this suspicious and unfriendly manner, it would make everyone angry and it would be their own fault. We were eager to understand them and none of us in these parts was interested in politics. It would be nice if they acted more openhearted for a change. They agreed to this but said that in their Army nothing was done without permission; the permission had not been granted as yet. All right, I said, but unless we can all circulate freely amongst each other there will be no trust and no confidence, and that will be terrible.

"It will be arranged in time, you will see," said the Colonel.

"Time is money," the interpreter remarked, knowingly.

In the morning the pontoon bridge was the center of interest. The day before, to the amazement of the GIs, some Russian soldiers had appeared and washed the boats which supported the wooden treadway. Today more Russians appeared, with pots of green paint, and painted the boats. Small fir trees were stuck up along the treadway and it was the prettiest bridge you could hope to see. Now in the early sunlight, a procession of thin, quiet displaced persons appeared; these were the Russians who had been taken into slavery by the Germans, and they were crossing the Elbe to go home. The Elbe is not very wide and the banks are soft green grass, but as soon as anyone crossed that bridge and disappeared up the opposite bank he might as well have gone to Tibet, because it was forbidden, unimaginable territory.

For a little while there was relative calm and we sat on a stone wall and watched the river and smoked and talked about nothing. Gradually the Russian Army began to cross the bridge to our side of the river. The Army came in like a tide; it had no special shape, there were no orders given. It came and flowed over the stone quay and up on the roads behind us like water rising, like ants, like locusts. It was not so much an army as a whole world on the move. Knowing nothing of the formation of the Russian Army (and never being told by the Russians), one does not know whether this was a regiment or a division or six regiments or six divisions for that matter, but it came on and on and on, inchoate, formless, and astonishing, and it was very noisy and slightly mad and it knew exactly what it was doing.

First came men, hordes of them, wearing tunics, greatcoats, baggy khaki-ish clothing, and carrying a light sort of tommy gun, pistols, grenades and generally assorted munitions. They did not seem to march and they did not seem to be numerically divided into groups; they were simply a mass. They looked tired and rather indifferent and definitely experienced. Then some trucks bumped over the bridge—God knows what sort of trucks, or where manufactured. Quantities of men rode on these, also women. These women were uniformed like the men, and equally armed, and were young, absolutely square in build, and tough as prize-fighters. We were told that the women were wonderful snipers and that they served as MPs. At this point a woman soldier arrived at the near end of the bridge, carrying two flags like semaphore flags, and took up her position. She was an MP, and with her flags and an air of authority she proceeded to handle this startling traffic.

A pack train now rumbled across the bridge. It consisted of beat-up carts and wagons and strong but shabby horses, and the drivers handled the horses with a competence that was inspiring and rather like the chariot races in *Ben Hur*. The pack train carried everything, bedding and clothing and pots and pans and ammunition and also women, because Russian women can go to war with their men, and it seems a reasonable idea. These were no glamour girls; they were peasants and they looked as if no hardship would be too much for them, no roads too long, no winter too cruel, no danger too great.

After the pack train, something like the first locomotive appeared. It was short and had a huge smokestack and it towed two huge wooden cars. The GIs on the wall above the river broke into applause, saying, "Here comes the motorized stuff." Men on bicycles pedaled across the bridge and more men on foot and then some trucks carrying pontoons. The noise was a splendid Slavic roar mixed with the clang of iron wheels on cobbles and occasional shouts which may have been orders or curses. There was no visible plan to this exodus and you felt you were watching a marvelously realistic movie about the Russian armies during the war against Napoleon. It was entirely unlike anything we had ever seen before and it would be impossible to describe the feeling of power that came from this chaos of men and materiel. We sat on our wall and thought how bitterly the Germans must have regretted attacking the Russians. We thought anyone would be extremely silly to bother these people; for in these great shapeless numbers they were as overwhelming and terrible as a flow of lava.

By miracle this welter of humanity vanished from Torgau, no one knows how, and proceeded to infiltrate inland to take up the Russian line along the Mulde River, some fifty miles west. I have no idea how this was done; it happened. It is to be noted that many of the men wore the medal of the Battle of Stalingrad, and the whole lot had certainly fought their way west for some three thousand miles, and probably pretty largely on their own feet.

It was lunchtime and the exodus stopped temporarily. "The show's over," said a GI sitting next to me. Then, summing up the whole matter, he said with awe, "My God." We walked back to the bridge which leads to the American side of Torgau. Two GIs were guarding the bridge, and a Russian soldier, aged about eighteen, stood across the street apparently guarding it also. Three Russian soldiers were leaning over the stone railing in the middle of the bridge and suddenly there was a loud explosion and a fountain of water coming up from the stream below.

"That's nothing," one of the American guards said. "They're

just throwing hand grenades in the water. They're crazy about that. I don't know what it does to them, but if you see one anywhere near a bridge he's pretty sure to throw a hand grenade in the water."

The Russian guard now crossed the street and said in a voice of wonder. *"Amerikanski?"* to which the GIs replied in a tone of equal wonder, *"Russki?"* We all shook hands.

"You can't turn around for Russians shaking hands," the short GI said. "Now this joe, for instance, he's been on this bridge all morning and this is the fourth time he comes over and says *'Amerikanski'* and gives us the handshaking treatment."

"It's to show we're allies," the tall GI explained.

"Sure," said the short one, "that's okay by me. I only ask myself how many more times today this joe is going through this routine."

"Look at the ambulance, will you?" said the tall one. We turned and saw something like a furniture van, painted green and with small red crosses on its side. It had stopped farther down the street and a band of wounded crawled, limped or hopped out. They had been packed in on a nest of quilts and mattresses and they disappeared into a house which may have been an aid station.

"That's the first ambulance I seen," the tall one said. "Seems like if you can walk you go right along in their Army. You see more guys with bandages on their heads. Don't seem to bother them none."

"I used to think we were rugged," the other GI said, "until I saw these Russkis. Boy, they're really rugged, I mean."

"They're crazy," the tall one said flatly.

"What's the matter?" I asked. "Don't you like them?"

"Sure, I like them. They seem like pretty good guys. They're crazy, that's all."

"I guess they'll push us back to the Rhine pretty soon," the short one said. "They certainly shoved a lot of men over this morning."

"Suits me," his colleague answered. "I hope they push us back quick. I hope they take all of Germany. They'll know how to handle it, brother. They really know. Suits me. What I want is to go home."

Dachau

May 1945

We came out of Germany in a C-47 carrying American prisoners of war. The planes were lined up on the grass field at Regensburg and the passengers waited, sitting in the shade under the wings. They would not leave the planes; this was a trip no one was going to miss. When the crew chief said all aboard, we got in as if we were escaping from a fire. No one looked out the windows as we flew over Germany. No one ever wanted to see Germany again. They turned away from it, with hatred and sickness. At first they did not talk, but when it became real that Germany was behind forever they began talking of their prisons. We did not comment on the Germans; they are past words, there is nothing to say. "No one will believe us," a soldier said. They agreed on that; no one would believe them.

"Where were you captured, miss?" a soldier asked.

"I'm only bumming a ride; I've been down to see Dachau."

One of the men said suddenly, "We got to talk about it. We got to talk about it, if anyone believes us or not."

Behind the barbed wire and the electric fence, the skeletons sat in the sun and searched themselves for lice. They have no age and no faces; they all look alike and like nothing you will ever see if you are lucky. We crossed the wide, crowded, dusty compound between the prison barracks and went to the hospital. In the hall sat more of the skeletons, and from them came the smell of disease and death. They watched us but did not move; no expression shows on a face

179

that is only yellowish, stubby skin, stretched across bone. What had been a man dragged himself into the doctor's office; he was a Pole and he was about six feet tall and he weighed less than a hundred pounds and he wore a striped prison shirt, a pair of unlaced boots, and a blanket which he tried to hold around his legs. His eyes were large and strange and stood out from his face, and his jawbone seemed to be cutting through his skin. He had come to Dachau from Buchenwald on the last death transport. There were fifty boxcars of his dead traveling companions still on the siding outside the camp, and for the last three days the American Army had forced Dachau civilians to bury these dead. When this transport had arrived, the German guards locked the men, women and children in the boxcars and there they slowly died of hunger and thirst and suffocation. They screamed and they tried to fight their way out; from time to time, the guards fired into the cars to stop the noise.

This man had survived; he was found under a pile of dead. Now he stood on the bones that were his legs and talked and suddenly he wept. "Everyone is dead," he said, and the face that was not a face twisted with pain or sorrow or horror. "No one is left. Everyone is dead. I cannot help myself. Here I am and I am finished and cannot help myself. Everyone is dead."

The Polish doctor who had been a prisoner here for five years said, "In four weeks, you will be a young man again. You will be fine."

Perhaps his body will live and take strength, but one cannot believe that his eyes will ever be like other people's eyes.

The doctor spoke with great detachment about the things he had watched in this hospital. He had watched them and there was nothing he could do to stop them. The prisoners talked in the same way—quietly, with a strange little smile as if they apologized for talking of such loathsome things to someone who lived in a real world and could hardly be expected to understand Dachau.

"The German made here some unusual experiments," the doctor said. "They wished to see how long an aviator could go without oxygen, how high in the sky he could go. So they had a closed car from which they pumped the oxygen. It is a quick death," he said. "It does not take more than fifteen minutes, but it is a hard death. They killed not so many people, only eight hundred in that experiment. It was found that no one can live above thirty-six thousand feet altitude without oxygen."

"Whom did they choose for this experiment?" I asked.

"Any prisoner," he said, "so long as he was healthy. They picked the strongest. The mortality was one hundred percent, of course."

"It is very interesting, is it not?" said another Polish doctor.

We did not look at each other. I do not know how to explain it, but aside from the terrible anger you feel, you are ashamed. You are ashamed for mankind.

"There was also the experiment of the water," said the first doctor. "This was to see how long pilots could survive when they were shot down over water, like the Channel, let us say. For that, the German doctors put the prisoners in great vats and they stood in water up to their necks. It was found that the human body can resist for two and a half hours in water eight degrees below zero. They killed six hundred people in this experiment. Sometimes a man had to suffer three times, for he fainted early in the experiment, and then he was revived and a few days later the experiment was again undertaken."

"Didn't they scream, didn't they cry out?"

He smiled at that question. "There was no use in this place for a man to scream or cry out. It was no use for any man ever."

A colleague of the Polish doctor came in; he was the one who knew about the malaria experiments. The German doctor, who was chief of the Army's tropical medicine research, used Dachau as an experimental station. He was attempting to find a way to immunize German soldiers against malaria. To that end, he inoculated eleven thousand prisoners with tertiary malaria. The death rate from the malaria was not too heavy; it simply meant that these prisoners, weakened by fever, died more quickly afterward from hunger. However, in one day three men died of overdoses of Pyramidon, with which, for some unknown reason, the Germans were then experimenting. No immunization for malaria was ever found.

Down the hall, in the surgery, the Polish surgeon got out the record book to look up some data on operations performed by the S.S. doctors. These were castration and sterilization operations. The prisoners were forced to sign a paper beforehand, saying that he willingly understood this self-destruction. Jews and gypsies were castrated; any foreign slave laborer who had had relations with a German woman was sterilized. The German women were sent to other concentration camps.

The Polish surgeon had only his four front upper teeth left, the others on both sides having been knocked out by a guard one day, because the guard felt like breaking teeth. This act did not seem a matter of surprise to the doctor or to anyone else. No brutality could surprise them any more. They were used to a systematic cruelty that had gone on, in this concentration camp, for twelve years.

The surgeon mentioned another experiment, really a very bad one, he said, and obviously quite useless. The guinea pigs were Polish priests. (Over two thousand priests passed through Dachau; one thousand are alive.) The German doctors injected streptococci germs in the upper leg of the prisoners, between the muscle and the bone. An extensive abscess formed, accompanied by fever and extreme pain. The Polish doctor knew of more than a hundred cases treated this way; there may have been more. He had a record of thirty-one deaths, but it took usually from two to three months of ceaseless pain before the patient died, and all of them died after several operations performed during the last few days of their life. The operations were a further experiment, to see if a dying man could be saved; but the answer was that he could not. Some prisoners recovered entirely, because they were treated with the already known and proved antidote, but there were others who were now moving around the camp, as best as they could, crippled for life.

Then, because I could listen to no more, my guide, a German Socialist who had been a prisoner in Dachau for ten and a half years, took me across the compound to the jail. In Dachau, if you want to rest from one horror you go and see another. The jail was a long clean building with small white cells in it. Here lived the people whom the prisoners called the N.N. N.N. stands for *Nacht und Nebel*, which means night and mist. Translated into less romantic terms, this means that the prisoners in these cells never saw a human being, were never allowed to speak to anyone, were never taken out into the sun and the air. They lived in solitary confinement on water soup and a slice of bread, which was the camp diet. There was of course the danger of going mad. But one never knew what happened to them in the years of their silence. And on the Friday before the Sunday when the Americans entered Dachau, eight thousand men were removed by the S.S. on a final death transport. Among these were all the prisoners from the solitary

182

cells. None of these men has been heard of since. Now in the clean empty building a woman, alone in a cell, screamed for a long time on one terrible note, was silent for a moment, and screamed again. She had gone mad in the last few days; we came too late for her.

In Dachau if a prisoner was found with a cigarette butt in his pocket he received twenty-five to fifty lashes with a bullwhip. If he failed to stand at attention with his hat off, six feet away from any S.S. trooper who happened to pass, he had his hands tied behind his back and he was hung by his bound hands from a hook on the wall for an hour. If he did any other little thing which displeased the jailers he was put in the box. The box is the size of a telephone booth. It is so constructed that being in it alone a man cannot sit down, or kneel down, or of course lie down. It was usual to put four men in it together. Here they stood for three days and nights without food or water or any form of sanitation. Afterward they went back to the sixteen-hour day of labor and the diet of water soup and a slice of bread like soft gray cement.

What had killed most of them was hunger; starvation was simply routine. A man worked those incredible hours on that diet and lived in such overcrowding as cannot be imagined, the bodies packed into airless barracks, and woke each morning weaker, waiting for his death. It is not known how many people died in this camp in the twelve years of its existence, but at least forty-five thousand are known to have died in the last three years. Last February and March, two thousand were killed in the gas chamber because, though they were too weak to work, they did not have the grace to die; so it was arranged for them.

The gas chamber is part of the crematorium. The crematorium is a brick building outside the camp compound, standing in a grove of pine trees. A Polish priest had attached himself to us and as we walked there he said, "I started to die twice of starvation but I was very lucky. I got a job as a mason when we were building this crematorium, so I received a little more food, and that way I did not die." Then he said, "Have you seen our chapel, Madame?" I said I had not, and my guide said I could not; it was within the zone where the two thousand typhus cases were more or less isolated. "It is a pity," the priest said. "We finally got a chapel and we had Holy Mass there almost every Sunday. There are very beautiful murals. The man who painted them died of hunger two months ago."

Now we were at the crematorium. "You will put a handkerchief over your nose," the guide said. There, suddenly, but never to be believed, were the bodies of the dead. They were everywhere. There were piles of them inside the oven room, but the S.S. had not had time to burn them. They were piled outside the door and alongside the building. They were all naked, and behind the crematorium the ragged clothing of the dead was neatly stacked, shirts, jackets, trousers, shoes, awaiting sterilization and further use. The clothing was handled with order, but the bodies were dumped like garbage, rotting in the sun, yellow and nothing but bones, bones grown huge because there was no flesh to cover them, hideous, terrible, agonizing bones, and the unendurable smell of death.

We have all seen a great deal now; we have seen too many wars and too much violent dying; we have seen hospitals, bloody and messy as butcher shops; we have seen the dead like bundles lying on all the roads of half the earth. But nowhere was there anything like this. Nothing about war was ever as insanely wicked as these starved and outraged, naked, nameless dead. Behind one pile of dead lay the clothed healthy bodies of the German soldiers who had been found in this camp. They were shot at once when the American Army entered. And for the first time anywhere one could look at a dead man with gladness.

Just behind the crematorium stood the fine big modern hothouses. Here the prisoners grew the flowers that the S.S. officers loved. Next to the hothouses were the vegetable gardens, and very rich ones too, where the starving prisoners cultivated the vitamin foods that kept the S.S. strong. But if a man, dying of hunger, furtively pulled up and gorged himself on a head of lettuce, he would be beaten until he was unconscious. In front of the crematorium, separated from it by a stretch of garden, stood a long row of well-built, commodious homes. The families of the S.S. officers lived here; their wives and children lived here quite happily, while the chimneys of the crematorium poured out unending smoke heavy with human ashes.

The American soldier in the plane said, "We got to talk about it." You cannot talk about it very well because there is a kind of shock that sets in and makes it almost unbearable to remember what you have seen. I have not talked about the women who were moved to Dachau three weeks ago from their own concentration camps. Their crime was that they were Jewish. There was a lovely girl from Budapest, who somehow was still lovely, and the woman with mad eyes who had watched her sister walk into the gas chamber at Auschwitz and been held back and refused the right to die with her sister, and the Austrian woman who pointed out calmly that they all had only the sleazy dresses they wore on their backs, they had never had anything more, and that they worked outdoors sixteen hours a day too in the long winters, and that they too were "corrected," as the Germans say, for any offense, real or imaginary.

I have not talked about how it was the day the American Army arrived, though the prisoners told me. In their joy to be free, and longing to see their friends who had come at last, many prisoners rushed to the fence and died electrocuted. There were those who died cheering, because that effort of happiness was more than their bodies could endure. There were those who died because now they had food, and they ate before they could be stopped, and it killed them. I do not know words to describe the men who have survived this horror for years, three years, five years, ten years, and whose minds are as clear and unafraid as the day they entered.

I was in Dachau when the German armies surrendered unconditionally to the Allies. The same half-naked skeleton who had been dug out of the death train shuffled back into the doctor's office. He said something in Polish; his voice was no stronger than a whisper. The Polish doctor clapped his hands gently and said, "Bravo." I asked what they were talking about.

"The war is over," the doctor said. "Germany is defeated."

We sat in that room, in that accursed cemetery prison, and no one had anything more to say. Still, Dachau seemed to me the most suitable place in Europe to hear the news of victory. For surely this war was made to abolish Dachau, and all the other places like Dachau, and everything that Dachau stood for, and to abolish it forever.

THE WAR IN JAVA

Peace was wonderful because no one got killed any more and, foolishly, in those early days we thought we had learned enough not to start killing again. During the war, the rule was never to discuss casualties; people mourned in silence. Grief was always there and always heavier but contained, from necessity. Now the survivors had time, suddenly too much time, to count their losses. In old-fashioned wars, men went off to fight and parents, widows, fatherless children wept for them. Since modern total war was first practiced in Spain, men could return safe from the battles to find their families and homes wiped out. Bombs, artillery, mines, deportation, hunger killed non-combatants and combatants alike. In its entire history, Europe had not known such appalling loss. By unspoken agreement, people kept their sorrow to themselves.

The past could not be changed and though it was no longer legally a crime in England to "spread despondency and

187

alarm," it was wrong to spread darkness of spirit. Everyone had his own share of memory to live with. And many had to live with the worst memory in all experience, the Nazi concentration camps; nothing else in war was as evil, as bestially subhuman. We did not talk of the dead and the destruction; we were determinedly cheerful about the present.

Still, peace did not feel quite natural or comfortable; one couldn't think what to do with oneself, having fixed one's mind for so many years on the single aim of finishing Nazism. Soon after V-E Day, a friend and I wandered around London musing on the question: what next? What next indeed? As a beginning, one might try to settle somewhere. I bought a little house in London that afternoon and imagined I had taken a sensible step in the right direction. An expert surveyed my property and said that a land mine which had dropped across the street, blowing a large gap in the row of houses, had also shaken my dwelling to its foundations and dry rot had set in everywhere and it wasn't the best bargain of the century. This type of news would alarm one normally, but seemed unimportant then. You couldn't buy paint or sheets or furniture anyway. Owning a house was the sort of nervous gesture one made, in an effort to convert oneself to peacetime use.

Then I decided I must go to the Pacific. I had had enough of the Orient in 1940—41 to last me for life but it was my duty (to whom?) to see this war through to the end. And it would be fun to stop in my native land-of-plenty, en route. America turned out to be an alien country, inhabited by strangers whose conversation enraged or bored me. The only comfort was to meet old war chums and drink and swap stories about our compatriots and their ordeals and sacrifices on the home front. The ex-captain of a P.T. boat, who transported Allied agents to German-held shores, and the ex-pilot of a Thunderbolt fighter-bomber, who flew close infantry support, and other similarly ex-employed citizens agreed with me that nothing good would come of such ignorance. America was isolated in its safety. Despite a massive dose of war reporting, by word and picture, the residents had no conception of war.

What was true more than twenty years ago is true now: a gulf as wide as the Grand Canyon separates America from all the people who have known war in their own countries. War, for Americans, is a fact but not a reality; it has not happened here in living memory. The history of the failed peace and the threatening future would be different if a few bombs had fallen on a few American cities during World War II. It is strange that too much safety should prove to be so dangerous.

The stunning news of the A-bombs, immediately followed by the stunning news of Japan's surrender, came over the radio in St. Louis where I was visiting my mother and dawdling on my way to the Orient. Like everyone else, I had no idea what these bombs were, but was deeply uneasy: since when did two bombs have such an effect? Innumerable tons of bombs had never produced final results. I remember walking up and down the poorish average-income streets of the city, ringing doorbells and asking housewives in curlers and men in undershirts what they thought; how about these new bombs, I kept saying, what do you think? They were uneasy too, and talked of saving our boys and bringing them home and it was fine the war was ended, but their faces and voices were troubled. People weren't throwing their hats in the air and shouting with joy over those bombs, even then, when wild celebration might have been expected.

As there was no war in the Orient, I went quickly back to Europe, where I belonged. London had become (and still is) my favorite city; the shabbiness, the ration cards, the marks of destruction by high explosive and fire, the weariness, the wit, the special gaiety of the brave, the absence of heroics formed a climate that I thought the best climate in the world. But I am a traveler by nature and profession, not a settler, and though, at last, my little London house was repaired and furnished, I doubt that I lived in it three months altogether.

The 82nd Airborne Division was the U.S. occupying force in Berlin; editors liked Berlin stories; we liked the Division. I drifted in and out of Berlin, it was a drifting period for ex-war correspondents. Berlin was a ruin, the buildings like huge decayed teeth, which did not sadden any of us. Berlin was also full of Germans whom we regarded with complete indifference and hardness of heart, feeling it correct for Germans to suffer a bit in view of the horrors everyone else in Europe had suffered at German hands. We were gay and lazy in Berlin; none of us knew what to do next.

189

Meanwhile men were again at war in Java. By then I scarcely knew how to write about anything else and I thought, mistakenly, that this was the tail-end of the war against Japan; so I went to Batavia. That war finally converted me to peacetime use, as I have noted earlier in this book. My memory is tricky, but I think I know the day when I decided to opt out of war for good. Two young English officers and I were driving in a jeep through jungly landscape, terrain where hidden small brown men could shoot at you or you might ride over a mine in the track. We were so profoundly sick of it all that we didn't care; we didn't care what anybody did to anybody else; if people were crazy enough to accept war, let them. Though I would not swear to this, I remember that they quoted poetry. The English have dazzling memories for poetry. This war around us was disgusting, but language remained beautiful, and poets were sane, unlike politicians.

The war in the Netherlands East Indies was an early example of continuous armed revolts against colonialism. My twenty-year-old report from Java strikes me now as a rather ironical pre-view of things to come. U.S. officialdom used to be enamored of Dr. Soekarno; you might have thought he was an Asian copy of Abraham Lincoln. Money was lavished on our splendid ally, that bastion of something or other, Dr. Soekarno. Then there was a row, probably about money, and Dr. Soekarno became a scoundrel, intriguing with the enemy, the Red Chinese. Power politics must be a fascinating game for power politicians. As we know, Dr. Soekarno's political games ended in a massacre, very pleasing to U.S. policy since the right (i.e. the left) side got massacred. I would bet that much of the killing in Indonesia was due to personal vendettas and xenophobia, and was a way to get rich quick by looting and expropriation. Dr. Soekarno was always exactly what he was in the beginning, a whizz-bang demagogue, an opportunist, just another little dictator. U.S. officialdom never tires of backing that type. Nor does U.S. officialdom take sufficient note of the writing on the wall, such as: Down With All Whites. I wonder what the phrase looks like in Vietnamese.

Java Journey

February 1946

Java is an island four times the size of Holland, shaped like a badly dented cucumber, and anchored between the Indian Ocean and the Java Sea, six degrees below the Equator. Now, more than half a year after the Japanese surrender, there is still war in this once-pleasant tropical island. Armed Japanese troops live comfortably in the interior, where the Allies cannot reach them, and thousands of Dutch civilians remain isolated in internment camps.

The "war" in Java is insignificant compared to the great battle against the Japanese which ended in the late summer of 1945. The Dutch and British lose a few soldiers killed and wounded each day; their self-appointed enemies, the bands of native Indonesians who fight for "freedom from white rule," lose many more. There is little glory for either side in this conflict.

For the most part, the Dutch now in Java have been here all during the Jap occupation, living under conditions which do not need to be described; the Jap camps are ugly familiar knowledge. They kept themselves alive on hope—hope of finding their families, their homes, their work and a quiet orderly pattern of existence. Instead, they find themselves still separated from their families, homeless, destitute, and accused of being foul imperialists who grind down native peoples. The injustice of this suffocates them. And they cannot seem to make their case heard, partly because they haven't a child's notion of the self-advertising which is propaganda, and partly because everyone is tired of everyone else's suffering.

191

When the Dutch came out of the Jap prison camps, the Indonesians greeted them with kindness and friendship, giving them fruit and flowers and clothes and even money. The Dutch were unprepared, emotionally and intellectually, for what followed. They claim that, if there had not been six weeks between the Jap surrender last summer and the arrival of the British in Java to take that surrender, the extreme Indonesian Nationalists would not have declared this republic, which the Dutch largely regard as a state of gangsterism.

Dutch women continue to live in the same camps where the Japs kept them; the men are crowded together into small private houses or in various barracks and offices. They are all threadbare and they exist on relief allowances from the Dutch government or on the small salaries they earn from official jobs, for which they may or may not be suited. Their plantations or factories in the interior are, of course, expropriated by the Indonesians; their former employment as civil servants does not exist; no European commercial concerns operate in Allied territory, for there is nothing to operate them with.

And, meantime, there are 30,000 Dutch nationals still held captive somewhere in the interior of Java and Sumatra, about whom little or nothing is known; and those bodies floating down the canals are Dutch bodies, and Dutch people cannot really feel safe anywhere. They look at the seedy ruin of their former colony, and remember it as flourishing and fine, and they do not understand why foreigners now say they were monstrous overlords, considering how the Indonesians thrived and multiplied, were spared famine, protected from disease and educated as much as they would take.

Few white men—probably less than twenty—have visited the Nationalists' Java, where for four years the Japanese carried on a successful anti-white "Asia for the Asiatics" campaign. Recently, eleven correspondents were permitted to travel 300 miles through this forbidden land.

In this curious war, trains run regularly between the hostile camps, so we departed from Batavia in two special cars attached to the daily Jogjakarta local. On board was Mr. Sjahrir, a modest, sincere, charming man somewhere under five feet tall, who is the Indonesian prime minister. He was going to the capital to consult the president of the Indonesian Republic, Doctor Soekarno. Doc-

192

tor Soekarno no longer visits any area held by the British and Dutch, which considerably delays all negotiations in this war, as Doctor Soekarno is the strong man of Indonesia and nothing can be decided without his consent. Traveling under Mr. Sjahrir's chaperonage is the one known way of visiting the interior with the prospect of remaining intact.

The prime minister's party occupied a sleeping car; the press traveled in one half of a chair car, with twelve plush seats and six folding tables among them. These elegant carriages were air conditioned. The windows were made of monstrously thick glass and would not open. The air conditioning did not work. In the vestibule at the end of our carriage eleven small brown people crouched, stood or sat upon one another; thirty men were wedged in the second half of our chair car. The rest of the train was covered with Indonesians like bunches of grapes, and the long string of cars was slowly and wearily towed by an old engine which burned teak wood.

Just outside Batavia, at the frontier between Allied territory and Indonesian territory, British Indian troops sauntered through the train, pretending to inspect us. A few kilometers later, Indonesian soldiers wandered in and out. We had passed through no man's land and the trip began.

There were only three guards in the vestibule of the prime minister's carriage, which was practically empty space compared to the rest of the train. A colleague and I opened the outer doors and sat on the steps, watching the cinders fly past. "Like tracer bullets," he said, in a voice homesick for all-but-forgotten battles. "Very pretty." At five-fifteen in the black morning we were informed that we were passing the Happiness Mountains. A length of fire hose coiled on the wall fell on my colleague, and subsequently the toilet started flushing itself and overflowing the hallway. That ended the first night.

The train stopped at a town called Kroja. Opposite the Kroja station lay and squatted Indonesians dressed in gunny sacks and looking like the skeletons of Dachau; they were scaly with hunger and raw with sores. We were told that these people had been taken for forced labor by the Japanese, and now they were trying to find their way back to their own villages. You see these unfortunate natives everywhere, in Batavia as well as in the interior. The other natives looked adequately dressed and healthy.

Then the train stopped again at Poerwokerto. There was a great crowd at the station; everyone wore a little swath of the national colors, red and white, sewed or pinned to him somewhere, and every male above the age of twelve seemed to be armed with a knife, a sword, a bamboo spear with a knife attached, a pistol or a rifle. They were a stony, unfriendly lot in this town, and their faces frightened us. The station walls were painted with slogans in English—FREEDOM—THE GLORY OF A NATION, and so on—though no one had been able to read them except ourselves and a press party which went by this way some months ago. Also, the passing trains were plastered with signs: WE WANT TO REIGN OURSELVES; HOSPITALITY FOR EVERYONE. Indonesians have a great talent and enthusiasm for slogans. All that morning we saw no one who laughed or looked happy, which was puzzling, as we had heard so much about the gay and simple Javanese.

It took eighteen hours to get to Jogjakarta; this is a trip which used to take eight hours before teak-burning engines and train inspections set in. There was a frowsy honor guard at the station to meet the prime minister, and the correspondents were met by a tiny tornado of a woman whom the English soldiers call Surabaya Sue, and who calls herself by a Balinese name, Tantri.

Miss Tantri is an Englishwoman, who speaks over the clandestine Surabaya radio and is a local version of that other famous broadcaster, Lord Haw-Haw. She is small, not young, not pretty, wearing her mahogany-red hair straight and with a square bang, and in this heat she has an energy that is terrifying. Before we got out of the station she told us that Soetomo, an Indonesian extremist leader, was sweet and delicate as a woman and wouldn't hurt a flea; that 10,000 Indonesian women and children had been killed by British bombs in Surabaya; and that the thousands of kidnappings and murders of Dutch in Java were all done by Dutch government agents. We got into a worn-out bus and were driven to the hotel.

En route we saw a discouraging slogan which said, DOWN WITH ALL WHITES.

Doctor Soekarno, the president of the republic, had bronchitis; the minister of defense was not visible; no one knew where Tan Malaka, the Communist leader, might be at present; we could not visit a T.R.I. training camp, as that was a military secret. The T.R.I. is the legal Indonesian army; the soldiers wear uniforms and have Japanese arms and obey the government. They are mainly Boy Scout age. There is also the People's Army, which wears anything and is armed with bamboo spears and trained in bands, and obeys whoever is training them. Then there are the *Pomoedas,* or Young Ones, who are a heritage of the Jap-trained youth organizations; these are adolescent guerrillas who are living happily off loot and mayhem. They obey their own gang leaders. Finally there are localized military groups such as the *Pembrontaks,* or Wild Bulls, around Surabaya, who seem to obey Soetomo, the rebel leader, and wear some sort of uniform and also have Jap arms. The Japanese army, before interning itself in great comfort in inaccessible parts of Java, complete with phonographs and refrigerators and plenty of food, gave most of its arms to these fiery young men. The Japanese can be highly gratified with the result.

On the way to Soerakarta, for the first time the land of Java did not look like an overcrowded tropical suburb. According to the 1941 census estimate, there were 390 people per square kilometer in Java. In England there were 182, and in the United States 15.7 persons per square kilometer. You are constantly aware here that there are far too many people around. But now between Jogjakarta and Soerakarta the land opened up in long sweeps of rice fields leading to ridged green mountains. Java began to look like a place worth fighting for.

Soerakarta is a prosperous, tidy town, little changed either by the Jap occupation or the present revolution. The streets are wide and shady, with European-style, roomy, cream-colored bungalows lining them.

That night the president was receiving, at the Sultan of Soerakarta's palace, some 300 administrators from all over Java. None of us had seen such a shining collection of American automobiles for a long time. Originally the Japanese stole these cars from the Dutch. Then the Indonesians took the cars from the Japs. These cars, plus expropriated Dutch houses and house furnishings, have considerably raised the living standard of Indonesian officialdom.

The administrators moved forward to the head of the room in groups of six and were presented to the President. Doctor Soekarno is tall for an Indonesian, with a serene, portentous face and a manner like royalty visiting hospitals. He wore the Mohammedan black cap and a black tie and white linen clothes, and he is

195

clearly the dominant personality in this country. He greeted his officials with the Indonesian salute, which is halfway between a military salute and the Heil Hitler flipper, and talked a moment, and then more men were presented. It was our turn at last. Not many facts are available in this emotional political situation, so we began asking the President questions. You always get an answer, because people are too polite to leave you unsatisfied, and probably one answer is as good as another, since no one can prove the contrary.

Doctor Soekarno told me that the Japanese exported 5,000,000 Indonesians for forced labor in the outer islands or Siam, and these have disappeared; and that a further 1,500,000 were used by the Japs as coolies in Java, and that hundreds of thousands of them died of bad treatment and hunger. His figures may not be correct—they are higher than any previously stated— but the fact remains that the native population suffered grievously during the Jap occupation.

What makes it so awkward is that this suffering proceeded under the aegis of Doctor Soekarno himself, who also felt impelled repeatedly to declare his gratitude to Japan and his admiration for the Greater East Asia Co-Prosperity Sphere and to decry the efforts of the western imperialist nations to defeat Japan. This awkwardness is now explained by saying that Doctor Soekarno merely used the Japanese to help the cause of Indonesian freedom, and that he always worked in the underground against Japan.

One morning two of us left a meeting where speeches were being made in Malay and walked out into the town. We did this without thinking, having forgotten our perilous white skins. Nothing happened. People stared a good deal, and in the market we collected as big a crowd as if we had been movie stars on Broadway. My colleague suggested that we were shattering illusions; the natives had been told the Dutch were all liquidated, and here were white, Dutch-seeming people back again.

We went into a drugstore, looking for coconut oil against sunburn and ammonia against lice bites, and found a family of white-skinned Eurasians dispensing medicines. They were very glad to see us, and very afraid. They did not want to talk too long or too openly, though we were their only hope of getting any news to their own people or any help. They said quickly that they were not interned, like all the other people of Dutch blood, because they

196

were the only trained chemists in the area. This had always been their shop; the Japanese, too, had allowed them to run it because they were necessary.

They told us also that there was a big internment camp three blocks from our hotel, and a small European-Dutch camp just down the street, and others we would find out about if we inquired at the Red Cross. They did not know what had become of any of their relatives—fathers, husbands, brothers—because these were either taken away to Siam by the Japs in 1942 or taken last fall by the Indonesians. It was this final imprisonment that was unbearable, and this last fear on top of the years spent fearing the Japs.

In the afternoon we insisted on seeing the Sinkokan camp, where some 600 Eurasian and Dutch women and children and old men were jailed. The camp was a horror. The Indonesians do not beat or torture or kill their Dutch prisoners; they simply neglect them to death. This comes not from cruelty, but from inefficiency. One starves as fast on a diet of 150 grams of rice a day, regardless of whether the starvation is according to plan or without plan. In the Sinkokan camp there were many cases of dysentery and beriberi; the people slept on damp cement floors without mattresses; their clothes were in shreds. The children were the saddest of all, squatting along the walls trying to heat up brownish patties of dry rice to make their meal more palatable. When we arrived, they went wild with joy, believing we were coming to free them.

Later, Soetomo was produced for us to interview. Soetomo, who is the great radio voice of Indonesia and a loudly blood-thirsty rebel leader, is twenty-five, very small, with delicate clawlike hands, beautiful teeth, large brown, somewhat mad eyes, and copious black hair.

He stated that the Dutch and British were not fighting seriously now because of the 15,000 or more Dutch nationals who were held in camps in the interior. Wherever these internees had been returned to the allies, as in Semarang and Surabaya, he said the allies came with bombers and cannon.

"Then the Dutch internees are hostages," one of the correspondents said.

"Not at all," said Soetomo.

The great event in Soerakarta was an evening meeting for 5,000 members of Indonesian schoolgirl organizations, at which Doctor Soekarno spoke. The meeting place was an open, whitewashed hall, sensibly and handsomely constructed, like all the prewar, Dutch-built public edifices—like the hospitals and schools and office buildings and sports stadiums and swimming pools. There could not be a more attractive audience, even rows of shining black heads and beautifully carved little brown faces.

Doctor Soekarno enthralled them from the beginning; he is a great orator. Without understanding a word, but watching his hands and following his voice and the eyes and faces of the children, one could feel his power, and one remembered Mr. Hitler and the organized children of Germany. However, to the credit of these people, when they are swept up in a wave of emotion they do not scream *Sieg Heil,* and become hysterical; they laugh. Laughter here is not mockery or amusement, but applause.

"What does he say?" I asked a Chinese next to me.

"He is talking about the ideals," said the Chinese, smiling. "It is all about the ideals. He just say, 'Our social ideal is an automobile for everyone.'"

There was another great crash of laughter.

"What now?"

"He say," the Chinese interpreted, "'Indonesia is the policeman at the crossroads of the Orient.'"

This sort of phrase apparently works anywhere.

Now there was a thunderclap of laughter and applause. The Chinese interpreted without being asked; he was flushed with excitement himself. "'I repeat again about the social ideal. It is not like in the old times of the kings. Everyone will have his electric light, his automobile and his bicycle.'"

Then they all sang Great Indonesia, to a variation of the tune of Boola Boola, and we went home.

In the train on the return trip, Johnny, an Indonesian poet, came and perched on the arm of my chair, like a very young, very thin bird. One of the great charms of the Indonesians is the place they give a boy like Johnny; they say he is good for nothing except to write poetry once in a while, but everyone loves him and even respects him, and he is supported by his friends, since he owns nothing and does not bother to earn money.

Now Johnny said, "What do you think? Will we get our independence?" For, despite all the shouting and slogans and the red-and-white flags, they do ask questions like that.

"Oh, sure," we said, both to cheer him up and because we

believe it. Obviously, in due course there will be no colonial empires anywhere. No one recognizes this more clearly than the Dutch in Java. The only point in question is the method of transfer.

"That's nice," Johnny said happily.

It is the idea of *Merdeka* that has got them, though it is hard to find out what exactly they think this *Merdeka*—Freedom—will mean. Naked, potbellied children stand along the roadside and pipe *"Merdeka,"* raising their clenched fists in salute. Coolies put down their loads and say *"Merdeka,"* as you would say "Hi, Mac." Neat, pretty Javanese young ladies, selling subscriptions for nonexistent newspapers in the cafés, smile and say *"Merdeka"* politely, like saying "Good-bye" or "Delighted to have met you." It is an immensely successful word. It sounds cheerful and appeals to everyone.

"What are you going to do, once you've got *Merdeka,* Johnny?" someone asked. You do find yourself peevishly wishing the Indonesians would be practical. "How are you going to make your country run?"

"Oh, I see," said Johnny, still happy as a lark. "As soon as we have our freedom, we will let the Dutch stay and help us."

INTERIM

The two articles that follow are not properly war reporting, yet I think they are essential to this book. When a war ends, it is not over. Unfinished business remains. Tragically, the greatest war of the world, to date, spawned almost ceaseless little wars; the business is still unfinished. These articles describe different efforts to prevent war.

The Nuremberg Trial set a precedent in history. Aggressive war was branded as a crime under international law and those responsible could not escape punishment by saying they had merely obeyed orders. That was a moral judgment and applies equally to all nations.

And then there was the Paris Peace Conference. The people of Europe were facing the seventh winter of hunger and cold, in threadbare clothes and unheated houses, and already our leaders were misguided by fear, already lining up for the next war. The shape of the future became clear, while our leaders talked of ways to arrange peace: East versus West, West versus East, madness again.

The Paths of Glory

November 1946

For ten months and ten days they sat there under the hard blue-white lights, and each one found an expression for his face which would last as long as the trial lasted. They were strange faces and told nothing.

Goering's terrible mouth wore a smile that was not a smile, but only a habit his lips had taken. Next to him Hess, with dark dents for eyes, jerked his foreshortened head on his long neck, weird, inquisitive and birdlike. Ribbentrop held his mouth pursed and sat rigid as the blind. Keitel was nothing, a granite bust badly made of inferior stone. Kaltenbrunner, whose face was terrifying even now when it could bring fear to no one, stared ahead with a flat, polite attention.

Rosenberg seemed smeared, a meaningless, soft face which had only silence to hide behind. Frank, sheltered by dark glasses, had a small cheap face, pink-cheeked, with a little sharp nose and black sleek hair. He looked patient and composed, like a waiter when the restaurant is not busy. Frick's gray-blond cropped head and lean, horsy face bent forward to listen, almost as if he were a visitor here. Streicher chewed gum, the long loose mouth working steadily, and his face too showed nothing; the face of an idiot, this one.

Funk, slumped in his chair, had a dog's face with dewlap jowls; he looked sorry for himself, ready to cry, sleepy and grotesque. Schacht sat very straight, disagreeable and righteous, with the lights shining on his éyeglasses and an expression of disapproval as hard as iron on that mean, down-curving mouth.

Behind them in the second row were the lesser men. There were the two nondescript admirals. Doenitz and Raeder; then the dreadful, weak face of Schirach (there were times when from the side Schirach looked like a woman who has suffered from imagined ailments all her life and blackened her family's existence with complaints); Sauckel, a puzzled stupid butcher-boy face; Jodl, held together by his military tunic; Von Papen, looking handsome and somehow crafty and careful; Seyss-Inquart, whom you could imagine as once arrogant and who now seemed made of wood and dull as wood; Speer, a technician turned criminal with a face you could see anywhere, in any subway, in any drugstore; Neurath, with the breeding and culture of his face only a deceit, and something gone bad beneath the good looks; Fritsche, the youngest, with a sensitive fox's face, vain perhaps, wearing a romantic sadness like a minor poet who has killed his mistress. None of them moved or looked at one another or changed his separate expressions.

They were just faces, some crueler than others and all more insignificant than you would believe possible. They were just men after all, with the usual number of legs, arms and eyes, born like other men; they were not ten feet tall and with the revolting masks of lepers.

You sat there and watched them and felt inside yourself such outrage that it choked you. These twenty-one men, these nothings, these industrious and once-confident monsters were the last left alive of that small gang which had ruled Germany.

The cowed and mindless people of Germany followed them, feared or cheered them, and because of their guiding brains—because of this unimposing gang—ten million soldiers, sailors, airmen and civilians are dead as victims of war, and twelve million men, women and children are dead in gas chambers and furnaces. In great common graves where they were shot, in the stockyards that were concentration camps, dead of hunger and disease and exhaustion, dead all over Europe. And all these deaths were horrible. What these men and their half-dozen deceased partners were able to do, no famines, no plagues, no acts of God ever did: they produced destruction as the world has never seen destruction. And there they sat behind their fixed faces.

Perhaps you think one might feel pity. We are not trained to gloat when we win, we cannot help feeling that the strong must have mercy on the beaten. But the pitilessness of these twenty-one men was so enormous, so beyond all human understanding, that one could feel no pity for them now.

It was a quiet court and a cold one. There was no anger here and no hate and no question of vengeance. Thirteen years of misery and crime can never be wiped out, twenty-two million dead will not live again. Nothing can correct what these men planned and ordered. This tribunal was gathered to judge, but above all, it was gathered to reaffirm and re-establish the rule of law between nations.

Everything about the trial at Nuremberg was unique in history; everything happened for the first time. Everyone present seemed to know that history was being made; everyone seemed to feel that responsibility and to find it heavy. The judges looked more tired than the men they were judging; the tables where the prosecution sat were crowded with the lawyers and advisers of four nations and they too seemed drained by fatigue.

The German defense laywers, in rows before the prisoners' dock, were pale and exhausted. For ten months, day after day, they had all listened to a record of such evil as truly darkens and sickens the mind. There was an atmosphere of long strain, of patience and determination, and there was a kind of grandeur about this room which history will note.

You turned a dial on the gadget fastened to your chair arm and tuned in on whatever language you understood. The best voice perhaps was that of Lord Justice Geoffrey Lawrence, president of the tribunal. Over the earphones you heard that slow, careful and immensely quiet voice reading without haste or passion, and you felt the dignity and the modesty of the man. He too looked tired and old, with the hard lights shining down on his great bald dome of a head. His voice was a symbol of what all civilized people want and mean by justice—something serene and unafraid and stronger than time. Something that will endure in honor. That voice was speaking for history:

"Planning and preparation are essential in the making of war. In the opinion of the tribunal, aggressive war is a crime under international law. According to the indictment, aggressive action was planned and carried out against Austria and Czechoslovakia in 1936–1938, followed by the planning and waging of war against Poland; and successively against ten other countries. Hitler could not make aggressive war by himself. He had to have the co-operation of statesmen, military leaders, diplomats and businessmen. That they were assigned to their tasks by a dictator does not absolve them from responsibility for their acts."

Those are clear words which anyone can understand. Aggressive war is a crime; the state is not some vague abstraction; the state is governed by men who are in authority over their fellows; they are responsible for their acts; if their acts are crimes, they are criminally responsible.

Wars do not just happen. And now there is a law against murder, for nations as for men. There is crime and punishment. The organizers of wars will no longer live in comfortable exile when the war is over, while the plain people build back their world, brick by brick, and mourn their dead.

The twenty-one remaining leaders of the German Nazi state were indicted at Nuremberg on four counts. The first was "The common plan or conspiracy," which in fact includes the other three charges of criminality. "The common plan or conspiracy" count states that these men planned consciously for a period of years to wage aggressive war and to employ—in the course of such war—every criminal means they could devise in violation of international treaties and agreements and national law, to insure their victory.

Their common plan began in the beer halls of Munich and proceeded through the Nazi seizure of power in Germany, continued with secret rearming and the deformation of the life of the German nation, the perversion of the German people, into undeclared wars whose full and monstrous horror has been exposed for the first time in the endless documents of this trial. The common plan was stopped forcibly by the Allied victory in 1945; otherwise we would all be living according to that common plan today.

The second charge against these twenty-one men was crimes against peace. War is the crime against peace. War is the silver bombers, with the young men in them, who never wanted to kill anyone, flying in the morning sun over Germany and not coming back. War is the sinking ship and the sailors drowing in a flaming sea on the way to Murmansk. War is the two wooden crosses with dog tags nailed to them at the road junction above Arlon. War is casualty lists and bombed ruins and refugees, frightened and homeless and tired to death, on all the roads. War is everything you remember from those long ugly years. And its heritage is what we have now, this maimed and tormented world which we must somehow restore.

The third count in the Nuremberg indictment was war crimes. Because men could not abolish war they tried at least to limit its horrors, and a body of common practice and custom had grown up since the eighteenth century, and had been modified in our time, which prescribed the treatment of prisoners, helpless combatants, civilian populations and property and neutrals in time of war. The German Nazi doctrine of total war had no use for these rules, which were binding on all. There is nothing gentle and little good about war; in the insanity of battle, prisoners have been shot by both sides. But Germans organized their crimes as if they were running a vast industry, and nothing was forgotten.

There were always the neat, formal orders, the interbureau notes, the reports, the polite or slightly bragging messages between the leaders. With the greatest order and system they organized the shooting of hostages, the "bullet decree" for escaping war prisoners, commandos and aviators, the failure to rescue and the attempted murder of survivors from sunken ships, the "night and fog" decree whereby anyone judged dangerous to the German regime was transported into Germany and ultimate death and no trace of his whereabouts or fate ever made known, the wholesale plundering of occupied nations whose people might starve as long as Germans lived, the vast and appalling herding into slavery of seven million foreign men, women and children.

At one time a German order appeared saying that "for the moment no more children will be shot." The demand for labor was growing hungrily and it had been discovered that children could be worked quite well.

The German Nazi state and its leaders have been mainly convicted from their own documents. It is impossible to quote here even partially the proofs of their crimes as recorded by themselves. But there are some few which must be mentioned.

On the subject of Russian prisoners of war captured in the early days of the campaign, Himmler said in 1943, "At the time we did not value the mass of humanity as we value it today as raw material, as labor. What is now deplorable by reason of the loss of labor is that the prisoners died in tens and hundreds of thousands of exhaustion and hunger."

Field Marshal Keitel in 1941 ordered: "It should be inferred in every case of resistance to the German occupying forces, no matter what the individual circumstances, that it is of Communist origin. The death penalty for 50 to 100 Communists should generally be regarded as suitable atonement for one German soldier's life." In Yugoslavia, a month later, 2,300 hostages were shot at one time in revenge for the killing of ten German soldiers and the wounding of another twenty-six. It was the same throughout Europe.

Himmler, in 1941, addressing SS officers on the necessity for obtaining more slave labor, said, "Whether 10,000 Russian females fall from exhaustion while digging an antitank ditch interests me only in so far as the antitank ditch for Germans is finished."

And so it goes, on and on, the disgusting record of brutality and murder. Frank, one of the defendants at this trial said in 1941, "As a matter of principle we shall have pity only for the German people and for no one else in the world."

The fourth count against the twenty-one defendants was crimes against humanity. The crimes against humanity are the extermination or attempted extermination of whole peoples and races whom the Germans decided were in their way. These people lived on land or owned property which the Germans desired; furthermore, the Germans regarded them as inferior. (In their own country, as a sideline, they exterminated 275,000 men and women who were described by them as "useless eaters"—the old, the feeble-minded, the incurably ill.)

They killed one third of the population of Poland and two thirds of the Jews of Europe; they tried systematically to murder the intelligentsia in occupied countries because these men would carry on the traditions of their people and keep alive their love of freedom.

Again the German leaders organized death as a mass industry. There were the great murder factories at Auschwitz, Belsen, Treblinka, Mauthausen, Sachsenhausen, Flosseberg, Neuengarme, Gusin Natzweiler, Lublin, Buchenwald, Dachau. These were the main plants, and in them some six million people were killed.

All the defendants knew of these places, some of them ordered their construction, directed their operations and used their services as a matter of routine. Imagine if you can, Kaltenbrunner, the Gestapo chief, a 42-year-old lawyer with a face of really deadly evil, giving luncheon parties in his Berlin home and over cigars and coffee explaining in detail the working of the gas chambers and crematorium ovens.

There is one heartbreaking and appalling piece of testimony which must be quoted here; it is the eyewitness account of a German who watched the mass shooting of Jews at Dubno. He describes the great open pit, already half full, and the new victims arriving by truck. They had to put down their clothes in fixed places, sorted according to shoes, top clothing and underclothing. Without screaming or weeping, these people undressed, stood around in family groups, kissed each other, said farewells and waited for the sign from another S.S. man who stood near the pit, whip in hand.

"During the fifteen minutes that I stood there," says the eyewitness, "I heard no complaint or plea for mercy. I watched a family of eight persons, a man and a woman, both forty, with their children of about one, eight and ten, and two grown-up daughters of about twenty or twenty-two. An old woman with snow-white hair was holding the year-old child in her arms and singing to it and tickling it. The child was cooing with delight.

"The couple were looking on with tears in their eyes. The father was holding the hand of a boy of about ten and speaking to him softly; the boy was fighting his tears. The father pointed to the sky, stroking his head, and seemed to explain something to him.

"The S.S. man at the pit counted off about twenty persons and instructed them to go behind the earth mound. Among them was the family I have mentioned. I walked around the mound and found myself confronted by an enormous grave. People were closely wedged together and lying on top of each other so that only their heads were visible. Nearly all had blood running over their shoulders from their heads. Some of the people shot were still moving. I estimated that the pit contained about one thousand bodies already. I looked for the man who did the shooting. He was an SS man who sat at the edge of the narrow end of the pit, his feet dangling into the pit. He had a tommy gun on his knees and was smoking a cigarette."

There were months of this testimony; all proved, all sworn to by witnesses, the witnesses checked and counterchecked, the documents verified. It is no wonder that in Germany you feel as if the very air you breathe is poisoned. The defendants, who knew all this at the time, and heard it repeated in this courtroom day by day, somehow still sat in their allotted spaces with the same fixed expressions on their faces.

The night before the verdict we decided to escape the cracked rubble that is Nuremberg. We would drive out into the countryside, which is sweet and richly green, and find a village and a pub and a meal and some beer. In Ansbach a boy offered to guide us to a café. He was tall and blond, twenty years old, with charming manners and blue eyes and white teeth. We invited him to eat with us.

We have all talked to many Germans since the early days of entering this country with the Army. I remember the very beginning when white sheets of surrender hung from every window and no one was a Nazi, and oddly enough vast numbers of Germans were half Jew and everyone had hidden a Communist, and all were agreed that Hitler was a monster.

Then, six months later, I remember that had changed and we heard how even during the worst period of the war they had butter and coal and clothes to wear and now (with an accusing look at us) there were none of these things. I remember my German driver eating a large white-bread sandwich and telling me bitterly that everyone was starving. But listening to this handsome boy in Ansbach was probably the most melancholy experience of all.

He had been a soldier since he was sixteen, in the Panzer grenadiers, which means that he was top-notch quality by German standards. He had been wounded three times, had fought against the English at Caen and on the Russian front. He said quite simply that Germany made war because England was ready to attack her. The Allied bombings, he said regretfully (for he did not wish to hurt our feelings), were not correct; they could not be forgotten: What did innocent women and children have to do with war?

"Then why do you suppose the German air force bombed Warsaw and London and Coventry first?" we asked. He was puzzled by this, but said there was probably a reason.

He went on to remark that this talk about the concentration camps was exaggerated and propaganda; he had seen people returning from "protective custody" to this very town and they were fat and sunburned.

There must have been some look in our eyes which stopped him, for he changed the subject by saying that it was wrong to kill the Jews, it was a mistake. On the other hand, said the boy, you could not help hating the Jews because they never did real work. In his life he had only seen the Jews changing money in a tricky way. Now Jews were returning to this town, and German families had to give them back their houses and sit in the street; no one spoke to the Jews.

Life was very hard nowadays, and there was little to eat. Of course you could buy whatever you liked on the black market. The black market was run by foreigners and notably by all these Poles. The Poles, he said, got many extra pairs of shoes from UNRWA and sold them and so grew into rich black marketeers.

The Hitler Jugend, he opined, had been a fine organization; they were given trips and concerts; they were taught culture. In the worst year of the war in Germany, everyone had everything he needed, but look at them now.

"Didn't you get all the things, the food and the clothes and all the little niceties, from Poland and France, Belgium and Holland?" my colleague inquired.

"No," said the boy proudly, "from Germany."

"Nuts!" said my colleague, who was beginning to feel sick.

At the end of the war, the boy continued, people hated Hitler because he had lost the war; but now they were beginning to see that Hitler was not really so bad, for things were much worse than when he had been running Germany. As for these trials, said the boy, Goering followed his ideas, he admitted it; he tried to do his best for Germany. The generals and admirals obeyed orders and should not be tried at all. But Funk, who had wept on the witness stand, was not a real German and whatever happened to him was all right. Anyhow, of course, the Allies would do whatever they liked at this trial since they had won the war.

When we left, the boy looked at us with hurt eyes, for he saw that he had not made a favorable impression though he had been so friendly and tried so hard to help us understand Germany.

I visited various responsible Germans, asking their opinion of the Nuremberg trial. There is no use in reporting those dreary interviews. One respectable businessman suggested that I consider

211

Nuremberg, bombed flat, and Hiroshima, wiped out. Apparently, he said, what the victors do is all right; only the vanquished are bad. The upshot of these conversations was that since the Allies have won the war they could hold a trial if they liked, but why didn't they just shoot the defendants without endless talk? The German people were sick of all these trials.

It took forty-seven minutes on the afternoon of October 1st to deliver sentence on the twenty-one German leaders. After it was over, there was an empty, stunned feeling in the courtroom, the judges filed out, the room was quiet, the trial was over, justice had been done. Justice seemed very small, suddenly; an anticlimax. Of course it had to be, for there was no punishment great enough for such guilt.

We must stand back from this trial to see it truly. At the end of his final speech the British Attorney General said: "The state and the law are made for man, that through them he may achieve a fuller life, a higher purpose and a greater dignity. States may be great and powerful. Ultimately the rights of men, made as all men are made in the image of God, are fundamental."

Eighteen nations are signatory to the charter under which this tribunal functioned. Eighteen nations are bound by the precedent this tribunal has set. Eighteen nations have agreed that the rights of man are inviolable and that aggressive war is a crime against mankind. This crime, together with all the evils flowing from it, is punishable by law. The men who labored so steadfastly and so honorably to set this precedent have committed a great act of hope. The hope is that this body of law will serve as a barrier against the collective wickedness, greed and folly of any nation. In these dark times it is only a hope. But without hope we cannot live. And in a time of doubt and suspicion, there is hope in the fact that men of four nations could work patiently together to brand evil and re-affirm the power and goodness of honest law.

They Talked of Peace

December 1946

On the street outside the great stone gate of the Luxembourg Palace, a very fat, violently blonde woman stood and stared. She had bare white legs and wore a black cloak and, underneath, a black lace dress that was both dirty and tattered. She had no age and no obvious profession; if she were a housewife, she must be married to a ragpicker; or perhaps she had once been an opera singer and had fallen into poverty, but retained the black lace.

She looked very strange indeed, and she represented the Public, for no one else—out of the millions in Paris—seemed interested, or could spare the time, to come to this street. Movie stars would of course always draw a big crowd; inside the Luxembourg the attraction was nothing but the politicians of twenty-one nations who were setting the pattern of peace.

From the courtyard behind the gate a voice announced over the loud-speaker: "Car 28, Brazilian Delegation . . . Car 47, Russian Delegation . . ." Only the blonde, and the cops who guarded the gate, watched the shining black cars which bore the delegates of the Peace Conference away to lunch.

This was the recess between the morning and afternoon sessions. The automobiles looked magnificent, rich and certain; the delegates did not look different from most of the people you see nowadays in the streets of any European capital, a little shabby but respectable, pallid, tired, and not very happy. After a while, the

213

astounding blonde shook her head—with wonder or with sorrow?—and walked away down the Rue de Seine.

At lunchtime, the enormous palace of the Luxembourg became like a theater when the curtain is down and the audience has left: the stagehands took over. I went upstairs to the Hall of Lost Footsteps where the big commissions on the Italian peace treaty held their meetings. At the doorway to this hall, I met two cops, for there were cops everywhere. The cops, who were proud of the Luxembourg Palace, offered to show me around.

The great conference hall is very grand, with much heavy gilt carving and a complete and depressing set of Gobelin tapestries around the walls, telling the story of the life of Orpheus in a million stitches. The cops extolled the beauty of the room and said it was a pity that the delegates did not like one another more, and have more pleasure, as it were, working in such a handsome place. "They don't like one another?" I said.

"Not at all," said the cops."How do you expect them to like one another when they agree about nothing?"

"Ah," I said wisely.

"In all cases," said the youngest cop, "when there is another war, poor France will get it in the neck as usual."

The cops advised me to pick up some lunch in the journalists' bar, which was a small white and gold salon, once no doubt the boudoir of a princess, where now a loud-speaker relayed, in three languages, incomprehensibly, the proceedings of the peace commission. There I met a lovely girl called Marie-Rose, with gay slanting eyes and black curly hair; she was twenty-one and an interpreter. She remarked that the last conference she interpreted for, which was an international gathering of meteorologists, was better than this one, because the men were scientists and therefore naturally more honest and serious than politicians.

She said this peace conference was on the whole a droll affair; the delegates insulted one another, without the slightest embarrassment. Her parents were stunned when she repeated the impoliteness of these peace gentlemen. There seemed no hope for the future at all, she said, but (for she was twenty-one and lovely and alive) perhaps all this cynicism and despair would finally lead to something good. How that was going to happen, she could not tell.

Presently the great sleek cars returned and the delegates clambered out of them. They gathered around the vast table in the gilded conference room, and if you did not see the little cardboard plaques stating the names of their countries, you could not have distinguished the Belgians from the Norwegians, the Czechs from the Yugoslavs, the Canadians from the Americans; they just looked like men, any men at all. The moment they opened their mouths, you realized your mistake: all men are not brothers, by a long shot. In the first place they did not understand one another's languages, and after that they did not understand, let alone trust, one another's thoughts.

They were talking, that afternoon, with the sun pouring in the windows, about a cable line between Yugoslavia and Italy; the Yugoslavs wanted to share the cable line or someone should pay reparations on it, or something of the sort. The conversation was slowed up because of being repeated in three languages, but it had the acrimonious tone of an argument with the waiter about a bill in a restaurant. The Yugoslav delegate was immediately contradicted by someone of the Western bloc. This happened in both directions, with such regularity that you would have been astonished only if a Western power suddenly said to an Eastern power, with a broad smile, "You are absolutely right, old boy," or vice versa.

Everyone had of course forgotten what drove the Yugoslav: his country is a ruin, one out of every eight people in it is dead, the cruelties of the Germans and Italians, aided by the Fascist Yugoslavs, have left their poison as all brutality does. The Yugoslavs had also clearly forgotten that the present government in Italy is a collection of decent men of good will; that Italy is now as impoverished as Yugoslavia (victor and vanquished starve with equal ease) and that it is pointless to go on loading a bankrupt country with charges which it will obviously never be able to pay.

The delegates went on talking about this cable line, drearily, carefully, almost hopelessly. The various spectators, press and visitors, sat on red plush benches and listened or sank into a lethargy produced by boredom and a desire to be someplace else.

On the bench beside me lay a booklet, entitled Fascist Italy in Ethiopia; someone had either lost it or simply left it, out of indifference. It was printed like a cheap advertisement for patent medicines, the pictures were blurred and no one had remembered to put captions underneath to explain them. The pictures showed, however, smiling, attractive young Italian soldiers, posing happily

215

for the camera, holding in their hands, by the black kinky hair, the decapitated heads of Ethiopians. That was all, and perhaps no captions were needed.

The Ethiopian delegates sat at the conference table and listened in silence. They are very nice people (and so are the representatives of the Italian Republic). The Ethiopians have wonderful names, the chief of their delegation is called Aklilour Habte-Wold, which means Crown of the Grace of our Lord; all their names mean something. I remembered a conversation with one of the Ethiopians, who said, "Here at this conference one sees only the interests of nations, and never humanity."

He had told me in a bemused voice that the Italians made a book to show the Allied delegates, and this book—full of beautiful pictures—established what a fine work Italy had done in Ethiopia, roads and hospitals and model farms and all the rest. The Ethiopian said sadly that they would really prefer to have been spared these improvements, and to have been left alive . . . I had been told how the Ethiopians computed their desired reparations; with innocence and sadness and humility, they decided that a human life must be worth about $500 to Western peoples, so they multiplied their dead by $500 . . .

The Dutch and the Norwegians had nothing much to do with the Italian peace treaties; they also listened and tried to vote for the best. They, too, are nice people and as puzzled as you or I. Both countries are making an enormous effort to rebuild the ruin of the war; both countries are slowly succeeding. A Norwegian said to me, "If we are left alone, we are all right; we work and we can live. We are happy together." And then he said, with sudden sorrow and passion, "There is no idealism left in the world; if a man spoke with ideals here he would be regarded as a fool."

A Dutchman had told me about Walcheren Island (where so many Canadians died to drive out the Germans) and he said not a tree was left alive in the flooded wasteland of Walcheren. But hundreds of thousands of Dutch people contributed a dollar each to buy a tree, and if there was peace and the island was not flooded again, the trees would grow. . . . The Dutch did not fear that anyone wanted to harm them, as they wanted to harm no one. It was the great nations who feared and made fear; and we looked at each other with sadness, for I belong to a great nation and am no different from him, and we knew it, and we knew that this was true of most of the people of the world.

In the mornings, the commission which discussed the political aspects of the peace treaty with Italy met in the same hideous, ornate room. The frontiers between Italy and Yugoslavia will get shifted around again. When you shift a frontier it means that a man with two cows and two children and a wife and a little plot of land, and another man who owns a small shop where he sells wine or shoes or pills or writing paper, will feel the change. One listened, as in a dream, to the strange remote talk which dealt in frontiers and not in human life. The American delegation, realizing that human beings had some connection with these frontiers, added an amendment to the peace treaty. As an amendment, it sounds reasonable enough to our ears; to the people of Europe it may easily seem like wearing a lucky charm against snake bite.

The American amendment says: "The state to which the territory is transferred shall take all measures necessary to secure to all persons within the territory, without distinction as to race, sex, language or religion, the enjoyment of human rights and of the fundamental freedoms, including freedom of expression, of press and publication, of religious worship, and of political opinion." This means that the 23,000 Yugoslavs, who find themselves Italian, and the 130,000 Italians who find themselves Yugoslav, according to the new frontiers voted at the peace conference, shall not be pushed around by either government. But no one believes in noble intentions written on paper.

I went to call on the Yugoslavs and they are very nice people. So are the Czechs and the Poles. I regret to say that I do not know the Russians. A young man of twenty-six offered me Yugoslav vodka, which is a potent drink, white, and tasting a bit like gasoline, and some pals of his came in and we argued about problems which our elders and betters never discuss so freely.

They said, with perfect candor, that the Yugoslav people were not in an uproar about all these frontier discussions. The Yugoslav people were completely occupied trying to rebuild their country. (Exactly like everyone else). Due to UNRWA, they are eating, though of course they could eat a good deal more, and because their factories are mostly gutted and they lack raw materials, there is a terrible shortage of clothing; besides, all communications are destroyed, and one third of Belgrade is gone, and countless villages burned.

The Yugoslavs were not discouraged by this devastation. They are full of faith and fire, they are young, the future can not possibly be as terrible as the past. They were very friendly, and very open and I said. "Why do you suppose it is necessary for our representatives to line up in blocs?"

They answered, sincerely, "It is the West which makes the bloc, not the East. Inside what you call the Slav bloc we vote, each one as we think right, but the others, they vote together, as they are told. We are not the satellites of Russia. Russia is our friend. Russia protects small nations. But we are ourselves, we are free." You do not have to believe this, but it is what *they* believe.

The Military Commission, which decided how many guns and planes, et cetera, the former enemy nations may retain, was a somewhat different outfit. The delegate-soldiers bowed and smiled to one another when they arrived in the morning, which was unusual in this peace conference. And one felt that they knew they were talking nonsense, so they worked honestly at the nonsense which was assigned to them, but they did not get into a temper over it. For surely, since the advent of self-propelled missiles and atom bombs, it was silly enough to discuss the piddling frontier fortifications of Hungary or whether Italy could have two, three or four warships, when one atom bomb did such final work at Bikini.

The soldiers, who make war when ordered to do so, seemed much more brotherly than their nonwarlike colleagues upstairs. They had little human jokes (and you can scarcely believe how attractive and encouraging a human joke was in the Palace of the Luxembourg).

One morning a photographer arrived with a camera and flash bulbs and got himself into position to take a picture of the Brazilian soldier-delegate. The Brazilian, who was sensibly reading the morning paper, did not notice this, until a Canadian officer leaned over and told him to smile at the birdie, and a low restrained giggle ran through the august military gathering. The soldiers knew very well that deciding to reduce fortifications, armies and battleships of a few small defeated nations was not going to make or save peace anywhere.

You see, it is very difficult. You and I are just people, and it is

218

easy for us to say, "We want peace, we want nothing else, the whole world wants peace." Why didn't those men in the Luxembourg set a good example? It is true that peace never seemed farther away than in the splendid halls of the Luxembourg. It would be wonderful if it were only the delegates' fault; because then we could fire them, we could say we want better, more competent men. It was not their fault. They were human beings, like you and me, just as anxious and twice as prejudiced.

They know that their people are exhausted, hurt and poisoned by war. They themselves were not living in some delicious Shangri-La during those cruel years. The Norwegian chief delegate spent the war in Sachsenhausen, one of the great death concentration camps of Germany. The second-ranking Dutchman was in a Jap prison camp in Java. Bevin was as vulnerable to the bombs that fell on London as any cabdriver. The Italian prime minister, who served his apprenticeship in a Fascist prison, took his chances in Rome like anyone else who opposed the Fascist and Nazi regimes. The Yugoslav, who is very young, went to prison as an anti-Fascist before the war, and fought as a partisan during the war. The Pole was imprisoned by the Germans in both wars. Bidault was probably more wanted by the Gestapo than any man in France. And so the list goes on.

In that they shared the pain of their people, these men are representative of their people. In democracies where the citizens may read, hear or say what they like, the leaders are no better and no worse than the followers. So perhaps, if we cannot blame the leaders because the job of peacemaking is a sorry mess, we can only blame ourselves.

Is it possible that all the people of the world paid too heavily for the war, so now everyone wants peace cheap, at bargain rates, or better still, letting the neighbor bear the cost? Is it possible that the poison which flowed from Germany has so infected and corrupted the world, that the people of the world are sick; and have neither the strength nor health to struggle for peace? An Italian asked me whether I believed that nations really wanted to live, and I said, "Of course," and then we both began to wonder. It will cost a great deal to live; it will mean great sacrifices.

The library of the Luxembourg is a beautiful room and no one goes there; it is full of sun and quiet and faces the ordered grace of the Luxembourg Gardens. From the windows you can see the people of France, who are not much different from any other people. Two young matrons knitted beside their baby carriages; a dreamy old gentleman was painting a water color; three other old gents sat on a bench reading newspapers and smoking their pipes with the great economy of tobacco; some workers, in blue overalls, arrived to eat their lunch in the sun. I wondered if they knew that they and all the ordinary people everywhere were much more important than the men sitting in Luxembourg. For in the end, the peace of the world is not in the hands of delegates but in the hands of all people everywhere. It is an almost overpowering effort to be just, informed, sane and strong when you are worried about a roof over your head, money for food, for the children's shoes, for coal, for a little fun, worried and harassed by the daily unending problem of living. But it is an effort that must be made, for lasting peace is not going to come of itself, nor cheaply, nor due to someone else.

The delegates to the peace conference sat in the Senate Chamber of the Luxembourg Palace and finished their voting on the five peace treaties; East versus West, West versus East, as before. The sleek black cars rolled into the handsome courtyard and the delegates drove away. The Conference of Paris of 1946 had come to an end. The conference never had power; it was intended as a great international debating society, giving everyone a chance to think aloud. As such, it served its purpose; like a giant alarm bell, it warned people everywhere that our world is dividing in two, cleft by fear and mistrust. The people, who made war with such extraordinary determination and courage, must make peace the same way—if nations want to live.

The astounding stout blonde was not in the meager crowd that watched delegates drive away. Peace was a hard business as she knew very well because she was the one who did the marketing; besides it was already getting cold and she had neither stockings nor coal for the winter. And everyone talked about the next insane war between Russia and America, so what was the use of anything? She thought this big expensive peace conference would make the world an easier place to live in, but the world seemed unchanged. She had lost interest for it was all too discouraging. She went down the block to a café, and drank cognac with friends and tried to forget her own and the world's problems.

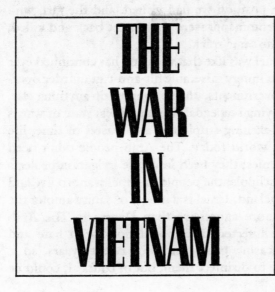

THE WAR IN VIETNAM

By the spring of 1949, Israel had in fact won its war of independence against the middle eastern Arab states but the Arab Legion was still raiding from behind high desert hills in the Negev and the Israeli army was dug into machine gun nests on opposite hills. The Negev was remarkable as geology, streaky sand hardened into stone, dead and empty, and the silence was very unpleasant. In war, there is a choice of two unpleasantnesses, exaggerated noise or exaggerated silence, and neither is desirable.

I remember being impressed and amazed by the equality of the sexes in Israel's army: every able-bodied Israeli, irrespective of age or sex, took eager part in protecting the new life on the old land. And I remember the well-known cold sensation in the back, riding in a jeep to an airfield from wherever we'd been, along the floor of the desert. A few hours later the Israeli

221

Major, whose gun position we had visited, and the girl, who was his second-in-command, were shot in the back and killed, when driving on the same track.

The war in Israel was like that then and has continued ever since in this form, a mingy miserable hit-and-run murder operation. The Arab governments, unable to agree on anything else, use Israel as a unifying scapegoat. That political state of war is one of the most sickening stupidities and wastes of time, life and money in the world today. The Arab people don't need armaments and armies; they need immense irrigation projects and hospitals and schools; the people of Israel want to live and improve their homeland. Israel is a model of sanity among the nations, and no more aggressive than Denmark. The Arab governments have infected their populations with hate and fear, through unceasing propaganda for twenty years, so it would take a while to disinfect them, but of course it could be done.

Whole populations never clamor for war: as proof, no population ever believes it has started a war. They are told and blindly respond to the same lie everywhere: the Russian soldiers in Finland were informed that Finland was attacking Russia; the Germans were sold the notion that a ring of hostile nations was poised to annihilate them; the Arab people are convinced that Israel—smaller than New Jersey with less than 3 million population—is preparing to conquer the vast neighboring Arab territories and take on some 50 million enemies; Americans are now solemnly warned that if "communist aggression" is not halted in a little underdeveloped country 10,000 miles away, America will be endangered.

I did not go to Israel as a war reporter, I went to see the young nation and wrote of it with such unrestrained enthusiasm that my article was never printed. Editors have to be careful about controversial subjects; the business department might announce a loss in advertising or subscriptions because some insignificant writer has been too outspoken.

After Israel, which was the briefest visit to a war, I declared a separate private peace. The world's woes seemed perverse and self-inflicted. I gave up reading newspapers as a matter of principle, listened to music instead of news bulletins, and was healthy and happy in Mexico. One day, a neighbor telephoned in high excitement to announce the outbreak of war in Korea. Five years after the end of World War II, we were engaged in large-scale international killing again. One could only pity all the people who had to fight or suffer that war and pity Korea, occupied by Japan since the Russo-Japanese war, liberated in 1945, and immediately divided by East-West fear into two Republics, both dictatorships.

The fear between our rulers, East and West, first visible at the Paris Peace Conference, had logically resulted in the first pointless East-West war. Tens of thousands of ordinary people, who had no genuine reason to fear each other would die though the rulers would remain safe, warm, well-fed honored for their misdirection which produces war, and incurably fearful.

As for me, I had seen enough dead bodies, and enough refugees, and enough destroyed villages and could not bear to see any more. It was useless to go on telling people what war was like since they went on obediently accepting war. To feel useless or helpless is the way most people feel, when faced with great public acts, and it is a bad way to feel but also an excuse. If you can do nothing to change events or rescue your fellow men, you are free to live your own life, and living one's own life is always more pleasant than the exhausted scrabbling role of a responsible citizen.

I based my life successively in Mexico, Italy, London and East Africa, beautiful places to live. I wrote fiction because I love to, and journalism from curiosity which has, I think, no limits and ends only with death. Though I have long lost the innocent faith that journalism is a guiding light, I still believe it is a lot better than total darkness. Somebody has to bring the news as we cannot all see for ourselves. Sometimes journalism was pure delight—weeks in the Serengeti; sometimes it was pure torment—Auschwitz and the Eichmann Trial.

I would never have chosen to go near a war again if my own country had not, mysteriously, begun to wage an undeclared war. Around February 1965, Vietnam became the urgent business of every American citizen. Americans do not notice the military activities of their government; such goings-on are specialists' jobs and anyhow far-off and who understands them. For years, America had been mixed up with an

223

obscure Asian country called Vietnam. I paid no more attention to this than did the majority of my compatriots, although
I had the impression that we inherited Vietnam from John
Foster Dulles whom I regarded as a national disaster. But there
were so many disasters that one could hardly concentrate on a
country whose very location was not clear in one's mind.

We were suddenly, enormously involved in a war, without
any explanation that made sense to me. Instead of reason and
fact, we got exhortation and propaganda. All the war reports I
could find sounded inhuman, like describing a deadly football
game between a team of heroes and a team of devils and
chalking up the score by "body counts" and "kill ratio." The
American dead were mourned, but not enough; they should
have been mourned with bitter unceasing questions about the
value of sacrificing these young lives. The Vietnamese people
were apparently forgotten except as clichés in speeches. American bombing missions were announced as if bombs were a
selective weapon, or as if only the proclaimed enemy lived on
the ground. Vietnamese civilians lived all over the ground,
under that rain of bombs. They were being "freed from aggression" mercilessly.

I did not want to learn about new techniques of warfare,
nor ever again see young men killing each other on the orders
of old men. Finally I went to South Vietnam because I had to
learn for myself, since I could not learn from anyone else, what
was happening to the voiceless Vietnamese people.

A New Kind of War

September 1966*

U.S. troops, upon arrival in South Vietnam, are read an indoctrination lecture of 30 mimeographed pages which is earnest, clear, and laudably humane. The following paragraphs seem best to sum up the whole:

"You and I know that we are here to *help* the people and the Government of South Vietnam. We know what our mission is: we are here to help save this valiant little country, and with it all of South-East Asia, from Communist aggression and oppression. In doing so, we will strengthen the security of the United States itself. And you and I know that we can't accomplish this mission without the support of the Vietnamese people. Everything we do to help win their support will help to shorten and win this war; and anything we do to alienate them will only weaken our effort at its most vital point. . . .

"From everything I've said, it should be plain to see that we're in a new kind of war. And the name of this new game is much, much more than just 'Kill VC' (Vietcong). We've got to kill VC all right; but there's a lot more to it than that. To really and truly and finally win this war, we must help the Government of South Vietnam win the hearts and minds of the people of South Vietnam."

*These six reports were written in London in September 1966 after returning from Vietnam.

In its simplest terms, this is the American doctrine in Vietnam; and though my contacts with any U.S. officials, civilian or military, were brief and glancing, I had the impression that all sincerely believed it, especially the central tenet: Americans are in Vietnam to help the people and they are helping the people. (The lecture defines "the people" as the peasants, 80 percent of the population of the country.)

The new port and old provincial capital of Qui Nhon was once a pretty seaside resort for the French rulers and a native fishing village with a population of 20,000. The population now is said to be 200,000. Statistics on the Vietnamese are honest guesses at best; too often they are propaganda nonsense. Qui Nhon is a huge U.S. military supply dump, shrouded in red dust from the grinding wheels of army transport, and suffocated in heat like glue. There are the usual tent cities of the soldiery, the claptrap bars and laundries and shops that spring up wherever Americans go, the resort hotels and villas turned into headquarters, messes and billets, and everywhere the shacks of refugees built of anything from paper to sheets of rolled beer tins. It is estimated that 72,000 refugees are huddled in the town limits but no one can keep count of the increasing hordes of uprooted peasants.

Each of the provincial capitals in South Vietnam has a free hospital for civilians. The Qui Nhon provincial hospital is crowded to bursting with wounded peasants, men, women and children of all ages, none of whom would be alive were it not for the New Zealand surgical teams which have served in this hospital since 1963. Those doctors and nurses are beyond praise.

A New Zealand doctor, who had more important work to do, led me on a fast tour of the premises. Four big two-storey buildings are connected by covered walks; each floor is a single ward. But the wounded peasants pour in day after day and week after week and the narrow cots, packed close together, are filled two to a bed, sometimes three to a bed; it is luxury to have a cot to yourself. In some wards the wounded also lie in stretchers on the floor, and outside the operating room and in the recovery room the floor is covered with them. Everything smells of dirt, the mattresses and pillows are old and stained; there are no sheets, of course, no hospital pajamas or gowns, no towels, no soap, nothing to eat on or drink from. The Vietnamese Government allows a free food ration for one meal per day for 287 patients; there are 500 patients. Far from home, often homeless by now, the relatives of the wounded must somehow provide what is needed, cook for and feed and wash and nurse their own. So the jammed wards are further jammed by grandparents caring for tiny children, teenagers caring for parents, a vast conglomeration of the semi-starved looking after the desperately hurt. Everyone, healthy and wounded alike, is thin; fragile bones and tight skin, and the controlled faces, the tormented eyes.

As the doctor walked quickly through the wards, the people spoke to him in Vietnamese which he does not understand. He smiled the warm, loving smile he reserves for his patients, patted an arm, and soothed and encouraged them in a language they do not understand. "We're very proud of him," said the doctor, stopping by the cot of an old man, aged in fact 61. "Took bomb bits out of his brain, chest and abdomen. He'll live; I even think he'll be quite normal." Farther down the ward, he waved amiably at a young man with a shock of stiff black hair, a narrow naked torso and a leg in plaster. "Yes, that's a handcuff," the doctor said. It looked like a leather bracelet chaining the wounded man to his cot. "Vietcong. We have quite a few. Fine people, rather better educated than the rest, cheerful, make the people laugh, good influence in the ward."

"Like to show you something," said the doctor, and we raced along the covered walk to the end of the hospital where a small smoke-blackened cavern was the hospital kitchen, flanked by six latrines. Four were boarded up, totally blocked by excrement; two open doors showed overflowing mounds of filth. "Facilities for the families," the doctor said.

Across the way there was a handsome building, rather like a roomy seaside villa, and I thought perhaps the doctors lived in it. "Put up by US AID for the relatives of the patients," the doctor said. "Marvelous dining room, screened, never used; they take food to their wounded and eat whatever's left over, squatting on the floor the way they always have. Bedroom—maybe 30 could sleep in it cheek by jowl, but there are about 600 relatives here, and they sleep on the floor beside their own people, have to, who else is to look after the patients at night? There's a fine bathroom over there, too, with two toilets, now locked. Solid feces. That big building is the storeroom for medicines. AID spent $2 million on fixing up this hospital."

* * *

I got an interpreter and went round the wards asking plain factual questions. The old are pitiful in their bewilderment, the adults seem locked in an aloof resignation, the children's ward is unbearable. No one protests or complains. We big overfed white people will never know what they feel.

A boy of 15 sat on his cot with both legs in plaster casts. He and his little brother had gone to the beach to mend nets; a Vietnamese patrol boat saw them and opened up with machine gun fire; his little brother was killed. The boat then pulled in to shore to see what it had bagged and found two children. The American adviser got the living boy to the nearest town, where a helicopter picked him up. His mother and older brother made their way here by motor-boat to nurse him. He is lucky; he has only been in this appalling place for two and a half months and will some day walk again. He said he did not know the beach was forbidden; that was his only comment.

The tiny children do not cry out in pain; if they make any sound it is a soft moaning; they twist their wounded bodies in silence. In the cot by the door is a child burned by napalm. He is seven years old, the size of a four-year-old of ours. His face and back and bottom and one hand were burned. A piece of something like cheesecloth covers his body; it seems that any weight would be intolerable but so is air. His hand is burned, stretched out like a starfish; the napalmed skin on the little body looks like bloody hardened meat in a butcher's shop. ("We always get the napalm cases in batches," the doctor had said. And there's white phosphorus too and it's worse because it goes on gnawing at flesh like rat's teeth, gnawing to the bone.) An old man, nearly blind with cataract, was tending this burned child, his grandson. The napalm bombs fell a week ago on their hamlet, he carried the child to the nearest town, and they were flown here by helicopter. The child cried with pain all that week, but today he is better, he is not crying, only shifting his body to try to find some way to lie that does not hurt him.

In theory, the peasants are warned of an air attack on their hamlet, by loud-speaker or leaflets 48 hours in advance, but as the military say, this is not always possible. Obviously I did not canvass the country, but I found no case in the hospitals I visited where this timetable was kept. In the areas called Free Air Strike Zones, or some such jargon, there is no warning and the people can be bombed at will day or night because the area is considered entirely held by Vietcong, and too bad for the peasants who cling to their land which is all they have ever known for generations. In this child's hamlet, the people were warned to leave by loud-speaker from the air in the night; but no one in Vietnam moves readily by night and besides, in the dark and the haste and the fear, how could they take with them their possessions which they value fiercely just because they have so few.

That night, the boy and his grandfather, his mother and older brother got away from the hamlet with two of their four buffaloes. The buffaloes were their only capital, their fortune, without the buffaloes they could not cultivate their fields. At first light, many of the peasants crept back to the hamlet to rescue more of their livestock and household goods. The old man, too blind to go alone, took the child with him to try to find their remaining two buffaloes. But the jet fighter-bombers came at once. The two buffaloes were killed by napalm, the old man said, and so were many of the people, and many were burned. No damages for lost property, death or wounds will be paid to these people, though the whole business of damages to civilians looks like another of the many dreams on mimeographed paper which characterize this war. But damages, if ever paid, are only paid for accidents; these people were warned, their hamlet was destroyed as an act of war.

The old man was penniless, of course; he was given 300 piastres, before coming here with the child, in part a contribution from the local authority, partly a gift from neighbors. Three hundred piastres is less than 14 shillings, less than $2.00. He had now 100 piastres left to feed himself and the child. One cannot know what will happen when that runs out; it is no one's duty to worry about him. In principle, a refugee gets 7 piastres a day from the Government for about a month; 7 piastres is a sum too small to describe in our terms, and will not buy one kilo of rice. The little boy's father had already been killed in the Vietnamese army; his mother and older brother are somewhere in a refugee camp.

Another child, also seven years old, had been burned in the same hamlet. His mother stood over his cot helplessly. The child was in acute pain; she had covered him with a light cloth and kept fanning the small body as if she could cool that wet, blood-red skin. She too had gone back to save more things from her house, cooking pots, rice, clothing. She said that the Vietcong overan their hamlet—which means that, in some force, guerrilla fighters moved into the area—in April, but were long gone; why destroy their houses and their possessions and their children now in August?

The Vietnamese are a beautiful people, especially the children. The most beautiful child in this ward was a little boy who looked about five years old, with plaster on both his legs to the hips. He and two little girls sat on the tile floor which is cooler, resting their heads against the side of a cot. They simply sat, motionless and silent; the girls were also in plaster, a leg, an arm. The boy's eyes were enormous, dark, and hopelessly sad; no child should have such eyes. The mother of the little girls, who had been wounded by our artillery, told the boy's story: he and his mother were going back to their hamlet from the town market in a minibus, the midget-sized tin trucks pulled by a Lambretta scooter which are the transport of the poor in this country. The bus was mined by the Vietcong. The child's mother was killed, and many of the others in the bus. His father had brought the child here, given this woman money to buy food and care for his son, and returned to his hamlet because he had to; there were other children at home.

If this hospital were unique it would be dreadful enough but there is every reason to assume that all the provincial hospitals are the same, crowded with non-combatants, under conditions suitable to the Crimean war. No Ministry keeps a record of civilian wounded, at least those who are able to reach a hospital. No official tries to discover from the survivors the number of civilian dead. But if any neutral harmless-looking observers went through the provincial hospitals and asked the people how they were wounded and who else in their family was killed, I believe they would learn that we, *unintentionally,* are killing and wounding three or four times more people than the Vietcong do, so we are told, on purpose.

We are not maniacs and monsters; but our planes range the sky all day and all night and our artillery is lavish and we have much more deadly stuff to kill with. The people are there on the ground, sometimes destroyed by accident, sometimes destroyed because Vietcong are reported to be among them. This is indeed a new kind of war, as the indoctrination lecture stated, and we had better find a new way to fight it. Hearts and minds, after all, live in bodies.

Orphans of All Ages

Soeur Jeanne is a big, burly, fair-skinned French peasant, with a strong face and quick blue eyes. She walks like a man and speaks her mind without fear. She has worked in Vietnam for twenty-seven years and can compare three wars in the same country. "No one ever troubled the sisters," she said. "Not the Japanese or Ho's soldiers. We were in the provinces when they were fighting the French." In the thick of it, therefore. Now she is in charge of an *asile* far out in the pitiable Saigon suburbs which are regarded as dangerous after nightfall. In central Saigon barbed wire, sandbags and sentries protect the dwellings and offices of the powerful, from the apartment-house barracks of American soldiers to the beautiful white palace of the President of the Republic. Soeur Jeanne, and the thirty-six Catholic nuns with her, are powerless and need no protection.

Soeur Jeanne's *asile* is a large compound with long one-storey stucco buildings forming a square around a new, cement-covered cistern. The gravel paths are raked, the strips of grass are well tended, a few trees give shade, the place is clean and quiet. It is also a sorrowful corner of hell, an orphanage for all ages, furnished with bare wood beds, 1,500 of them, each one a home for the homeless, the destitute, the sick, the abandoned. "There never was such misery as now," Soeur Jeanne says. "This last year."

The crêche is an enormous room half-filled by cots for babies. The babies are tiny, wizened, soft skeletons, with pain already marked on their faces. They are too weak to move or cry.

231

"Starved," Soeur Jeanne said. "All the little ones come to us sick from hunger. What can you expect? The people are too poor."

There are ten children's orphanages in Saigon alone, and orphanages throughout the country, and no reason to think that each does not receive its terrible quota of the newly-born and starving. In another suburb, in an orphanage for 675 children, a gentle barefooted Vietnamese nun showed me their crowded babies' ward. By local standards this is a wonderful orphanage because, helped by foreign charities, it can provide some modern medical care. A three-weeks-old boy was being fed intravenously and the nun said his mother had brought him here four days ago, just not dead. "They bring many, many. The father is killed in the war, the woman has four children, seven children, she is too poor. The mothers cry, when they give us their children. They cry very much."

In Soeur Jeanne's crêche, beyond the cots of the babies, small children crawled on the floor, or sat with outstretched legs, or stood alone; all thin, all silent, all with dark, sad eyes. Soeur Jeanne said: "The misery, the misery. Everything is here. War orphans. War wounded. Tubercular. Crippled by polio. Deaf and dumb. Blind. Children of lepers. Children of refugees who cannot feed them. Men do not see the real misery of war. They do not wish to. Why don't they do something for the poor people of Saigon? It cannot go on like this."

But it never stops. Officially, 80,000 orphans are registered now, which means in institutions, and an institution is the last desperate resort. The Vietnamese exist as all-inclusive families, and they love children. No one could guess how many orphans are sheltered by relatives. The Ministry of Social Welfare predicts an average of 2,000 more orphans every month. Is it not strange that we count and proclaim only military casualties? These homeless children should be listed as wounded; and wounded forever.

The school-age children were down the road at a school where the nuns teach. Older girls and women sat or lay on the hard wood beds in their building; they have nothing else to do, month after month. Most of the adults are too sick or frail or old or handicapped to work. The relatively able do maintenance jobs around the *asile* and are rewarded by an extra food ration. The Vietnam Government contributes twelve piastres a day per person, which would not prevent general starvation. Soeur Jeanne must eke out that unreal allowance with gifts and by begging. But occupational therapy, proper medical care, any amusement are not even dreamed of: hunger rules.

Soeur Jeanne speaks in detail and with love of the gift-givers: "Embassy ladies"; a young Vietnamese army doctor who comes "from goodness of heart" every week on his day off, to treat her children; an American major who drove and unloaded on his own, two truck-loads of Christmas treats (which all the Vietnamese expected, from reading promises in the papers, and few received). These and others are remembered in the nuns' prayers. And Soeur Jeanne speaks with contempt of the privileged Vietnamese. "We have never seen a Vietnamese lady here. The rich in Vietnam have no conscience."

Soeur Jeanne talked encouragingly in Vietnamese to a girl of about sixteen, and slowly as if her back had been broken, the girl tried to raise herself to a sitting position. "Hysterical paralysis," Soeur Jeanne said. "Her mother was killed in their hamlet, bombs; and the girl was left alone with her father. It is curious for only two to remain in a Vietnamese family. Then one morning the girl woke and her father was dead; I don't know how. She became completely paralyzed at once, but she moves a little more every day."

Farther down the long room, a middle-aged woman babbled and laughed, and a little girl of six or seven tumbled over her bed, merrily; I thought they were playing. Souer Jeanne made a quick gesture towards her head. She smiled at this cheerful pair and said, "They have lost their reason, poor things. They are harmless and happier here; I do not want to send them to the horrible Government lunatic asylum. Many women have gone mad from their sufferings; children too."

An old woman greeted Soeur Jeanne as they all did, if awake, or not lying numb in sickness. Soeur Jeanne patted her scrawny shoulder and pointed to the shelf under the bed. "It is all they own in the world." Neatly arranged, on the shelf that is part of the bed, were a cooking pot, a tin plate, a bowl, a rolled mat, folded rags of clothing, a coolie hat. By the door, the last bed belonged to a woman more emaciated than the others. She stared at the wall unmoving. "Yes," Soeur Jeanne said. "Lost in darkness. She has not spoken since she was brought here."

*　　*　　*

Soeur Jeanne was proud of the new cistern, her achievement. At the corners of each building a tank, the size of a telephone booth, collected rainwater, hardly sufficient for 1,500 people. "Can you imagine how it was when the poor people wept and implored me for a drop of water and I had none?" In a test of the drinking water of all the world's capitals, according to a Vietnamese doctor, Saigon city water proved to be the most polluted. Besides it is not piped to the slum suburbs; the impure water must be brought in tins. Soeur Jeanne began to build her cistern and ran out of money; anxiously, she wrote her first and only letter to US AID, which was not answered. "I'd like to know where those millions of AID are," she said.

I could not explain that to Soeur Jeanne or anyone else. An honest, neutral, talented economist is wanted to study and describe the economy of South Vietnam. All I know is that there are 922 US AID personnel (civil servants) in Vietnam, and 221 AID "contractors", people employed by AID for their special skills. From June 1955 to July 1966, the dazzling sum of $3,005,600,000 was allotted for aid to South Vietnam. The major outlay, two billion dollars' worth, financed commercial imports "to keep the economy viable." The rest was divided between Food for Peace and Project Assistance, or varied direct help to the people. The US AID budget for this fiscal year is estimated to be $700,000,000. The war seems to have caused a bit of a boom all the way from Japan to Thailand; and the well-connected are certainly making a lot of money in Vietnam. But is any economy viable when most of the nation is undernourished and mothers give their starving babies to orphanages?

"Embassy ladies" rescued Soeur Jeanne and finished her cistern. Though the diet of the *asile* is distressingly inadequate, the people now have enough water to drink.

Old men lay wrapped in scraps of blankets under the eaves of a building. "Beggars," Soeur Jeanne said. "The police arrest them. Beggars should not be seen. I cannot take them all but they are better here than in the filthy gaol. The old sleep. They will stay until they die."

We entered a huge room, packed with men; old, middle-aged, and young, and everyone ill. A tall lean nun, another marvelous woman, led a fragile young man toward us and said to Soeur

Jeanne: "He is back from the hospital and more sick than when he went." Soeur Jeanne explained: "Tubercular, we have hundreds. Once they know they have this disease, they search and search to be cured. This boy left us to go to the tuberculosis hospital in Saigon. But the hospital can only keep them three weeks, and the people always return thinner." She shook her head and sighed. Standing at this door, the whole compound was in sight. "La misère," Soeur Jeanne said, "La misère."

Tuberculars live, eat, sleep alongside those who still have sound lungs, here and elsewhere, in the slums, the villages, the refugee camps. "It is like an epidemic," a Cuban doctor told me; he was a newcomer to Vietnam and stunned by what he found in a hamlet clinic. "Out of forty people, eight have tuberculosis. I have seen things I would not believe; pus running from the neck of a child." A Vietnamese doctor in Saigon said: "It increases every day, the people's resistance is lowered. What will stop it?" The answer is: nothing. Poverty breeds tuberculosis. And the hospitals are already overcrowded with civlian war-wounded.

Soeur Jeanne walked with me to the gate of the *asile*. Across the unpaved roads, the slum hutches spread in length and depth as far as we could see. Many of those next to the road are shops, square booths displaying cheap shabby wares, the essentials of life. At night, these shops become homes, and large families sleep somehow among the stock of cotton cloth and pots and candles and dried beans and kerosene. Soeur Jeanne considered the view which faces her every day, and spoke her mind.

"Think of the heat the people have to suffer in those disgusting little houses. When there is plague or cholera among them, they hide it. How could they live if they are put in quarantine for forty days? Ports, roads, all very nice; what does it mean to those miserable people? With the bombing, there will be more and more refugees. They come to Saigon if they can because it is the safest place. And the hunger grows. They will win this war only if they feed the people. They could start here in Saigon. Certainly there is a grenade now and then; it is also occasionally dangerous in Paris and London. The people need soup kitchens and ration cards, they must have them. And someone," she said, speaking from her heart, "who cares for human misery."

Saigon Conversation Piece

People do not rush about in Vietnam airing opinions. Of course there's a war on; moreover a new kind of war. The people of Vietnam, in the North and the South, have never had a free representative government. Their first chance for a nationwide direct vote was due to them in 1956, under the terms of the Geneva Accords. Diem (our man in Saigon at the time) refused to honor this agreement; his decision has been justified ever since in millions of words. Failing that vote, we still do not know what the Vietnamese people think and want. Doubtless they keep their opinions to themselves in the North as they do in the South.

The South Vietnamese press is tightly censored but the grapevine works. The existence of political prisoners is no secret, though only the Ministry of Justice could provide statistics; how many now and since the state began, the years of their confinement, their mortality. Freedom is a word often used in official speeches. Semantic confusion? Free enterprise mistaken for freedom? Surely freedom can be defined in language as clear as the Boy Scout's oath: freedom of thought, word and non-criminal deed. Vietnamese are understandably careful of talk, remembering Diem's police and noting the present hazards.

Introductions to Vietnamese private citizens from their London friends passed me through the barrier of silence. I liked and admired these people who trusted me with their opinions. Even if they had not asked for anonymity, the need is obvious. They were middle-aged to old, experienced in three Vietnam wars;

236

by occupation, respected members of the liberal professions; Buddhists, Catholics, unaligned. They are the new inflation-poor; their basic problem is money for food. Usually we spoke French, a few knew English, and we spoke alone, without worrying witnesses. By their acts, class and personalities, they refute any suspicion of being pro-Vietcong. They could be described as the best kind of patriots, moved by concern for their fellow-citizens, their beautiful country and their civilization.

The adults frequently mentioned students but were not able to arrange a meeting with them. Students are unwilling to talk to strangers; they have had too much trouble, too early. No Vietnamese government has regarded them as a suitably consensus-minded unit. In a last-ditch attempt to hear something straight from the educated young, I accosted two boys near a library, and we chatted in a nest of bicycles.

We were walking along Tu-Do Street in search of a quiet place to stop. This used to be Saigon's Bond Street. It is now a semi-red light district, crammed with bars, GIs and bar girls (who are another item in the human cost of war). My companion, like all responsible Vietnamese, loathes Tu-Do Street as a disgrace to his nation.

"In my village, 100 years of French rule have left no trace. Three to five years after the Americans go, it will be the same thing. They are a ripple on the life of the country. The people have great patience and the structure of the family stays intact. The people and the life here are the result of 2,000 years of adaptation to our milieu. Americans call us lazy. We can do nothing, but we resist by doing nothing. . . . The peasants do not want the Vietcong or the Vietnam Government or the Americans; they want to be left in peace to cultivate their land and elect their village chiefs and assess their collective tax. No one *asks* the peasants what they want because they're afraid to.

"We should have our own kind of socialism. We haven't the resources for the American capitalist system. . . . I'm sure the Americans will invade North Vietnam and this poor country will become a second Spain, a testing ground for everyone's weapons. . . . The Government? Clowns, pimps, crooks. The elections are meant to give some sort of legal basis to this regime. The U.S. likes a puppet Government. *Of course* honest elections would be possible, if anyone wanted them. . . . They all talk peace with the lips but not with the pocket. Why should this war end? It is too good."

The room felt as calm and remote as a cloister except when jet fighters screamed overhead. We drank pale tea, the least expensive token of hospitality. He was gentle and very small. Compared to the Tanagra refinement of the Vietnamese, we are overweight, unlovely giants.

He said: "We have become too intelligent at the sacrifice of our souls. There will be payment. Who made the H-bomb? Not God. Man has turned into a devil for man. . . . False prosperity in the cities, misery in the countryside. The peasants either stay and risk their lives to cultivate their fields, or flee to the cities. They are given a miserable little aid for a month; then they can perish. . . . The rulers, the highly-placed, profit from this war to enrich themselves.

"If elections had been held in 1956, Ho Chi Minh would have won. The Japanese, the French, now the Americans are afraid of a true representation. I believe the majority here are nationalists. But it must come to an honest vote. And if there are no nationalists and the majority want the Communists, then let it be so. It is *our* country. . . . Nationalist? It means anti-Communist, anti-Ho Chi Minh. And for liberty and freedom of expression. But we do not have freedom of expression.

"Unfortunately we are between two great power blocs. Vietnam is the waiting room for the next war. I think that this will end in the Third World War and a sea of fire. Humanity is *one*. Each of us is responsible for his personal actions and his actions towards the rest of humanity. All we can do is hold back our own brand from the fire—pull it back—do not add to the flame."

Old, spotted, scuffed chairs in a room that was an enlargement of a passage; more weak tea; and a wonderful man. He said, smiling, "In Vietnam, all honest men are poor. . . . To win the hearts and minds of the people, first you must have a heart yourself and also a mind. It takes time, patience and moral courage. . . . Some American soldiers should stay here for the big battles but all the rest should be done by Vietnamese. In Indonesia, communism was defeated without a single American soldier.

"The Vietcong gave the peasants land. That is what they really want. Then the landlords returned with the government soldiers and took back the land or collected old taxes. And now the bombs. It is only surprising the peasants do not all go over to the Vietcong."

He spoke in detail of wide-spread, small-scale corruption; how the poorest and most defenseless in Saigon are cheated. "If you steal a million, you live in a palace; if you steal an egg, you go to jail.

"Anti-Communism is becoming something like a business—like owning a coal mine. You put on a sign saying 'Anti-Communist' and you make a lot of money. It doesn't matter what else you are. Anti-Communist, good: but *for what?* Nothing else is offered. The French were crooked and cruel and the Americans say nothing. Diem was also and the Americans say nothing. All is good for the Americans if it is anti-Communist. But the Vietnamese people know it is not good. . . . These are very nice, decent people, not stupid, hardworking. They do not ask much, only a little justice. All people are the same everywhere. They know what is justice and what is injustice."

Some plain citizens in Saigon, horrified by the war's increasing destruction of their people and their country, decided to act on President Johnson's famous speech at Johns Hopkins University. ("And we remain ready, with this purpose, for unconditional discussions.") A year ago, these simple folk wrote a petition, proposing an immediate ceasefire on both sides and discussions between North and South Vietnam. They circulated their naive petition openly in the streets of Saigon and it appealed to the average public. Within a few weeks, they had 6,000 signatures; whereupon the leaders were arrested.

A middle-aged school teacher was sentenced to 25 years' hard labor but he has heart disease, so hard labor is commuted and he shares a cell, 24 by 16 feet in size, with 20 to 30 other political prisoners. Two more received sentences of 10 to 15 years. Their families can visit them once a week. To preserve their men from hunger sickness, the wives must find money for extra food bought in the jail canteen. And, finally, three were expelled to North Vietnam; a mystery I did not comprehend. They were not North Vietnamese themselves and their families have heard nothing for over a year.

The voice broke off in a short bitter laugh. "If you talk pure patriotism here, you become a prisoner; and if you speak of 'humanity,' you are a Communist." Warm rain poured down and swept garbage in a river along the curb. I was badly scared and glad to leave. My presence and questions were dangerous to a tired, harmless Vietnamese, now living in dread of the police, because President Johnson can propose "unconditional discussions" but Vietnamese, who hunger and thirst for peace, cannot.

Middle-class Vietnamese cling to their status by wearing neat, fresh, though cheap clothes. The new poor, whom I saw, were paper thin. This man put four lumps of sugar in his cup, no substitute for a solid meal.

"In Vietnam, everyone suspects everyone else. Even so, I defend the government, we must have it for stability. But, you see, the government has no confidence in the people who have no confidence in the government. Our rulers like to be flattered, they surround themselves with yes-men. Twenty percent of their minds wants to help the country; 80 percent wants to make money. . . . I am pro-American, they have good intentions. Many of their theories don't work in practice but they are modernizing the country, giving us factories and roads and ports. The people are too ignorant to appreciate that.

"Scandinavian socialism is the ideal way of life. The North Vietnamese have not understood how to exploit the economic suffering of the people" (he gestured towards his stomach) "but they will learn. . . . Here everyone still calls Ho 'Monsieur.' They call our own leaders *ces mèques*." (Those thugs. I startled him by laughing; typical of South Vietnam's black humor.) "Ho is respected because of defeating the French. And all the same, it is amazing the way he stops the Americans. Nationalism enters into it, a sort of pride. But Communists have no sense of the dignity of man. For that, I detest them; as a Catholic. Thought his government has no feeling for the individual either. . . . My greatest fear is a world war. We would all be annihilated. *No*, the human race is not mad. The rulers are mad."

* * *

They leaned on their bicycles, polite but uneasy. The smaller boy said, "We must enter the University by the time we are twenty-one, not later. It lasts three years. No, the government does not help us with money. Most of us work to continue our studies. Afterwards, if we are able to teach, we hope for three more years exemption, but we can be called up any day. The military service is four years for everyone. So we start life at thirty years old, or older. That is why many students are disillusioned."

Did they discuss the war among themselves? The other boy said, "With close friends, yes. It is very difficult in a large gathering. Do you understand? It is not a democracy here." Then they looked at me, with suddenly alarmed eyes, said "Au revoir," got on their bikes and rode quickly away.

The first reason for hating all dictatorships, Fascist, Communist and in-between, is that people under such rule are afraid to talk. It is like being afraid to breathe. Remember the noble four freedoms of our youth; freedom of speech and expression, freedom of religion, freedom from want and fear? At least the Vietnamese can pray, however they choose, for peace.

Open Arms for the Vietcong

"Open Arms" (Chieu-Hoi in Vietnamese) is a joint U.S.-Vietnam Government program for persuading Vietcong to rally to the Vietnam Government; in short, to defect. If the figures can be believed (a permanent *if* in this war), 39,349 Vietcong have "rallied" to the Government, from the middle of February 1963 to the middle of August 1966. This can be considered a great success. US AID is involved in the program, but my mind boggles as I read the mimeographed pages which explain the bureaucratic set-up of "Open Arms," with the committees, the representatives; the affiliated organizations and their representatives; and the resultant interminable reports, in four to forty copies, circulated among people already drowning in reports. Paper-pushing is a major activity of this grotesquely top-heavy, overstaffed war.

A US AID official, in one of their giant offices in Saigon, said that he calculated it cost $1,000 per head to get a Vietcong to rally/defect, whereas it cost about $1 million per head to kill a Vietcong, so he reckons that "Open Arms" is sound economics. This is a peculiar war: the primary object is not to win territory but to destroy enemy bodies. It is the first war on record where "body count" and "kill ratio" define a victory. "Open Arms" is a welcome change; their victory is a count of live bodies.

242

The principal means of persuading Vietcong to defect is by leaflets, dropped in millions all over the country, and by loud-speakers from the air, which promise rewards while playing on the fear of our bombing and the hardships of guerrilla life. Once a Vietcong, male or female, manages to pass safely into Vietnam Government hands, he or she is taken to an "Open Arms" camp for interrogation on military information and the structure of the Vietcong in the countryside. The Vietcong are not all guerrilla fighters: they have a complete civilian organization too, and I am told they also push papers.

Re-indoctrination lectures follow; we call it brainwashing when the Communists do it. In the central "Open Arms" camp in a Saigon suburb, this torture by boredom goes on for eight hours a day for a month. My nice Chinese girl interpreter asked the bright-est-looking of the young Vietcong peasants how it compared with what they went through on their side. "He says it's about the same, maybe longer here, but the content is different."

The "Open Arms" camp at My Tho, a provincial capital in the southern Delta, was smaller and happier than the Saigon camp. The ralliers have a vegetable garden and a fish pond and chickens and some of their families have joined them. Life is bearable for Vietnamese peasants only if children are waddling and gamboling around. Though useless to question the ex-Vietcong standing in a respectful body in their lecture hall, I did ask if any of them had ever been in a hamlet bombed by napalm. One boy at the back shyly raised his hand. How many dead? The answer: Six, two Vietcong and four peasants. In his Vietcong career, had he found that more Vietcong or more peasants were killed by our bombs and artillery? More peasants, he answered at once, because there are more peasants than Vietcong. Q.E.D.

In My Tho, a beautiful young Vietnamese woman, educated in Washington, DC, and married to an American, acted generously as my interpreter and hostess. All day long, she and I and a Vietcong peasant woman, Miss Phuong, who had defected three days ago, sat in Mai's front room, drank tea, soda water, orange squash, and heard Miss Phuong's life story. When the helicopters rattled and banged deafeningly overhead, we waited in patient silence; everyone learns to do that.

Miss Phuong was corpulent, muscular but well padded; the only peasant of that shape I saw in Vietnam. She was a spinster, probably aged 35, though she looked older: at 35 peasant women are apt to have seven children. Her voice was like the silver cooing of a dove, her laugh a tinkle. Her profile was attractive but her full face was not; her eyes were bloodshot, wary and cold. Only surprising that she did not look half-mad.

Miss Phuong and her fiancé were in the resistance, the war against the French. In 1954, when the country was divided by the Geneva Accords, her fiancé went to North Vietnam with the People's Army, and though she never heard from him again, Miss Phuong remained faithful. By profession, she was a successful midwife and owned a little hamlet clinic; a jealous rival denounced her to the Diem government of South Vietnam, for lacking a permit. I gather a tax wangle was involved. She was jailed for 45 days. After this alarming experience, she found that Diem had ordered her hamlet to move into a new fortified hamlet intended to separate the peasants from the Vietcong. She borrowed 40,000 piastres, a fortune, to build another clinic but the money ran out before it was finished.

At this point the Vietcong contacted her and told her she would never be able to make a living in that hamlet and besides would surely be put in jail again for debt, and so—for these simple material reasons—she joined the Vietcong, and became a nurse. From 1960 to 1964, she looked after sick and wounded Vietcong in various parts of the province. Then she resigned. Her reasons were fascinating: the Vietcong would not let her become a member of the Party because they said she was petit bourgeois. (We have been given to understand that the Vietcong are all Communists.) Only Party members got real benefits; she was tired of working hard for no benefits to herself or her family. Besides, she bitterly disapproved the sexual liberty of the Vietcong cadres (civilian administrators) who slept with girls without being married; that outraged her own virtue. She retired to her parents' hamlet; there was no fighting in her area.

Early this year, without warning, the hamlet was bombed, with regular bombs and phosphorus; everything burned, the orchards were destroyed and 20 people were killed or wounded. About 20 Vietcong cadres were in the hamlet but as they had no property or families to look after, they could run to safety. After this first bombing, our planes came over to broadcast the "Open Arms" propaganda, and some Vietcong guerrillas shot at the planes. From then on she could not count the number of bombings, and artillery fired on them every night. They brought their wounded here, to the provincial hospital in My Tho. People lived in camouflaged shacks in the rice paddies as their one hope of survival.

Were they free to move to Government-held hamlets? Oh yes, she said, but only those went who had relatives there, or family in the Vietnam Government army, or a profession or money; about half of the people had now resettled in Government territory. The poorest peasants stayed behind. They did not believe they could find work anywhere else, they said they were farmers, it was all they knew how to do, and whether they lived or died they would stay on their land.

Life was terrible in the hamlets: the Vietcong collected heavy taxes, 30 percent of whatever you had, money or rice; both sides drafted the boys; the people could not grow vegetables for fear of bombing, and could only keep a few chickens and a pig; they were hungry and always afraid; the Vietcong cadres were getting mean and superior; if the guerrillas came and shot at aircraft you were sure to be badly bombed at once.

But still the poorest of them clung to this fearsome hopeless life in their own hamlets, which must prove that word spreads through Vietnam by grapevine, and the peasants have heard of the wretched conditions of refugees. How do the people feel about the Government, I asked. Her dove voice changed, it became suddenly emphatic and louder. Mai translated: "She says they hate both sides. They don't care which side wins. They only want peace so they can work in safety." In Miss Phuong's position, "they" was a wiser word than "we."

Too casually, I asked whether she was not afraid the Vietcong would punish her family for her defection. For answer, she wept. Tears for her own family, hatred of both sides, terror of our weapons, a longing for peace were Miss Phuong's real emotions; conceivably, they are the real emotions of most Vietnamese peasants. In time, it should be possible to drive all the peasants from the land and thus starve out the dedicated hardcore Vietcong. It would also starve out the nation. From the air, abandoned rice paddies look like scraps of sand.

"But things like that, you know must be
At every famous victory."

The Uprooted

An official U.S. press handout says "The Government (Vietnam), when it first built the camps, did not want to make them too attractive for fear that a class of professional refugees would emerge." This is black humor, often to be found in press handouts; the Vietnam Government need waste no time worrying about the lure of refugee camps. Camps are everywhere but not all refugees live in them; acres of rickety hutches grow around Saigon and the two big towns I visited, and are certainly not exceptional. Statistics on the number of refugees vary and conflict; propaganda and bureaucracy add their muddle to the genuine disorder of flight. It is safe to say that millions are uprooted in Vietnam and that the escalation of the war produces a tragic escalation of refugees. They run for their lives and then, indomitably, they struggle to go on living.

A young Vietnamese journalist, my interpreter for the day, drove with me across the bridge to the Saigon suburbs, an area deemed perilous after dark. We drove for several miles beside the wide brown river, past small tumbledown houses, but there were trees, and a few roaming farm oxen, and a welcome sense of space and quiet. Then we abandoned the car because the road had become a rutted stream bed. We walked on a muddy path inland from the river, trying to find the refugee camp.

Where did the Government "first build the camps?" On acres of an old dump heap, rows and rows of sagging tiny shacks appeared to be floating on mud and green stagnant water. Lesser rows of unfinished cement-brick houses flanked the shacks. The acrid smell of garbage lingered in the air. A group of under draft-age boys and small children was gathered beneath a dirty piece of canvas supported on poles. The "recreational facilities?" They were repairing an antique bicycle. We asked for the camp leader.

A fine-looking young man in a clean white shirt and dark trousers presented himself; he was 23 years old, the chief of the 2,325 people living here, and a phenomenon. He was a second-year student in the Science Faculty at Saigon University, and hoped to become a teacher of science. Considering where and how this boy has lived, his achievement ranks as a great moral victory.

He took us to a large home-made, high-ceilinged shed, built of corrugated tin and odd bits of lumber; it serves as the camp office, schoolroom and church. Then the monsoon storm broke and the hammering of rain on the tin roof was like helicopters overhead. Sun on these tin roofs, a modern improvement from America, guarantees a dull oven heat in refugee quarters; I had not thought of the alternative, this maddening noise.

We shouted at each other; during the heavier bursts of rain, we shrugged, waited, and shared my cigarettes. The shouting talk revealed that these refugees were North Vietnamese Catholic peas-ants. They had migrated south in a body, with their priest, in 1954 when the Geneva Accords divided the country—the agreement then being, as we know, that neutral observers would supervise a vote of all Vietnamese in 1956, to unify the country and choose their Government. The mass transfer of Catholic hamlets from North to South in 1954 was caused by fear that a Communist regime would outlaw their religion. So this group moved to central Vietnam and built new hamlets. A tremendous effort, clearing land, planting fields, digging irrigation ditches, making homes, with only their arms and their will to help them.

In August 1965, the Vietcong "overran" their hamlets. This word is in frequent use in Vietnam and I still do not understand it. From wounded peasants in hospitals, I gathered that a force of Vietcong guerrilla fighters comes to a hamlet, probably takes a toll of rice or other supplies, and disperses away from so obvious a target. I asked the camp leader to explain, and my interpreter-colleague said: "He says the real danger is the presence of the Vietcong nearby because then the area is a battleground."

Whatever "overran" exactly means, the result is certain: bombing by our planes. "A small number were dead or wounded," said Tri (not his correct name), my interpreter. The people fled, a second time, and were generously assigned this dump heap.

In May 1966, eight months after their arrival, the Government (actually US AID through Vietnam Government agencies) supplied cement bricks, some wood, tin roofs, and Government technicians as advisers. The refugees, having already built their miserable hovels out of rolled beer tins, or any other junk they could scrounge, were now to build their permanent houses. The young camp leader said it cost 10,000 piastres of their own money to put up a house; they haven't the skill to work with these unfamiliar materials and must hire help, and provide the extras— window glass, doors, I presume.

By January 1967, they expect to complete their homes, at least those who can save the money. And they will not move again; they feel happier here because it is safe (so much for the Vietcong-menace-in-the-suburbs). The peasants have become laborers and are mostly employed by Americans on military or civil construction work, and in service jobs.

But no one had thought about water when they were led to this unwanted field of rubbish. In the monsoon, the people put tins outside their doors and collect rain water; in the dry season they must walk "a far way" down the road to buy it, 10 piastres a day for water, carried home in discarded kerosene tins. No electricity, of course, and one does not discuss latrines, an indelicate subject. At the end of the camp, I saw a row of four doors which might have been the plumbing arrangements.

Now, since the downpour had stopped, we would pick our way through the muck and the filthy puddles and visit homes. The splendid young student guided me first to their showplace; two houses—one room in each—whitewashed inside and out, with cement floors, glass windowpanes, and a few pieces of new furniture, as beautiful to them as Chippendale. A calico curtain on a wire separated the front sitting room from the bedroom section, with its standard communal wood-slat beds. Two brothers and their young families and relatives lived in these clean neat rooms; one, a soldier home on leave, beamed with house-pride. The absent brother sold soft drinks in the Saigon streets, until the night curfew. A young sister was fiercely sweeping out rainwater which had surged through the woven reed door on to their precious cement flooring. The camp leader's face was alight with pleasure, with hope. "He says all the houses will be like this," Tri interpreted. Only these two families were installed in their new homes.

Again we tiptoed through broken shards of china, tin cans, mounds of indecipherable refuse. "Mosquitoes?" I asked, noting the tracts of green water. No one took the point. "A U.S. civilian medic team comes once a week," Tri reported. "The camp leader says the biggest sickness is diarrhoea." From which babies here often die. "And the people are underfed."

We stopped at the first miserable shack because I could not bear to walk farther. It was about eight by ten feet in size, nearly filled by two beds, reeking of poverty, with dingy rags of clothing hung on nails, and the battered household goods on a narrow shelf. A woman, who looked 55 and was perhaps 35, drained, exhausted, gaunt, lived here with seven children and her husband. By trade, he repaired clocks and watches, but was ill and, besides, could find no work.

Three young children lay on the bare boards of the beds, silently; yes, they were sick. She didn't know what their sickness was, but she could not give them enough to eat. Only her teenage daughter had a job, miles away. "Maybe two hours to go there, two hours to come home," Tri said. The girl earned 80 piastres a day, 48 U.S. cents, 3 shillings and threepence, the entire income for the family. Occasionally, food is distributed by the Catholic charities, otherwise there is no direct aid. "How will she ever get one of the cement houses?" I asked. "She says she hopes the priest will help her."

Walking back to our car, from this not "too attractive" camp, Tri said with passion: "If everybody in Vietnam had such a house as those new ones, the Vietcong would be defeated. We cannot win this war without a social revolution. The profiteers should be shot. Now. All of them. US AID has made us an import economy. We do not need those things—television, a big American car. We should have our own factories for the small things people need. It is very bad. The young men behave so immorally because they do not care. They do not believe in anything, not even the future."

Tri belongs to the middle-class new poor, and has the Westernized romantic conception of government as the servant of the people. I wonder how long it takes for the idea of *noblesse oblige,* or *richesse oblige,* or simple conscience to penetrate the minds of a ruling class. Tri himself, poor and honest and a journalist, a resident of Saigon, visited for the first time that day the city hospital, the children's hospital, the Red Cross amputee center, this refugee camp, because he went with me. The gulf between the suffering people and the higher to highest members of Vietnam society is as wide as the Rift Valley.

In every camp, the children hem you in, shouting gaily: "Okay! Okay!" It is the one American word they know and the least fitting. These children were meant to be beautiful and happy; their beauty is spoiled because they are ill fed and dirty. It is not the refugees' fault that they are overcrowded in wretched shacks or sheds, too poor to buy soap, and deprived of an adequate water supply. Many of the children are made repellent by contagious skin diseases, some have cataracts, some are crippled by war wounds, some deformed from birth due to the undernourishment of the mother. Still, laughing, eager for fun, they shout "Okay!" In the Saigon children's hospital, a grand Scots nurse said: "I don't care about this war, I think it's daft. If they want to fight, let them. But they ought to take all the children away to a safe place. I never saw such brave children in my life."

At a Catholic camp in central Vietnam, the camp leader, wearing the black cotton peasant uniform, told me that 2,300 people lived here and named the date of their exodus: April 20, 1965. A "battle" around their hamlets, bombs, their houses burned: how refugees are made. (Vietnamese, who should know, say that all peasants dig slit trenches in the earth floors of their houses; no use against direct hits or napalm or white phosphorus, yet their only chance for protection against bomb or shell fragments.) This camp had received some help in 1965 (the visible US AID tin roofs anyhow), but none this year.

All the refugees I saw earned their scant livings in any way they could. Since the able-bodied men are drafted into the Vietnam army, the women are the main wage earners, doing heavy coolie labor, market merchandising for a profit of pennies, laundry work for the Americans if lucky.

The camp leader said, casually, that they had had cholera and plague in this camp but were now vaccinated. Plague is beyond my imagination, but I will never forget one close sight of cholera in China: a peasant woman staggering towards us like a drunk, then vomiting a torrent of blood, and falling in it, unconscious or dead. It is amazing that the refugees stay sane. First the bombs, perhaps the "battle" around them, their casualties, their naked helplessness; then the flight, leaving behind everything they have worked for all their lives; then the semi-starvation and ugly hardship of the camps or the slums; and as a final cruelty, the killing diseases which only strike at them.

An American colleague told me that, in 1958, the World Health Organization reported less than 300 cases of plague throughout the world. But since January 1966, the Vietnam Ministry of Health had counted 2,002 plague cases in South Vietnam. Cholera must be more prevalent; you cannot enter South Vietnam without a certificate of cholera vaccinations.

I would not have realized what the refugees have lost if a priest had not shown me his hamlet, an hour's drive from the town. The hamlet was a delight and a beauty; like any other, the priest said. The small thatched-roofed houses are made of adobe and cool; wooden pillars support a porch; wooden shutters keep out rain. Each house is set in a bouquet of tropical greenery, each has its garden. There are trees everywhere and running water, and quiet and cleanliness. Narrow shaded paths link the houses and church and schoolroom and orphanage. The peasants were poor, but never hungry. And they lived with dignity in their own ancient way; and as they can still laugh, they must be a naturally merry people, capable of happiness.

A U.S. official handout on refugees, dated June 1965, is positively bursting with cheerful propaganda and self-felicitation. It quotes the Vietnam Minister of Social Welfare as saying: "We are providing every assistance as needed." Was it true then, though it is patently untrue now? Propaganda may work with everyone else but never with the refugees themselves. One of the statistics, official if not necessarily accurate, is: 1,300,000 refugees in the last two years. The meaningful words are "the last two years."

These peasants had survived the Vietcong since 1957, on

whatever terms, hostile or friendly, and the war however it came to them. But they cannot survive our bombs. Even the Catholic refugees did not leave their hamlets until bombs fell. We are uprooting the people from the lovely land where they have lived for generations; and the unprooted are given not bread but a stone. Is this an honorable way for a great nation to fight a war 10,000 miles from its safe homeland?

Real War and the War of Words

On the first of August, 399 representatives of the news media of the world were accredited to the U.S. military command in Saigon. That's everybody: the entire staffs in Vietnam of newspapers, magazines, radio, TV, news photos, newsreels. There are also large governmental information services, Vietnamese and American, as well as the Vietnamese press, including three English-language newspapers. It might be termed saturation coverage for a small country and a small war. Unfortunately the one man who could report this war with shining intelligence is dead: George Orwell. He understood propaganda as if he'd invented the technique; how it is made and used and why. For there are two wars in South Vietnam: the real war and the propaganda war. We don't have to worry about Communist propaganda; we agree that's nothing but a pack of lies.

253

The principal manufacturers and consumers of propaganda on our side are American; George Orwell would understand the reason. I can merely attempt to classify it, from my brief experience, in two groups: the fear syndrome, which magnifies the Vietcong's lethal threat to everyone in Vietnam, civilian and military; and the cheer syndrome, which optimistically falsifies the conditions of Vietnamese civil life.

The fear syndrome, by exaggerating Vietcong power for destruction, misplaces the real pain of the real war, and is immensely dangerous. It leads to hysteria, to hawk-demands for a bigger war; it pushes us nearer and nearer to World War Three. The fear syndrome in no way serves the American cause; it can only jeopardize more American lives, with the ultimate risk of jeopardizing all life.

Before going to Vietnam, I had many unanswered questions, but was obliged to make my picture of this war, like everybody else, from a composite of news reports and the pronouncements of American leaders:

> Vietcong assassinations and atrocities. Grenades thrown continuously on the helpless populace. The countryside and the roads strewn with mines. Vietcong raids on the towns at any moment. All the young American soldiers open to massacre in the jungles, or to incessant surprise attacks wherever they were quartered. Snipers following every move. Terror by day and night. Saigon a city of awful hazard.

If this picture of the war was my private invention, I would now think myself certifiable; but it is not. It is average American, perhaps average British, too; the result of fear syndrome propaganda.

This is not a war of "unparalleled brutality," as we have been told. One day of Auschwitz was far more brutal than everything the Vietcong have done to date or anything they could possibly do in the future. Atrocities are vile and horrifying wherever committed, and nothing condones them, not ever. But unless we crave the propaganda of fear, we have to keep a grip on reality. The Vietnam Ministry of Information gave me their material on Vietcong atrocities, a sheaf of photographs and two illustrated booklets; in all 61 pictures of mutilated dead, too dreadful, too inhuman to look at. For us, aimed and savage murder is more appalling than the impersonal death dealt out by the machines of war. A knife in a man's hand is more evil than a bomb fragment, possibly even more fearful than napalm or white phosphorus. Vietnamese speak of Vietcong "executions" and mean a bullet.

The official Ministry of Information figure for all civilians murdered by the Vietcong, from 1962 until June 1, 1965, is 5,942. American soldiers, briefed on arrival in Vietnam, are informed that, since 1957, the Vietcong have killed 13,000 local officials. There is no way, of course, to check these divergent figures (as there is no way to check civilian casualties inflicted by our side, in acts of war or by accident). Whatever the number of the dead, it is a crime and a tragedy to kill a single Vietnamese noncombatant. But the important point is that this is a nation of fifteen million people and it would long since have fallen apart if the fear-syndrome propaganda was true; the country would have been paralyzed by terror.

Refugees are proof of fear and there may well be three million displaced people in Vietnam by now; but how many fled from the Vietcong and how many more have fled from our bombs and artillery, or from battles on their doorsteps, is anybody's guess. The refugees, crowded in and around the big towns which we hold, are surviving unjustifiable hardship but at least they feel physically safe. Town residents go about their work with no panic dread of Vietcong terorism or raids.

Millions of peasants remain on the land despite the Vietcong. The roads are unsafe for all civilians at night; in daylight, limited stretches are secure. The Vietcong, unpredictably, mine roads, bridges, and territory they wish to interdict. They also dig "spy traps," bamboo spikes planted in pits. Peasants, like soldiers, know these scattered perils, and are rightly afraid of travel. But they do travel; and continue to cultivate their land and bring their produce to market. Since peasants are no more inclined to suicide than anyone else, the real risks must be recognized as present and potentially lethal, but not fear-syndrome overwhelming. When and wherever a grenade is thrown or a mine explodes, the people bury their dead, take their wounded to hospital if they can, and get on bravely with their lives.

Saigon is by no means a city of awful hazard. Grenades are the

255

exception not the rule, just as murder is the exception not the rule in our cities. Central Saigon looks messy, busy, booming, with shops, restaurants and bars everywhere, and phalanxes of street vendors, but it still has charm: a street with flower booths like the Madeleine in Paris, trees, a view of ships on the river.

The streets are blocked by traffic jams, hardly possible if grenades were usual. The intrepid poor ride bicyles, the GIs favor bicycle rickshaws when not roaring around on Japanese motor bikes, the medium Vietnamese bourgeoisie have motor scooters, the rich have cars, the little blue taxis are filthy inside and scarred outside, there are Lambretta buses, jeeps, army trucks and the limousines of officialdom, Vietnamese and American. By day, the city is so noisy that you rarely hear our jet fighter-bombers thundering overhead, though at night they sound like a steady passage of freight trains across the sky.

Well-to-do Vietnamese and foreigners live in comfortable flats, villas or hotels; food and drink are copious; and money will buy every luxury from a Jaguar ("delivered stateside," the sign says) to diamond jewelry and portable TV sets. The heat is ghastly; the privileged have air conditioning. And the ravishing, reedlike Vietnamese girls float through this city in their beautiful national dress, the audai, and by their presence and bearing make all terror-talk seem absurd.

What haunts and hurts the people of Saigon, the vast majority, is not Vietcong terrorism but poverty. Perhaps a million and a half newcomers, displaced people, have poured into Saigon because it offers safety and the hope of earning more money. A tidal wave of inflation has swept the country, and a weird economic miracle is in progress. Any Vietnamese private citizen will tell you that, since the American invasion, the rich are getting richer and the poor poorer. The poor could scarcely look more ragged or more emaciated. They live in pitiful, sweltering shanty towns on the outskirts of the city, Vietcong-infested and ominous areas according to the fear-syndrome. Evidently they are less troubled by the Vietcong than by hunger.

In Saigon, during the period of August 17 to September 4 which I can vouch for, the Vietcong mortared a U.S. motor pool near the airport; a grenade was thrown at a jeep, wounding four Americans and a nearby market woman; and a grenade was thrown at a police post but that story is not clear. Saigon is the capital of a country at war; to Londoners who remember the blitz and the V1s and the V2s, it would seem a fortunate city.

Luckily, Vietnamese do not believe propaganda; they believe what they know from their own experience, and that is terrible enough. But Vietcong-fear-syndrome propaganda is an insult to the incredible courage and endurance of the Vietnamese people. And it deforms our understanding of all their varied anguish. Misunderstanding alienates; it does not "win the hearts and minds of the people."

On August 16, at a press conference on his ranch, President Johnson said: "The United States has never had a more efficient and courageous fighting force in the field than the men who are serving us at this hour in Vietnam." The fighting force in the field more than deserves the President's fullest praise, and it is heart-breaking that the killed-in-action figures have risen from *one* in 1961, to 3,036 from January 1 to August 27 of this year, climbing slowly for four years, then fast for one year and almost eight months to reach a total of 4,470.

But it might be comforting to correct the impression, which I know I shared with many, that *all* the 300,000 U.S. servicemen in Vietnam are constantly endangered by Vietcong and North Vietnamese guerrilla fighters. Old Vietnam hands estimate that between 65,000 and 75,000 men, of all branches of the service, are the U.S. fighting force in the field and they say that this is a higher percentage of combat personnel than was achieved in World War II.

Since this is not a war of position, with two opposing armies trying to conquer territory, the entire fighting force in Vietnam is not in steady contact with the enemy. On the ground it is a war of patrols, hunting out the enemy, ambushes, pitched battles whenever units of Vietcong or North Vietnamese are found. Like a deadly game of hide and seek, in real danger every minute. Jungle fighting must be the worst. "Thorns as big as a pencil," a soldier said. "I never saw anything like it before." The French used to call it, with horror, a "dirty little war" when they were fighting it. In the air over North Vietnam, where there are flak, missiles, and enemy fighter planes, it becomes the sort of war we know too well in this disastrous century.

The majority of the 200,000-plus servicemen, who are not the fighting force, are dotted around the country, sensibly aware that the country is not guaranteed Vietcong-proof; but good soldiers never inflate alarm. They are suffering heat in the lowlands, malaria in a coastal zone, the nagging discomfort of tent camps, doing their jobs—endless dismal army jobs—building, hauling, guarding, pushing papers, and surviving the boredom which commanders never talk about though it is one of the heaviest hardships of war. A grim, dull life in an alien land.

There's something very nice and normal in the fact that every American I saw, under the rank of colonel, announced to a day when his Vietnam year would end. On the milk run army plane, which flies from Saigon to the big towns in central and northern Vietnam, the boy next to me was reading a Western but looked up from his paperback to say, "This is a C-130, it's a little bit more safer." (An aviation buff, a connoisseur of planes.) "I got 72 more days here, then home. Work in a depot, this town we're coming to. Easy job." Lovable young soldier, propaganda-free.

Fear-syndrome propaganda does a grave disservice to the men in uniform. If they believe any of it, they are forced to overcome not only the strain of real war but the debilitating strain of induced fear. Moreover, it is an insult to the men in uniform (as it is to the Vietnamese people). By implying that the Vietcong constantly menace life everywhere, this propaganda debases the valor of the actual fighting forces who are constantly menaced. And by misrepresenting true hardship, such propaganda downgrades the wearing, daily, stoical endurance of the mass of support troops. There are many different kinds of heroism in this country, and honor is due them all. But honor based on the real war, not the propaganda war. Being neither George Orwell, nor an authority on power politics, I fail to understand why sober accuracy would not be better for everyone, inside and outside of Vietnam, if we earnestly desire to limit and end this war.

The cheer syndrome, or the optimistic falsifying of the conditions of Vietnamese civil life, does not affect the safety of the world. It really doesn't affect the life of the people in Vietnam either, it merely conceals that life. The serious aspect of this ballyhoo is that it discredits both the American and Vietnam Governments in the eyes of the Vietnamese people. Trust and loyalty are not won by propaganda but by promises kept and help given. If tough, honest criticism replaced the cheer syndrome, Vietnamese life might improve and one could argue that real improvement of the life of the people would be more helpful in ending the war than bombs.

The way it works appears to be a sort of tennis match between Vietnamese and American authorities; they bat cheer syndrome between them. This must be a performance for export as you cannot, for instance, convince 1,027 refugees, living in a little camp without latrines and a nearly dry well, that "the camps are being improved, recreational facilities are being added, and attention is being paid to the educational needs of the young." If refugees read Government handouts they would be astounded. I specially enjoy the one about a mythical refugee who received a plot of land and the cheer syndrome sum of 3,500 piastres (£7, less than $20) and built a five-room house; he must be the best-housed peasant in all South Vietnam.

"Social revolution" is a favorite cheer syndrome phrase but it can only impress the outside world, since even so tiny an indication of social revolution as food rationing does not exist in South Vietnam. University students, who get no assistance from their Government and are "suffering" ("hunger" is a shameful word for the middle class), are not applauding cheer syndrome reforms.

"US AID is a long pipe," a fine Vietnamese said to me, "with many holes in it. Only a few drops reach the peasants." Or the millions in need, in spite of the millions of dollars and the good intentions. But cheer syndrome propaganda is a net, and the American Government is caught in it; to maintain the export idea that we are guests, practically servants of the Vietnamese Government, US AID direct relief funds are channeled through various Vietnamese Ministries. "If the Americans want the people to get rice," said a Catholic priest, "they must give it out themselves."

It is not all words, there are American-inspired deeds, but they are modest compared to the amount of cheer syndrome propaganda and money and bureaucracy involved. However, the superb cheer syndrome effort of the late elections seems to have gone over with a bang, outside Vietnam. The foreign public does not notice oddities: in advance, the Vietnam press stated that a 70 percent turnout of voters would be a triumph. Four hours after nearly five million people allegedly went, with no compulsion, to over 5,000 polling booths, the wondrous figure was announced—a 70 percent turnout; later upped to 80 percent. Nor does the foreign public

259

understand the gimmicks built into the plan for this new Vietnamese Constitution. Pity the poor Vietnamese who cannot eat or wear or shelter under cheer syndrome propaganda, and have never had a freely elected Government in 2,000 years. "The Government ignores the people," said a Vietnamese journalist. "And the people ignore the Government." The perfect epitaph for cheer syndrome propaganda?

I date from an older America and I remember with longing the day when a President said to the American people, "We have nothing to fear but fear itself." That wasn't any form of propaganda, it was truth, and is just as valid now if only we knew it. I wish I could ask George Orwell's opinion, but it seems to me that propaganda is a sign of fear. We ought to give the Communists a world-wide monopoly of propaganda and let them founder in it; not us.

Postscript

June 1987

Two years ago I read Barbara Tuchman's splendid book, *The March of Folly,* an account of the way various rulers, ancient and modern, like dinosaurs plodding to the asphalt lake, blundered into willful, self-destructive conflicts. The chapter that most interested me is called "How America Betrayed Itself in Vietnam." I brooded on the verb, thinking "dishonored" would be better because my view of Vietnam is not centered on what America did to itself but on what it did to the Vietnamese people. Perhaps "betrayed" amounts to the same thing.

Reading along, I came to these sentences: "Americans who had never before seen war now saw the wounded and homeless and the melted flesh of burned children afflicted thus by their own countrymen. When even the *Ladies' Home Journal* published an account with pictures of napalm victims, McNaughton's hope of emerging 'without stain' vanished."

The name McNaughton meant nothing to me, presumably he was an important American in government, but I knew he had never set foot in Saigon. The dullest observer would have seen the stain in half an hour. With surprise, I realized that the "account" was mine and I had entirely forgotten it. Miss Tuchman was impressed by where it was published: the *Ladies' Home Journal* being an old, mass circulation, middle-American, super respectable magazine. Her time reference was therefore late 1966 and I think she was wrong about what Americans had seen by then on their TV screens. Bombed, burning villages as part of war, yes; and

261

stunned peasants straggling away from them; but none of the rest. TV cameras did not go into refugee slums or orphanages or civilian hospitals. And nobody showed the faces and bodies of napalmed children. The most famous and effective TV picture of the war—a little girl, naked but sheathed in napalm fire, running down a road—set off shock waves much later. Having registered these thoughts, I forgot it all again; the "account" had been long lost anyway in the chronic confusion of my papers.

Now that article for the *Ladies' Home Journal* has surfaced from a buried file. I see why I forgot it. The sugar coating on the pill sickened me at the time and still does. The illustrating photograph was the narrow perfect body of a boy, aged around five, with a long deep red gash, shaped like a quarter moon, in his back; shell fragment, probably. By Vietnamese standards the child was hardly wounded; the gash was not even infected. Few people have seen what napalm does and neither the *Ladies' Home Journal* nor any other American magazine could have published then (or now?) photographs of its effect on human flesh. Napalm was our weapon and we used it wholesale in Vietnam.

My six reports in the *Guardian,* London, were models of tact and self-censorship. Even liberal readers in Britain were not prepared for the full true story. The official American version of the war, as a generous effort to save the South Vietnamese people from communism, had been a public relations triumph. To dispute it, by showing what the war was actually doing to the South Vietnamese, risked the label of communist propaganda. I wanted to be read, to be heard, and knew I had to write carefully. There are smarmy sentences in those reports that I wrote with gritted teeth.

Everything I described in South Vietnam was there for anyone to see, open, obvious, and had been for well over a year at least, before I arrived in the country. I cannot explain to myself why the hundreds of correspondents in Saigon ignored this side of the war unless they thought it unimportant, uninteresting, not the proper concern of war correspondents, or realized how unwelcome such information would be to their editors and public at home.

Those toned-down reports in the *Guardian* proved to be too much and too soon. They enraged the South Vietnamese foreign office and no doubt their American counterparts. They earned me the unwanted, and I believe unique, distinction of being placed on a South Vietnamese press blacklist. Though I tried for years, I could never get a visa to return to South Vietnam. Appeals for help to American authorities were useless: I was told politely that after all the South Vietnamese ran their own affairs. The messenger who brings bad news is not popular.

I went to America in October 1966, trying to talk to anyone who would listen to me. I remember vaguely a meeting in the editorial offices of the *Ladies' Home Journal* where I explained that there were no politics in this, it was purely humanitarian. The editors risked patriotic condemnation and lost subscribers. Freedom of the press is another illusion we live by. Freedom to write certainly, but getting your words printed is something else. I had no new facts and readers will find repetitions but I am including the piece as it was published, complete with their title and editorial comment. This book is a record and this article is a record of exactly how much and how little unpopular truth could be told to a large American audience at that time. It is worthwhile to remember that I was writing what I had learned in August and September 1966, and nothing changed in the next eight years and eight months, or rather only for the worse.

"Suffer the Little Children..."

January 1967

It's time to talk of the Vietnam casualties nobody dares talk about: the wounded boys and girls

We love our children. We are famous for loving our children, and many foreigners believe that we love them unwisely and too well. We plan, work and dream for our children; we are tirelessly determined to give them the best of life. "Security" is one of our favorite words; children, we agree, must have security—by which we mean devoted parents, a pleasant, settled home, health, gaiety, education; a climate of hope and peace. Perhaps we are too busy, loving our own children, to think of children 10,000 miles away, or to understand that distant, small, brown-skinned people, who do not look or live like us, love their children just as deeply, but with anguish now and heartbreak and fear.

American families know the awful emptiness left by the young man who goes off to war and does not come home; but American families have been spared knowledge of the destroyed home, with the children dead in it. War happens someplace else, far away. Farther away than ever before, in South Vietnam, a war is being waged in our name, the collective, anonymous name of the American people. And American weapons are killing and wounding uncounted Vietnamese children. Not 10 or 20 children, which would be tragedy enough, but hundreds killed and many more hundreds wounded every month. This terrible fact is officially ignored; no Government agency keeps statistics on the civilians of all ages, from babies to the very old, killed and wounded in South Vietnam. I have witnessed modern war in nine countries, but I have never seen a war like the one in South Vietnam.

My Tho is a charming small town in the Mekong Delta, the green rice bowl of South Vietnam. A wide, brown river flows past it and cools the air. Unlike Saigon, the town is quiet because it is off-limits to troops and not yet flooded with a pitiful horde of refugees. Despite three wars, one after the other, the Delta peasants have stayed in their hamlets and produced food for the nation. Governments and armies come and go, but for 2,000 years peasants of this race have been working this land. The land and their families are what they love. Bombs and machine-gun bullets are changing the ancient pattern. The Delta is considered a Vietcong stronghold, so death rains from the sky, fast and indiscriminate. Fifteen million South Vietnamese live on the ground; no one ever suggested that there were more than 279,000 Vietcong and North Vietnamese in all of South Vietnam.

The My Tho children's hospital is a gray cement box surrounded by high grass and weeds overgrowing the peacetime garden. Its 35 cots are generally filled by 55 little patients. One tall, sorrowing nun is the trained nurse; one Vietnamese woman doctor is the medical staff. Relatives bring their wounded children to this hospital however they can, walking for miles with the children in their arms, bumping in carts or the local buses. Organized transport for wounded civilians does not exist anywhere in South Vietnam. Once the relatives have managed to get their small war victims to the hospital, they stay to look after them. Someone must. The corridors and wards are crowded; the children are silent, as are the grown-ups. Yet shock and pain, in this still place, make a sound like screaming.

A man leaned against the wall in the corridor; his face was frozen and his eyes looked half-mad. He held, carefully, a six-months-old baby girl, his first child. At night, four bombs had been dropped without warning on his hamlet. Bomb fragments killed his young wife, sleeping next to her daughter; they tore the arm of the baby. As wounds go, in this war, it was mild—just deep cuts from shoulder to wrist, caked in blood. Yesterday he had a home, a wife, and a healthy, laughing daughter; today he had nothing left except a child dazed with pain and a tiny mutilated arm.

265

In the grimy wards, only plaster on child legs and arms, bandages on heads and thin bodies were fresh and clean. The children have learned not to move, because moving hurts them more, but their eyes, large and dark, follow you. We have not had to see, in our own children's eyes, this tragic resignation.

Apparently children are classified as adults nowadays if they are over 12 years old. During a short, appalled visit to the big My Tho provincial hospital, among hundreds of wounded peasants, men and women, I noted a 13-year-old girl who had lost her left foot (bomb), sharing a bed with an old woman whose knee was shattered; a 14-year-old girl with a head wound (mortar shell); a 15-year-old girl with bandages over a chest wound (machine-gun bullet). If you stop to ask questions, you discover frequently that someone nearby and loved was killed at the same time, and here is the survivor, mourning a mother or a little brother; loneliness added to pain. All these people suffer in silence. When the hurt is unbearable, they groan very softly, as if ashamed to disturb others. But their eyes talk for them. I take the anguish, grief, bewilderment in their eyes, rightly, as accusation.

The Red Cross Amputee Center in Saigon is a corrugated tin shed, crowded to capacity and as comfortable in that heavy, airless heat as an oven. Two hundred amputees, in relays, have lived here. Now 40 Vietnamese peasants, male and female, ranging in age from six to 60, sit on chromium wheelchairs or their board beds or hobble about on crutches and, though you might not guess it, they are lucky. They did not die from their wounds, they are past the phase of physical agony; and in due course they will get artificial arms or legs.

The demand for artificial arms and legs in South Vietnam may be the greatest in the world, but the supply is limited; for civilians it had run out completely when I was there. These maimed people are content to wait; Saigon is safe from bombs, and they are fed by the Red Cross. To be certain of food is wonderful good luck in a country where hunger haunts most of the people.

A girl of six had received a new arm, ending in a small steel hook to replace her hand. Bomb fragments took off the lower half of her arm and also wounded her face. She has a lovely smile, and a sweet little body, and she is pitifully ugly, with that dented, twisted skin and a lopsided eye. She was too young to be distressed about her face, though she cannot have felt easy with her strange arm; she only wore it to have her picture taken.

An older girl, also a bomb victim, perhaps aged 12, had lost an eye, a leg and still had a raw wound on her shoulder. She understood what had happened to her. Since the Vietnamese are a beautiful people, it is natural that they should understand beauty. She hid her damaged face with her hand.

A cocky, merry small boy hopped around on miniature crutches, but could not move so easily when he strapped on his false, pink-tinted leg. Hopefully he will learn to walk with it, and meanwhile he is the luckiest person in that stifling shed, because the American soldiers who found him have not forgotten him. With their gifts of money he buys food from street vendors and is becoming a butterball. I remember no other plump child in South Vietnam.

A young Red Cross orderly spoke some French and served as interpreter while I asked these people how they were hurt. Six had been wounded by Vietcong mines. One had been caught in machine-gun cross fire between Vietcong and American soldiers, while working in the fields. One, a sad reminder of the endless misery and futility of war, had lost a leg from Japanese bombing in World War II. One, the most completely ruined of them all, with both legs cut off just below the hip, an arm gone, and two fingers lopped from the remaining hand, had been struck down by a hit-and-run U.S. military car. Thirty-one were crippled for life by bombs or artillery shells or bullets. I discussed these figures with doctors who operate on wounded civilians all day, and day after day. The percentage seems above* average. "Most of the bits and pieces I take out of people," a doctor said, "are identified as American."

In part, it is almost impossible to keep up with the facts in this escalating war. In part, the facts about this war are buried under propaganda. I report statistics I have heard or read, but I regard them as indications of truth rather than absolute accuracy. So: there are 77 orphanages in South Vietnam and 80,000 registered orphans. (Another figure is 110,000.) No one can guess how many

---

*Editorial cowardice: the word was *about* as next sentence shows—and is the truth.

orphaned children have been adopted by relatives. They will need to build new orphanages or enlarge the old ones, because the estimated increase in orphans is 2,000 a month. This consequence of war is seldom mentioned. A child, orphaned by war, is a war victim, wounded forever.

The Govap orphanage, in the miserable rickety outskirts of Saigon, is splendid by local standards. Foreign charities have helped the gentle Vietnamese nuns to construct an extra wing and to provide medical care such as intravenous feeding for shriveled babies, nearly dead from starvation. They also are war victims. "All the little ones come to us sick from hunger," a nun said, in another orphange. "What can you expect? The people are too poor." The children sit on the floor of two big, open rooms. Here they are again, the tiny war wounded, hobbling on crutches, hiding the stump of an arm (because already they know they are odd): doubly wounded, crippled and alone. Some babble with awful merriment. Their bodies seem sound, but the shock of war was too much for their minds; they are the infant insane.

Each of the 43 provinces in South Vietnam has a free hospital for civilians, built long ago by the French when they ruled the country. The hospitals might have been adequate in peacetime; now they are all desperately overcrowded. The wounded lie on bare board beds, frequently two to a bed, on stretchers, in the corridors, anywhere. Three hundred major operations a month were the regular quota in the hospitals I saw; they were typical hospitals. Sometimes food is supplied for the patients; sometimes one meal; sometimes none. Their relatives, often by now homeless, must provide everything from the little cushion that eases pain to a change of tattered clothing. They nurse and cook and do the laundry and at night sleep on the floor beside their own wounded. The hospitals are littered with rubbish; there is no money to spend on keeping civilian hospitals clean. Yet the people who reach these dreadful places are fortunate; they did not die on the way.

In the children's ward of the Qui Nhon provincial hospital I saw for the first time what napalm does. A child of seven, the size of our four-year-olds, lay in the cot by the door. Napalm had burned his face and back and one hand. The burned skin looked like swollen, raw meat; the fingers of his hand were stretched out, burned rigid. A scrap of cheesecloth covered him, for weight is intolerable, but so is air. His grandfather, an emaciated old man half blind with cataract, was tending the child. A week ago, napalm bombs were dropped on their hamlet. The old man carried his grandson to the nearest town; from there they were flown by helicopter to the hospital. All week, the little boy cried with pain, but now he was better. He had stopped crying. He was only twisting his body, as if trying to dodge his incomprehensible torture.

Farther down the ward, another child, also seven years old, moaned like a mourning dove; he was still crying. He had been burned by napalm, too, in the same village. His mother stood over his cot, fanning the little body, in a helpless effort to cool that wet, red skin. Whatever she said, in Vietnamese, I did not understand, but her eyes and her voice revealed how gladly she would have taken for herself the child's suffering.

My interpreter questioned the old man, who said that many had been killed by the fire and many more burned, as well as their houses and orchards and livestock and the few possessions they had worked all their lives to collect. Destitute, homeless, sick with weariness and despair, he watched every move of the small, racked body of his grandson. Vietcong guerrillas had passed through their hamlet in April, but were long since gone. Late in August, napalm bombs fell from the sky.

Napalm is jellied gasoline, contained in bombs about six feet long. The bomb, exploding on contact, hurls out gobs of this flaming stuff, and fierce fire consumes everything in its path. We alone possess and freely use this weapon in South Vietnam. Burns are deadly in relation to their depth and extent. If upwards of 30% of the entire thickness of the skin is burned, the victim will die within 24 to 48 hours, unless he receives skilled constant care. Tetanus and other infections are a longtime danger, until the big, open-wound surface has healed. Since transport for civilian wounded is pure chance and since the hospitals have neither staff nor facilities for special burn treatment, we can assume that the children who survive napalm and live to show the scars are those who were least burned and lucky enough to reach a hospital in time.

Children are killed or wounded by napalm because of the nature of the bombings. Close air support for infantry in combat zones is one thing. The day and night bombing of hamlets, filled with women, children and the old, is another. Bombs are mass destroyers. The military targets among the peasants—the Vietcong—are small, fast-moving individuals. Bombs cannot identify them. Impartially, they mangle children, who are numerous, and guerrilla fighters, who are few. The use of fire and steel on South Vietnamese hamlets, because Vietcong are reported to be in them (and often are not), can sometimes be like destroying your friend's home and family because you have heard there is a snake in the cellar.

South Vietnam is somewhat smaller than the state of Missouri. The disaster now sweeping over its people is so enormous that no single person has seen it all. But everyone in South Vietnam, native and foreign, including American soldiers, knows something of the harm done to Vietnamese peasants who never harmed us. We cannot all cross the Pacific to judge for ourselves what most affects our present and future, and America's honor in the world; but we can listen to eyewitnesses. Here is testimony from a few private citizens like you and me.

An American surgeon, who worked in the provincial hospital in Da Nang, a northern town now swollen with refugees and the personnel of an American port-base: "The children over there are undernourished, poorly clothed, poorly housed and being hit every day by weapons that should have been aimed at somebody else. . . . Many children died from war injuries because there was nobody around to take care of them. Many died of terrible burns. Many of shell fragments." Since the young men are all drafted in the Vietnam army or are part of the Vietcong, "when a village is bombed, you get an abnormal picture of civilian casualties. If you were to bomb New York, you'd hit a lot of men, women and children, but in Vietnam you hit women and children almost exclusively, and a few old men. . . . The United States is grossly careless. It bombs villages, shoots up civilians for no recognizable military objective, and it's terrible."

An American photographer flew on a night mission in a "dragon ship"—an armed DC 3 plane—when Vietcong were attacking a fortified government post in the southern Delta. The post was right next to a hamlet; 1,400 is the usual number of peasants in a hamlet. The dragon ship's three guns poured out 1,800 bullets a minute. This photographer said: "When you shoot so many thousand rounds of ammo, you know you're gonna hit somebody with that stuff. . . . you're hitting anybody when you shoot that way. . . . a one-second burst puts down enough lead to cover a football field. . . . I was there in the hospital for many days and nights. . . . One night there were so many wounded I couldn't even walk across the room because they were so thick on the floor. . . . The main wounds came from bombs and bullets and indiscriminate machine-gunning."

A housewife from New Jersey, the mother of six, had adopted three Vietnamese children under the Foster Parents Plan, and visited South Vietnam to learn how Vietnamese children were living. Why? "I am a Christian. . . . These kids don't ask to come into the world—and what a world we give them. . . . Before I went to Saigon, I had heard and read that napalm melts the flesh, and I thought that's nonsense, because I can put a roast in the oven and the fat will melt but the meat stays there. Well, I went and saw these children burned by napalm, and it is absolutely true. The chemical reaction of this napalm does melt the flesh, and the flesh runs right down their faces onto their chests and it sits there and it grows there. . . . These children can't turn their heads, they were so thick with flesh. . . . And when gangrene sets in, they cut off their hands or fingers or their feet; the only thing they cannot cut off is their head. . . ."

An American physician, now serving as a health adviser to the Vietnamese Government: "The great problem in Vietnam is the shortage of doctors and the lack of minimum medical facilities. . . . We figure that there is about one Vietnamese doctor per 100,000 population, and in the Delta this figure goes up to one per 140,000. In the U.S., we think we have a doctor shortage with a ratio of one doctor to 685 persons."

The Vietnamese director of a southern provincial hospital: "We have had staffing problems because of the draft. We have a military hospital next door with 500 beds and 12 doctors. Some of them have nothing to do right now, while we in the civilian hospital need all the doctors we can get." (Compared to civilian hospitals, the military hospitals in Vietnam are havens of order and comfort. Those I saw in central Vietnam were nearly empty, wasting the invaluable time of frustrated doctors.) "We need better facilities to get people to the hospital. American wounded are treated within a matter of minutes or hours. With civilian casualties it is sometimes a matter of days—if at all. Patients come here by cart, bus, taxi, cycle, sampan or perhaps on their relatives' backs. The longer it takes to get here, the more danger the patient will die."

There is no shortage of bureaucrats in South Vietnam, both Vietnamese and American. The U.S. Agency for International Development (US AID) alone accounts for 922 of them. In the last 10 years, around a billion dollars have been allotted as direct aid to the people of South Vietnam. The results of all this bureaucracy and all this money are not impressive, though one is grateful that part of the money has bought modern surgical equipment for the civilian hospitals. But South Vietnam is gripped in a lunatic nightmare: the same official hand (white) that seeks to heal wounds inflicts more wounds. Civilian casualties far outweigh military casualties.

Foreign doctors and nurses who work as surgical teams in some provincial hospitals merit warm praise and admiration. So does anyone who serves these tormented people with compassion. Many foreign charitable organizations try to lighten misery. I mention only two because they concentrate on children. Both are volunteer organizations.

Terre des Hommes, a respected Swiss group, uses three different approaches to rescue Vietnamese children from the cruelties of this war: by sending sick and wounded children to Holland, Britain, France and Italy for long-term surgical and medical treatment; by arranging for the adoption of orphans; and by helping to support a children's hospital in Vietnam—220 beds for 660 children. This hospital might better be called an emergency medical center, since its sole purpose is to save children immediately from shock, infection and other traumas.

In England, the Oxford Committee for Famine Relief (OXFAM) has merged all its previous first-aid efforts into one: an OXFAM representative, a trained English nurse, is in Vietnam with the sole mission of channeling money, medicine, food, clothing and eventually toys (an unknown luxury) to the thousands of children in 10 Saigon orphanages.

Everything is needed for the wounded children of Vietnam, but everything cannot possibly be provided there. I believe that the least we can do—as citizens of Western Europe have done before us—is to bring badly burned children here. These children require months, perhaps years, of superior medical and surgical care in clean hospitals.

Here in America there are hopeful signs of alliance between various groups who feel a grave responsibility for wounded Vietnamese children. The U.S. branch of Terre des Hommes and a physicians' group called The Committee of Responsibility for Treatment in the U.S. of War-Burned Vietnamese Children are planning ways and means of caring for some of these hurt children in the United States. Three hundred doctors have offered their skills to repair what napalm and high explosives have ruined. American hospitals have promised free beds, American families are eager to share their homes during the children's convalescence, money has been pledged. U.S. military planes, which daily transport our young men to South Vietnam, could carry wounded Vietnamese children back to America—and a chance of recovery.

The American Government is curiously unresponsive to such proposals. A State Department spokesman explains the official U.S. position this way: "Let's say we evacuate 50 children to Europe or the United States. We do not question that they would receive a higher degree of medical care, but it would really not make that much difference. On the other hand, the money spent getting those 50 children out could be better used to help 1,500 similarly wounded children in Vietnam. It seems more practical to put our energies and wherewithal into treating them on the scene in Vietnam." The spokesman did not explain why we have not made more "energies and wherewithal" available to treat the wounded children, whether here or in Vietnam. Officially, it is said that children can best be cured in their familiar home environment. True; except when the home environment has been destroyed and there is no place or personnel to do the curing.

We cannot give back life to the dead Vietnamese children. But we cannot fail to help the wounded children as we would help our own. More and more dead and wounded children will cry out to the conscience of the world unless we heal the children who survive the wounds. Someday our children, whom we love, may blame us for dishonoring America because we did not care enough about children 10,000 miles away.

Last Words on Vietnam, 1987

Forgetting is a normal human activity, although the usual result of forgetting mistakes and craven deeds is to repeat them. The collective forgetting of nations is something else: an unvoiced agreement to forget shame. Consensus amnesia was the American reaction, an almost instant reaction, to the Vietnam war. Perhaps the type of shame was divided as the country once divided: shame of defeat, the self-proclaimed patriots' view; shame of the war itself, the anti-war protesters' view. Amnesia worked well and unjustly for about twelve years. In American public consciousness twelve years is an aeon.

Amnesia erased the Vietnam veterans, all 2.8 million men; the small proportion of combat troops, who had a brutal record, together with the majority, non-combat support troops. Except for professional soldiers, marines, air force and sparse volunteers, amnesia deleted the fact that the huge majority of the veterans had been forcibly drafted and the huge majority were America's least privileged citizens, not exempt from Vietnam duty through attendance in college. Amnesia spared the men at the top, the men responsible for the war: the nation forgot to blame them. Amnesia even effaced the past. Whatever became of the rules governing nations that were established at the Nuremberg War Trials? The formal proscription, agreed by the U.S., against "the common plan or conspiracy," "crimes against peace," "war crimes," and "crimes against humanity." And amnesia simply blotted out the people of Vietnam, Cambodia and Laos.

Amnesia was convenient. Evidently it has served its purpose. Now America is standing tall, a remarkable feat that must astound backward foreigners. America can be proud. America is strong, as well it might be considering the Pentagon's budgets. America is not going to be pushed around by anyone again. (Did Vietnam invade America?) The outcome of the war is irrelevant to the unblemished high ideals that directed America into the war. The new look is righteousness. For a generation that had no experience of it, and for those Americans who cannot bear the thought that America was ever defeated, the Vietnam war is being rehabilitated.

To the extent that the President gives an emotional lead to the country, President Reagan stars in the revised Vietnam scenario. The key line in the change-over from amnesia to grandeur is President Reagan's "that noble cause." He has commended a comically grotesque movie hero, a Vietnam veteran called Rambo, as a model of American patriotism, the can-do man out there fighting single-handed to rescue imaginary American war prisoners from swarms of present-day murderous Vietnamese. The film itself would strain the credulity of a sensible five-year-old, but the country did not fall about laughing over Rambo. The scenario of Vietnam as a fine if failed crusade against communism suits a belligerent American attitude toward the rest of the world. The world is separated into enemies or followers. America is the biggest, the best, and knows best too. America is never wrong.

Again, Americans hear echoes of the Vietnam doctrine. Anti-communism is a religious faith, the President is its prophet and his supporters in government are its missionaries. True Americans believe without question in the faith and their President. Americans who oppose this doctrine as intrinsically wrong and dangerous to America and the world are unpatriotic, disloyal, heretics and (proof of sin) soft on communism. In a last effort to keep some of the record straight, I want to recall the real past, as I knew it.

Millions of Americans actively reviled the Vietnam war. (So did a multitude of non-Americans, objecting throughout the world.) In the early years of the war, when the voice of conscience was not loud in the land, the war-lovers named the war-haters "bleeding hearts," a sneering vulgarity that was new in the American language. Bleeding hearts increased in such numbers that two successive administrations saw them as enemies of the state and employed the FBI and the CIA to spy on American citizens exerting their legal right to protest against an illegal war. The police were freely and often violently used on anti-war demonstrators.

The homefolks were not alone in decrying the war. Veterans, returned from Vietnam and finished with their military service, declared their loathing of the war too. Passionate events marked the long passionate years of dissent. Two stand out as unique in American history. At Kent State University in conservative Ohio, a mass of students protesting peacefully if noisily were fired on by the National Guard. Four Americans, two girls and two boys, were killed for expressing their opinions. A thousand Vietnam veterans, wearing their old left-over uniforms, among them young men in wheelchairs, gathered at the Capitol in Washington and threw their war ribbons and medals on its steps: no fiercer gesture of contempt can be imagined. A civil war of conscience raged in America. The people who believed that America was about principles against the people who believed that America was about power.

I don't know when the phrase, "the most powerful man in the world" became automatically attached to the President of the United States. Did it begin with President Eisenhower or with President Kennedy? It has done no President good. On the contrary. A politician elevated to the highest office scarcely needs encouragement to egomania. The Imperial White House is not a good idea either.

The first and to date worst (though not last) result of the overweening use of Presidential power was the Vietnam war, a Presidential war. Not sanctioned as the constitution requires by Congress, it was waged on the strength of the famous Tonkin Bay Resolution, passed by Congress. Congress was stampeded into giving President Johnson an unprecedented authority by the report of a second attack on two American destroyers by North Vietnamese gunboats, 30 miles off the coast of Vietnam. It never happened, it was a non-incident. A lie. The first attack had been harmless to American lives though insulting to American destroyers. The whole episode remains in doubt.

Washington waded into the Vietnam war with buoyant arrogance. Geopoliticians, those ominous fortune tellers, predicted that China would conquer all Southeast Asia if communism were not defeated in Vietnam. After which, the imagined threats were legion. Apparently no one stopped to think about the Vietnamese, who had already fought the Japanese and the French to get what they wanted: freedom from foreign domination. The Vietnam war would also prove to the world that the U.S. government had an iron will and "credibility," that mysterious word, and could be counted on to protect its allies, including an outstandingly corrupt puppet Asian dictatorship, masquerading as a democracy. In a horrifying way the Vietnam war was a show-off war, based on an ignorant fallacy.

Old-fashioned American ideals about the right of peoples to self-determination had been sloughed away in 1956 when the Vietnamese were denied the right to vote on their future. An international treaty, approved by the U.S. government, guaranteed this right. But we live in the tough real world now, don't we; we're not playing marbles, we're playing Superpowers.

Then the War in Vietnam ended. It seemed to leak away. After twelve years of covert two-faced involvement in Indo-China, and ten years of all-out American war, it was over. *And no one was responsible.* The grandees in Washington and Saigon—the politicians, the policy-makers, the planners, the administrators, the generals—just walked off. Nobody even said, "I'm sorry."

Fifty-eight thousand twenty-two Americans died in Vietnam, in combat and from non-combat hazards. 300,000 Americans were wounded; we are never told details of wounds and do not know how many of these were maimed for life. The war caused a special kind of casualty: trauma, men who came back physically intact, but could not live with their memories, with themselves, the mentally wounded. They had seen and done atrocities; it was an unclean war from the sleazy black market atmosphere of Saigon up to the burning hootches. American soldiers did not decide the methods for fighting the Vietnam war. Body counts and kill ratio dictated the methods. Those Americans who collected enemy ears and enjoyed the liberty to destroy—as in "search and destroy"—are chilling compatriots.

One pilot felt such revulsion from the murderous bombing of Vietnam that he refused to go on and was treated in military hospitals as insane, until his final discharge. Pilots and air crews in Vietnam distributed wholesale death and destruction. In scale, they

277

committed far worse atrocities against helpless civilians than the infantrymen—napalm, white phosphorus, Agent Orange, anti-personnel bombs, the earth-shaking horror of carpet bombing—but were not condemned like the soldiers on the ground who committed atrocities by hand. Perhaps, after the war, some of them thought about it and condemned themselves; perhaps not.

These men were all obeying the orders of their superiors. The orders to bring to mind the Nazi theory of the successful practice of war: *schreklichkeit,* frightfulness. Frightfulness was defeated in Europe as in Southeast Asia. Aside from the irreparable damage it did to three Asian countries, I think it did irreparable damage to America in history.

The American army in Vietnam was an army of occupation, victims and victimizers both. Victims because they were wrongly sent 10,000 miles from home, to take part—even as mildly as storekeeper, clerk, cook—in a political war of aggression. Victimizers because they looked on the Vietnamese as a lesser breed, close to non-persons, gooks, sneaky, no doubt Vietcong at heart, acceptable as laundresses and bar girls. From this outlook, the hamlet barbarities were not unnatural.

The soldiers I saw in Vietnam and the American soldiers I knew in the Second World War in Europe might have come from different countries. Perhaps this is how you can tell a just war from an unjust war. Vietnam veterans felt bitterly that they were blamed for a rotten lost war. The blame was never theirs. The leaders should be judged; they led into evil. There have been no questions, no accounting to the American people. No one is responsible.

After long delay, a Vietnam War Memorial stands in Washington. Perhaps it was intended as part of the new gilding of the Vietnam war. I have not seen it except in photographs but I have heard much about it. I think it is inspired, I think it is perfect. That long handsome black stone wall condemns the war in Vietnam man by man, one at a time, name after name. The war is real because those names belonged to real men who lived with their names to identify them, and are now dead. I am told that people walk along the wall, reading names, and weep. So they should. Weep in sorrow, but also in anger. Why are these men dead? By what right and for what reason, were they sent off to be killed? The Vietnam memorial is a lesson in stone: mourn the dead, never excuse the war. Beware the glorifiers, for they will lead into evil again.

The American war in Vietnam destroyed three ancient civilizations. They had survived through millennia everything history can do, which is always plenty, but they could not survive us, who understood nothing about them, nor valued them, and do not grieve for them.

The whole of Vietnam, Cambodia and Laos is a war memorial. The Vietnamese have never been able to count their dead and wounded. Cambodians, subjected to 3,500 secret bombing raids, and Laotians who got whatever we were doling out, are a separate and unknown casualty toll. Outside opinion suggests two million Vietnamese dead and 4.5 million wounded. Given our weaponry and their lack of medical care, a tragic number of these must be amputees, the blind, the napalm deformed. Soldiers of the South Vietnamese Army, the Vietcong, the North Vietnamese Army account for a heavy share of the dead; no one can say how many hundreds of thousands. The bulk of the Vietnamese dead were peasants—more old men than young, women of all ages, children—who died of hunger and disease, died in massacres, died because they lived on that day's battleground, died because nightly "interdiction" artillery sprayed random shells over the countryside. Mainly they died under the fire and steel that rained from the skies. Vietnam is a small country, slightly larger than Norway. American planes dropped more tonnage of bombs on Vietnam, North and South, than was dropped in all theatres of war by all air forces in World War II.

We left behind in South Vietnam six and a half million destitute refugees, uprooted from their ancestral lands and traditions, with no homes to return to. Based on South Vietnam's official wartime Ministry of Health figures (surely not an overestimate) and projecting from their own forecasts, we left behind a pathetic army of some 300,000 orphans. There is no data that I know of to describe the conditions in North Vietnam but ten years of saturation bombing must have inflicted the same suffering.

Vietnam veterans deserve reparation, not re-packaging. Amends in care and money, according to need. A lot of generous rhetoric is floating about these days but not much else. It is infamous that the government left veterans, afflicted (like the Vietnamese) by the effects of Agent Orange, to struggle alone for compensation from the chemical manufacturers. Need exists; reparation is owed.

279

The Rambo re-packaging would be a bad joke (and surely is to Vietnam veterans) were it not that American teenagers, watching "Rambo II," have been heard to greet the film with screams of USA, USA, USA. As political indoctrination of kids, "Rambo" is unsound. More thoughtful re-packaging presents Vietnam combat troops as unfortunate young men fighting under horrendous conditions with great bravery, discredited by a few sadists and killers among them. This is a much happier image of themselves for Americans but it is full of peril: if the men were heroes, then the war tends to appear heroic. And it was not. It was a dirty big war like the dirty little war the French fought first.

In Vietnam war movies I have seen and the books I have read, Americans are the subject; the Vietnamese people and their country are background. This egocentricity implies that America and Americans were the major victims of the war. There has also been an odd note of self-pity in all these accounts of the war. Where is the pity for the Vietnamese? Where is there any sense of the war as a crime against the peasant people of Vietnam? Nobody deserves reparation more than the Vietnamese. We savaged them though they had never hurt us; and we have made no reparation to them, nothing.

We are the richest people in the world and they are among the poorest and we cannot find it in our hearts, our honor, to give them help—because the government of Vietnam is communist. And perhaps because they won. Vietnamese peasants are still punished for Superpower politics. They endured years of torment beyond our imagining, and kept their finest human qualities: kindness, dignity, courage. They are admirable people. What is the matter with us that we do not see our obligation to them? Have we forgotten our own humanity?

We could economize on our new MX ten-warhead nuclear missiles, for we certainly have enough already, turn over the saved billions to the Red Cross and ask it to manage a giant aid program for the impoverished people of Vietnam. Money is the least we can do. Instead, ever since the end of the Vietnam war, U.S. governments have harried the Vietnamese, economically and politically, with tireless spite. The U.S. has thus forced Vietnam into complete dependence on the Soviet Union; then castigates Vietnam. U.S. policy is nothing more than malign ill will toward a small distant country foundering in hardship because we ruined it and have

280

done our best to keep it ruined. And China is our new ally in the persecution of Vietnam: the convoluted glory of geopolitics.

Vietnam is rarely in the news today, but a few years ago I saw a glimpse of it on TV: a children's hospital in Saigon, a shed. The little bodies were crowded three to a narrow wooden plank bed, just as they were in 1966. The doctor said sadly that he had few medicines, really nothing at all.

It is almost twenty-one years since I was in Vietnam and I can not forget any of it and never will, because I am American. The Presidents did not worry about the likes of me when they dumped a lifelong load of shame to fall where it might on the citizens. I remember with fury how we were lied to. Lyndon Johnson won a landslide election by promising not to send American boys to do the job Asian boys should do, though already the plans were made for sending American boys. Richard Nixon won a landslide election by promising that he had a plan to end the hated war, then proceeded to enlarge it for four years. American democracy needs an overhaul, re-tooling, there isn't much value in elections if the voters state their purpose at the polls and are promptly cheated afterwards.

It is not easy to be the citizen of a Superpower, nor is it getting easier. I would feel isolated with my shame if I were not sure that I belong, among millions of Americans, to a perennial minority of the nation. The obstinate bleeding hearts who will never agree that might makes right, and know that if the end justifies the means, the end is worthless. Power corrupts, an old truism, but why does it also make the powerful so stupid? Their power schemes become unstuck in time, at cruel cost to others; then the powerful put their stupid important heads together and invent the next similar schemes. A Saigon doctor, a poor man serving the poor, understood more about the real world than the power men in the White House. "All people are the same everywhere. They know what is justice and what is injustice."

Lest we forget.

THE SIX DAY WAR

In June 1967, Israel was the hero of the western world. The Six Day War was a famous victory, unmatched in modern warfare. The David and Goliath aspect of this conflict aroused great admiration. Considering Goliath's superior force, it looked beforehand as if David might not make it. The western world had been talking worriedly and to no purpose for weeks while the Arab armies massed and tension soared, but talk would not save Israel; very comforting, very helpful that Israel managed to save itself. Israel had to win. Losing meant the end of their people and their state.

On May 27, 1967 President Nasser of Egypt announced: "Our basic objective will be the destruction of Israel. The Arab people want to fight." He added, a day later, "We will not accept any co-existence with Israel . . . The war with Israel is in effect since 1948." On May 30, he proclaimed: "The armies of Egypt, Jordan, Syria and Lebanon are poised on the borders of

Israel . . . while standing behind us are the armies of Iraq, Algeria, Kuwait, Sudan and the whole Arab nation. This act will astound the world. Today they will know that the Arabs are arrayed for battle, the critical hour has arrived."

Like an echo, on May 31, the President of Iraq declared: "The existence of Israel is an error which must be rectified. This is our opportunity to wipe out the ignominy which has been with us since 1948. Our goal is clear—to wipe Israel off the map." Cairo Radio, "The Voice of the Arabs," then the premier cheer-leader, outdid itself by bellowing "Slaughter, Slaughter, Slaughter," a delirious cry taken up by huge crowds in the Cairo streets.

This confidence in victory was based on simple arithmetic. The Arab armies on its borders outnumbered Israel's three to one; they had the same three to one superiority in tanks, combat aircraft and heavy artillery. Israel's regular army was 40,000, enlarged by reservists to a fighting force of about 48,000. Israel's citizen army, reservists, women to age 34 and men to age 54, moved into support: signals, transport, supplies, medics, engineers. But it was the Israeli pilots and tank crews who guaranteed the triumph of David over Goliath.

Twice before and again after June 1967, the Arab governments ignored the U.N. armistice terms as soon as the ceasefire was in operation. In 1967, having provoked and lost the war, they immediately demanded the return of the conquered territories, though they refused absolutely to negotiate peace treaties with Israel. There is something childish or lunatic in this, as if the Arab leaders thought war was a fatal game of marbles: just because you won doesn't mean you can keep my marbles, give me back my marbles right now until we get ready to play another game . . .

The area of the four Arab nations ranged around Israel was 677,000 square miles. Israel, in its vulnerable wasp shape, covered 8,000 square miles. The population of those four Arab states was 46,100,000; in Israel there were 2,300,000 Jews and about 350,000 Israeli Arabs. Nor was Israel valuable property; no oil, no diamonds, no gold, mainly fruit and vegetables, an agricultural miracle. No sane mind could conceive any threat, by the tiny state of Israel, to the safety and well-being of this enormous Arab land and human mass.

I think that if Israel did not exist, the Arab leaders would have to invent it. It is the single imaginary enemy that unifies all their people. The Moslems of the Middle East quarrel among themselves, mistrust, assassinate, plot coups, change alliances, kill each other with ferocious energy; they can agree on nothing except their nourishing hatred for the Jews of Israel.

In 1967, with every reason to do so, Israelis still did not hate the Arabs. I noticed this detachment with wonder in 1949, after the new state had fought off six attacking Arab armies determined to annihilate Israel at birth. It seemed to me that Israelis didn't think much about the Arab states until they had to, in case of war. PLO terrorists were something else. Men who plant bombs in a school bus, in a movie theatre, in a market, kill unarmed civilians—men, women, many children—and then run for it, that is different. Those men they loathed.

I came to that war late. I was in the Midwest, in America, held up for some forgotten reason, when the war began. I hurried and arrived in Israel on the fifth day. After the sixth day, for several weeks, I retraced the war.

I wish I had notes and photos but have only these disjointed memories of that singular journey, seeing the whole shape of a war, a still life of death and destruction. In the Sinai, dead bodies of Egyptian soldiers like dark rag bundles and the nauseating stench of death. A vast line of guns, buried in the sand, with the long heavy barrels above ground, pointing at Israel. They were captured at night by Israeli paratroops crossing the dunes on foot to attack the gun crews from the rear, in the trenches. Mines piled beside the roads; found, lifted, stacked by Israeli engineer companies.

Flies like moving black clouds; they settled on your body, they flew into your eyes and mouth. Painful dry heat, blue-white sky, glare; lukewarm rationed water. Tanks, burned, crashed on their sides, skewed with broken treads, everywhere, hundreds of them, strange black dead monsters. Clusters of boots, scattered on the sand, torn off by the Egyptian troops, in retreat or surrender. Handsome civilian cars, headed toward Egypt, smashed by machine gun fire: these were the private cars of Egyptian officers, escaping on their own, and vengefully destroyed. The Israelis had a special contempt for those cars. More pitiful dark rag bodies.

In the middle of nowhere, in the sand emptiness, a contingent of Israeli troops, very young. No combat troops look well dressed, but the Israelis were outstandingly tatty. Sneakers rather than boots, unbuttoned khaki shirts hanging over unmatching khaki pants or pants cut off to shorts, hatless or floppy canvas hats, dirty, casual. The officers wore no insignia and nobody in the Israeli army seemed to salute. Officers and men knew each other well and called each other by their first names. The citizen army was already being sent home, where there was work to be done, within days of the victory, but at that nowhere place the troops were waiting for orders around a communications van. Two small pretty fair-haired girl soldiers hopped out of the van. These gentle-voiced soldiers, with pony tails and unforgettable soft black ballet slippers, operated the radios, reservists in the Signal corps.

On the Suez Canal, at Kantara, a group of Israeli soldiers, rumpled and in a rage, were glaring across the Canal. They said they were not sending back any more Egyptian prisoners—they had watched and those bastards on the other side took the poor guys off and *shot them*. They were not sending any more until the Red Cross or somebody came and checked it out; what kind of people did that to their troops?

Somewhere in the desert I saw a missile installation. I had never seen one of these things before, as long as a railroad car, very beautiful and sleek in its underground silo. I don't know what kind it was nor why still there but everyone was glad it was, unused.

Somewhere else, in the Negev probably, there was a big P.O.W. camp, Egyptian prisoners whom the Israelis were eager to return; hundreds of them with shaven heads, sitting about looking depressed. They were guarded by a few uninterested Israeli soldiers. The prisoners, though glum, must have been delighted to receive water and food but no other attention. They had been told that the Israelis mutilated and killed their prisoners and would have believed this since they were instructed to show no mercy to captured Israelis.

On the West Bank near a bridge in the Jordan Valley, discarded boots littered the ground but no dead bodies; the

Arab troops had escaped into Jordan. Mixed with boots, a mess of blown paper, Arabic newspapers, comic books, whatever. The cartoons were self-explanatory. The Nazi image of the Jew, fat, swarthy, with a great hook nose and slobbery lips. I had seen the same kind of art work, in 1961, in all the Palestinian refugee schools in Jordan and Lebanon, schools financed by the United Nations Relief and Works Agency. Along the road to Jericho, full ammunition boxes abandoned by the Jordanian army. Stenciled on them the American flag with the clasped hands of friendship. On the Golan Heights, silence in the abandoned positions from which Syrian guns had shelled Israeli settlements in the Galilee valley below for eighteen years. The Golan was a cliff-top Maginot Line, artillery in solid bunkers, connecting trenches, mine fields, barbed wire. Tired troops captured that fortified frontier after non-stop fighting on other fronts. The Israelis took heavy casualties.

Long after the war, reading a technical report of the operation confirmed my still-life impression that the Six Day War was an unparalleled military achievement. If war is forced on a nation, then it is admirable to conduct it with supreme skill, speed, courage and a determined effort to spare civilians. No soldiers can have been more profoundly motivated than the Israelis. The Arab armies were fighting for slogans; the Israelis were fighting for the existence of their country.

Israel was remarkably sober about its victory. The people were grateful to their brilliant fighting men who had saved the nation; their borders were now safer than ever before. But 766 young Israelis had been killed and more than 1,000 badly wounded. And they knew this was not the last war against the Arabs, whose leaders were indifferent to their casualties and would not make peace.

Immediately the war was over Arab propaganda swung into action. Word of Israeli outrages was sent abroad and published without verification. Hospitals and refugee camps had been bombed, thousands of Arab civilians had been killed in the towns; the Israelis were mass murderers. I knew this was a lie and set out patiently and carefully to collect the facts. Not that the lies don't stick, or that people do not believe them with enthusiasm. But at least you can keep the record straight, however modestly. By the time my articles appeared, in late

July 1967, Israel was no longer the hero of the western world; it was already being blamed for this and that, a perpetual nagging. Israel is a hopeless failure at propaganda.

Israel is unpopular just now. It generally gets a bad press unless the world is dazzled by some fabulous act of daring, like the rescue of its hijacked citizens in Uganda. Or the Six Day War. Then the world applauds ecstatically for a time, and relapses. A double standard of judgment applies to Israel; Israel must be one up on Caesar's wife, while anything goes for its Arab enemies.

For the first time, in 1977, Israel elected a right-wing chauvinist government, as if no other democracy ever indulged in such an aberration. This government allowed grievous mistakes which divided Israelis among themselves. Blaming them for what they did and did not do, the outside world never takes into account the unique pressures that must affect Israeli actions and judgment: the relentless hostility of the Arab states, always increasing Arab armament, decades of terrorist attacks at home and abroad. It would be surprising if Israel did not have a siege mentality, knowing that it can rely only on itself.

Outside public opinion has no influence on how Israel manages its primary business, which is to survive. Israel is the size of Massachusetts, of Wales, half of it the Negev desert. If the country had been safely at peace, since 1948, it would have been sufficient glory to build farms and factories, universities and hospitals, museums and theatres, schools, houses; a modern civilized democracy. Israelis have not lived in peace, not for one year in their short history, and the strain tells on the people. My belief in Israel is unwavering and I do not expect it to be faultless, unlike any other state. I have never forgotten Dachau, nor the soul-sickening testimony by Jewish concentration camp survivors that I heard hour after hour at the Nuremberg Trials and the Eichmann Trial. I have not forgotten a nightmare day, spent with a former prisoner, in the haunted emptiness of Auschwitz. And I am angrily impatient of those who do not know or care to remember the suffering and the endurance that founded Israel. Nazi Germany made Israel essential, the safeguard against a repetition at any future time of the ugliest crime in history. And of the shameful reluctance beyond Germany to give shelter to escaping Jews.

Her neighbors oblige Israel to waste resources and time on military strength. Israelis are not fond of being warriors; they have no choice. But Israel is far more than a bulwark. It produces funny wine and good books, scientists, musicians and farmers of genius. It may have the highest I.Q. per capita in the world. It is brave. It is there to stay.

Casualties and Propaganda

July 1967

For the best part of a month I have been listening to Palestinian Arabs in West Jordan and the Gaza Strip. It always started well; Arabs have charming manners, though somewhat less charming to their own women, and are often fine to look at. Wherever we were, we sat in a circle, group formation, drank coffee from tiny cups, and conversed like reasonable people. Then suddenly all was lost.

"Bethlehem was bombed all day!" one cries. But there is Bethlehem, intact and rosy in the afternoon light. "The Jews came to every house in Nablus, shooting. Our youths defended their homes. Two hundred were killed, women, children, boys, at least 200." And there are the houses, solid, unmarked, of cut stone, and on a later visit, calmer counsel reduced the number of civilian deaths to 19: still incredible. Where? How? We agree there was no fighting here. We agree that the town is untouched except for a few buildings at the southern entrance. We agree that this damage is minimal. Yes, the "youths" were probably "shooting a bit" from the now lightly pock-marked police post out there, perhaps also from the nearby buildings. No records; no circumstantial evidence. It is comforting to feel certain that people are alive and well, whom propaganda has killed.

In a Gaza Strip refugee camp, a very fat, pleasant-faced old man, surrounded by his buxom wife and eight stout healthy off-spring, announced with terror, "The Jews shoot every man, woman and child they see in the street." He had witnessed this

291

crime? No. Then he must have heard the shots? No. The camp was an oasis of peace; not one shot had been fired anywhere near it; and the Israelis, poised to kill, were five dusty young soldiers, sitting on a wall across the main road, as guards for the large camp warehouse.

There is logic in this new post-war Arab propaganda. Before the Third Arab-Israeli War, intoxicated by every propaganda drug, these Arabs truly expected to wipe out Israel. For once, they had reason to believe their propaganda, considering the beautiful billionaire Russian weaponry of the Egyptians, and the size and might of the Arab armies. Even as civilians, they could hope to take some part in the glorious victory, since the Jordanian and Egyptian governments distributed weapons lavishly to the population in West Jordan and the Gaza Strip.

If the Six Day War can be made to seem a nightmare, a hell of fire and flying steel, if their sufferings were unparalleled, defeat becomes justified. And the Israelis become more hateful, evil, ruthless. The roles are reversed: David is changed into Goliath. This logic clearly dominates official Arab propaganda. It accounts for the casualty figures put out by Jordan (an original claim of 25,000 civilian and military deaths lowered to 15,000) and for reports of "the fury of war," peril and shattered homes, which drove 200,000 refugees to seek safety across the Jordan River. The land must lie in rubble, for propaganda purposes.

Happily for the Arabs in the war zones, and heartening for us all, the fact is that the Third Arab-Israeli War, the Six Day War, scarcely touched the Arab civilian population. I am not talking about Arab emotions, I am talking about real war: death and destruction. The difference is self-evident, like the difference between civilian life in London and New York during World War II.

Before this recent conflict, an estimated 1,500,000 civilians lived in West Jordan, the Gaza Strip, Syrian hill villages within the Syrian Maginot Line and the adjacent Syrian garrison town of Kuneitra, and two Egyptian towns on the edge of the Sinai desert. Those were the Arab civilian war zones. Some 410,000 Israeli citizens also lived in war zones: on their side of Jerusalem, under sweeping Jordanian artillery fire for 52 hours; on populous Israeli farm land along the entire Syrian frontier, shelled by Syrian artillery for four days; in the narrow waist of Israel from Tel-Aviv to

Letanya, hit by sporadic Jordanian artillery fire for two days. Nearly two million civilians were therefore at risk.

I submit that a total of *two hundred civilians,* Arab and Israeli, everywhere, throughout the war, is the highest conceivable number of noncombatants killed.

All the dead are to be pitied and mourned; none should be exploited for propaganda. In my opinion, that death toll is still too high; I am glad to think that fewer human beings lost their lives. (The military casualties are tragic enough.) But I accepted Arab statements on the spot, even though they denied the evidence before our eyes. I checked at hospitals, talked with Arab mayors, ordinary Arab residents, priests, UNRWA (United Nations Relief and Works Agency) staff, and scoured the war zones to see the actual damage of war in cities, towns, villages, refugee camps.

From England eastwards around the world to Japan, adults remember civilian war as bombing from the air: a horror. The people of Vietnam know this sort of war, with agony. Bombs are the mass destroyers of civilians and their homes. In the entire Six Day War, the Israeli Air Force dropped 10 to 15 light bombs on one civilian target, the Syrian garrison town of Kuneitra.

Kuneitra (population 30,000) lies immediately behind the fortified Syrian hills, a Middle Eastern Maginot Line. The Israeli Army and Air Force attacked these positions and Kuneitra on the fifth day of the war. Below Kuneitra, the Syrian villages between the military strong-points were vacated before the battle began. It is unlikely that the Syrian Army Command, in its minor Pentagon headquarters at the edge of Kuneitra had not also evacuated the army families from the town. Kuneitra was deserted when the Israeli Army entered it on the afternoon of the sixth and last day of the war.

Twice, the Israeli Air Force operated in civilian inhabited areas. Israeli planes gave close support to infantry fighting on the hills behind Jerusalem, and again on the road to Gaza town. No one denies the accuracy of the Israeli Air Force; bombs did not rain by accident, away from the military targets, all over helpless civilians.

After bombing, the doom of civilians is to live on a battlefield, pounded by artillery and overrun by soldiers fighting in the streets and through their houses. In West Jordan, civilians live in Jerusalem, in nine small towns, 20 refugee camps, and some 350 rural

293

settlements. The war was 70 hours long. The Jordanian Legion and the Israeli Army fought in only three inhabited areas: Jerusalem, mainly on the surrounding hills (civilian deaths, 25); a border town Qualquilya (15): a border village Ya'Bad (16). The passage of war caused civilian deaths in Jenin (2), Nablus (19), Tulkarm (30), Ramallah (2), Bethlehem (7), and the village of Beit Mersem (1). All refugee camps were intact. Israeli civilian war deaths were in Israeli Jerusalem (15), in the remaining Israeli war zones (8). Artillery fire destroyed Israeli property and farmland; people stayed in shelters.

In the Gaza Strip, civilians live in three towns, eight refugee camps, and in innumerable single farmhouses and clusters of houses. During approximately 28 hours of war, the Israeli Army and combined Palestine Liberation Army and Egyptian units fought along the road from the Strip's southern entrance into the southern section of Gaza town. No refugee camps were hit. Judging by visible war damage, hospitals, talks with refugees, I conclude that 10 civilians is the highest probable death toll.

Significantly, neither the Egyptian nor Syrian governments made any claim of civilian deaths when announcing their combat casualty figures. The heaviest battle of the war was fought in the Sinai desert, away from all civilian habitation. On the edge of the Sinai desert, the town of El Arish lay outside the battle zone, undamaged. Entered on the sixth day of the war, the town of Kantara on the Suez Canal was almost totally evacuated. It shows signs of small arms sniping at its entrance on the desert side. For 38 hours, Israeli and Syrian forces fought in the military positions on the Syrian hills, in gun emplacements, bunkers, trenches and in three deserted villages between these positions. Early witnesses and later observation indicate there were no civilians in the battle zone during the hours of combat and that the estimated 300 civilians now in Kuneitra returned to their homes, as the whole Druse population returned to its villages, after the ceasefire.

Possibly, but one can hope with reason not probably, there could have been 50 more civilian casualties in damaged private cars and isolated buildings along some major roads in West Jordan and the main Gaza road. A 19-year-old Israeli soldier, hitch-hiking back to his post in West Jordan, explained this war perfectly. "The General say and every soldier understand we fighting armies not peoples." It was a war between armies, mercifully remote from the people.

Fortunately, Israelis are not addicted to propaganda. Propaganda is the begetter of hate and hate is the begetter of killers. Perhaps, as time goes on, the Arabs in Israeli-held territory will decide that peace is more rewarding than propaganda. There are hopeful signs: Bethlehem is a joyous boom town, full of Israeli tourists; and the Israelis cannot squeeze into their municipal swimming pool in Jerusalem because it is full of Arabs.

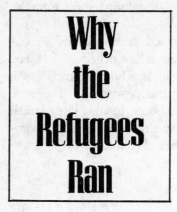

Why the Refugees Ran

July 1967

Between Jericho and the unpleasant milky blue of the Dead Sea, close to the Allenby Bridge over the Jordan River, there are four Palestinian refugee camps. The valley is green with orange groves and fields; the hills behind are eroded gray limestone; now, in summer, the heat is a weight to carry. Imagination leaps from the term "refugee camp" to the picture of a little Belsen, hordes of hungry idle people penned in by barbed wire. The camps are nothing like that. They are simply poor Arab villages or small towns, all different, as the houses in them are all different. If there is enough land for the refugees to plant trees and grow grape arbors and flowers, they look liveable and cheerful; if cramped for space, they look like rural slums. But the residents have one great advantage; UNRWA (United Nations Relief and Works Agency) runs a welfare state for its charges, the Palestinian camp refugees. Native Arab poor enjoy no such special care.

The largest refugee camp in Jordan, Aquabat Jaber, near Jericho, covers 700 acres of ground. It is a well-organized small town, with nine schools, 323 shops, cafés, a post office, sports grounds, a clinic compound, mosques, and—most important—232 taps for unlimited clean water. As in all camps, the houses and their little walled patios are built of what UNRWA sorrowfully describes as "mud brick." Mud brick is adobe, the traditional building material of peasant and working-class Arabs, Mexicans, Vietnamese and

296

others who live in a hot climate; adobe serves as natural air conditioning.

Aquabat Jaber and the neighboring Jericho camps are now ghost
towns though probably most of the residents will filter back. No
other mass exodus happened anywere else in West Jordan and it is
fishy. The lightning war was not heard even as a passing bang in
this valley. The camp leader, himself a Palestinian refugee, is a
choleric fat man, a powerful UNRWA administrator, feared and
obeyed by his people, as I remembered from a visit years ago. Why
didn't he prevent this panic flight? We insisted that there must have
been some sort of trouble to drive the people away.

"No, no. The battle lasted an hour, far off," the camp leader
said. "There was nothing here. No, no, the Israeli Army did not
come here at all; everything is all right; everything is correct. There
are plenty of supplies. There is no trouble."

Since non-war had been followed by instant peace, why did
the refugees run? "People talk," the camp leader said. "There were a
lot of stories. Political party people spread rumors. They said all the
young men would be killed. People heard on the radio that this is
not the end only the beginning so they think maybe it will be a long
war and they want to be in Jordan."

A group of sullen young men were sitting in a café; they tuned
in to Radio Cairo as we passed. Perhaps Radio Cairo and all it
stands for, Arab politics and propaganda, are the true reason for
the first frantic rush of camp refugees into a second exile across the
Jordan. They were not escaping the danger of war, nor fleeing their
shattered homes. There are 20 UNRWA refugee camps in West
Jordan; not one of them was touched by the war; not one resident
was killed. (Statement made by UNRWA's chief representative in
West Jordan, during an interview on July 4 at Kalandia, which
confirmed my own observations.)

By their location, I calculate that nine of the camps cannot
have heard or seen the war. In all cases, the war passed them by
quickly on the roads; whereupon the refugees set off for the Jordan
River. This second exile is doubly sad because so needless. Again
they have left behind the homes they had built, the furniture and
possessions they had collected, to live—we read—under tents,
stupefied by glaring heat and dust, exhausted, once more self-
uprooted.

I suggest that blind fear of the Israelis, not the dangers of war, was their driving emotion. Radio Cairo had promised destruction of the Jews. King Hussein's last broadcast before his ceasefire is memorable. "Kill the Jews wherever you find them. Kill them with your hands, with your nails and teeth." Now the Jews had won, so the Jews would kill them instead.

The majority of Palestinian refugees do not live in camps. Any of these, like any other Arabs who were exposed to actual war, may have decided to escape immediately lest the fighting go on or start again and trap them in danger. Perhaps some of the first wave of refugees had valid, political reasons for leaving, unlike the later waves of stoical departing Arabs.

In the last few weeks, neither fear of war nor fear of reprisals nor family nor financial complications explain the smaller but steady flow of people plodding over the Allenby Bridge, no matter what the waiting hardships of exile. "They don't feel secure," said an intelligent Palestinian woman on UNRWA's staff in Hebron. "They don't know what is going to happen next. They want to be among Arabs." She surprised me by remarking that the local Israeli military commander had been "very kind to UNRWA, very gentle and helpful," amazing words for an Arab to use about a Jew. The commander had provided a car for their work, and truck transport for refugee women, children and old people to the Allenby Bridge. I surprised her by remarking that this truck transport, a gesture of decency in the white heat of summer, had been transmuted through propaganda into forced expulsion. If the Israeli Army had tried at any moment to prevent the exodus, that would have been treated as forced detention.

Hopefully, the Jordanian and Israeli governments will be able to co-operate, without mutual paralyzing suspicion, on the return of all those refugees who choose to come back to West Jordan. UNRWA's "educated guess," here, is that 100,000 of its West Jordan refugees are now on the east bank, including those who were working in Jordan before the war. It would be wise and restful not to harass Israel for an overnight solution of the 19-year-old Palestine refugee problem. With time, work, and money, the Israelis will manage simply by treating their acquired Palestine refugee population as people, not as political pawns. During these 19 years, Israelis have gained much useful experience through resettling half a million Jewish refugees who fled to Israel from the Middle Eastern Arab countries.

Thoughts on a Sacred Cow

July 1967

After 19 futile years, there is at last a chance for three-quarters of the Palestinian refugees to escape imprisonment in the Palestine Refugee Problem. They are now beyond the effective reach of Arab politics, in West Jordan and the Gaza Strip. With moral and financial support from the West, Israel could work out their permanent self-sufficient settlement in both areas, which are in fact their native soil. But no solution is possible without the cooperation of the refugees and of UNRWA (United Nations Relief and Works Agency), their long-time official guardian.

What about UNRWA? UNRWA is the governing power for 20 refugee camps in West Jordan and eight camps in the Gaza Strip. Its actions and attitudes, filtering down from the top through all its staff, influence refugee actions and attitudes.

Israeli co-operation with UNRWA was immediate and obliging. One does not feel that the cordiality is reciprocated. Since I was in the Gaza Strip, the UNRWA high command there has changed and no doubt improved. In West Jordan, it seems to me UNRWA is making heavy weather of the Arab defeat, without justification.

Their 20 refugee camps are happily intact, untouched by war. Supplies have not run out and new shipments will arrive on schedule through an Israeli port. Their Jerusalem office building was fought over and war damaged but they have adequate temporary office space in the elegant UNRWA technical school farther out of the city. Their published and private statements suggest obstacles and hardships that cannot be located on the ground. The peace is really as surprising as the war.

UNRWA has always been treated like a sacred cow. No one has ever made a careful neutral study of the organization, totting up its succeeses and failures and examining its methods, its finances and its political fall-out. (I expect to be accused of blasphemy as I write.) UNRWA is a bureaucracy composed of 11,419 Palestinian refugees and 118 Americans and West Europeans who are understandably and necessarily devoted to Arabs, converts to a cause. Of course this bureaucracy, itself preponderantly Arab, would have welcomed an Arab victory and is far from joyful over the reverse. Of course UNRWA's foreign administrators could not have operated in Arab countries for 17 years unless they accepted and supported the Arab governments' political position on Palestinian refugees.

But has this bias, however understandable, been the best way to help the refugees themselves? Ritually, annually, succeeding UNRWA Commissioner-Generals deplore the fact that Israel does not commit suicide by repatriating all Palestinian refugees. That is official Arab doctrine; return to Palestine or nothing. Yearly, the refugee population grew, and fortunately thrived, with UNRWA's care and because the refugees fend for themselves. Neither official Arab doctrine nor UNRWA's acceptance of it changed.

For 2,300,000 Israeli Jews, 1,300,000 hate-indoctrinated Arabs (taught hate steadily in UNRWA schools as well) make a pretty big Trojan horse. Clearly Israel was not going to commit suicide. If UNRWA could not devise, if the Arab governments would not agree to any program except repatriation, UNRWA had to accept tacitly the official Arab alternative: war to recover the Palestine homeland. Was UNRWA totally opposed to that unique solution for a refugee problem?

UNRWA's reports and handsome publicity brochures are the basis for soliciting governmental and private contributions to UNRWA. They paint a heart-rending picture. As a side effect, UNRWA thus confirms Arab propaganda. The refugees must be kept desperate, in fact or on paper, or the Palestine Refugee Problem disappears. Without the Palestine Refugee problem, there is no

proper Arab excuse for war with Israel, since Israel impinges on no
vital Arab interest.

Year after year, UNRWA states that 40–50 percent of the
refugees are destitute or near destitute ("without resources" in my
dictionary); 30–40 percent are partially self-supporting; and some
10–20 percent are all right. Yet UNRWA does not give money to
refugees. Its direct aid is a monthly ration of flour, pulses, sugar,
rice, oil amounting to 1,500 unbalanced calories a day. If the
destitute, without resources, had nothing else to live on they would
long since be dead, instead of having a higher birth rate than other
Arab peasants, and healthier children.

Over half the refugees live outside the camps, in private dwellings; they must be more than partially self-supporting to pay for
rent, clothing and food (aside from UNRWA rations). Someone in
each family has to work for money, and they do, and their work has
benefited the "host" countries. Poverty is endemic in the Middle
East (while the Arab governments waste vast wealth on arms);
Palestinian refugees, like non-refugees, have to combat the general
affliction and the special restraints put on them by Arab politics.
But UNRWA's picture of them does not stand up to common sense
or the refugees themselves in the flesh.

During the past 19 years, 67 governments, including Israel
(but never once the Soviet Union, the Arabs' friend) and innumerable private charities have contributed to an average of some $35
million annually to UNRWA for the support of the Palestinian
refugees. This money is spent on goods and services and amounts
to Big Business, however you look at it. The Palestinian refugees
have been a vested interest as well as a propaganda weapon.

Three fourths of the refugees can now be given a new deal.
UNRWA, in West Jordan and the Gaza strip, needs a fresh international staff, people who are favorable neither to Arabs nor Israelis
but strictly concerned with the refugees as human beings. The
dispassionate newcomers should then screen UNRWA's enormous
Palestinian refugee staff.

And finally, there must be an accurate census of the Palestinian
refugees, forbidden by the Arab governments all these years, so
that instead of a propaganda numbers game, true need is defined
and adequate help given. It really is the limit that a man, living on
his native soil, among his own people, speaking his own language,

the owner of a large Jerusalem hotel, a travel agency, and a house in the suburbs, is classed as a Palestinian refugee.

For 19 years, Arab politics have demanded a Palestinian Problem. Two generations of Palestinian children have had to learn from refugee teachers in UNRWA schools how and why they were a Problem. Being a Problem doesn't come naturally. During the same years, unaided by UNRWA but inhindered by politics, some 35 million other refugees all over the world have bravely and quietly solved their problem and made new independent lives.

WARS IN CENTRAL AMERICA

Most Americans, including me, knew little or nothing about Central America. It is well off the tourist beat, which stops at Mexico. The countries were known as banana republics, a contemptuous description of their economy and their governments. That has now changed, thanks to the President of the United States, who appears obsessed with the area and makes dramatic statements on El Salvador and Nicaragua that bear no relation to facts. The President justifies his policies and actions by declaring that the guerrillas of El Salvador and the Sandinista government of Nicaragua are Communists. As a result, Congress cannot be relied on to obstruct the President, for fear of being branded "soft on Communism". It would be less damaging for an American politician to be accused of cannibalism.

The former American Ambassador to the United Nations, paramount theoretician of the present American administra-

303

tion, enunciated a new American view of the world. There are two kinds of dictatorship, the lady proclaimed; *totalitarian*, Communist and utterly abhorrent, and *authoritarian*, right wing, maybe not all one could wish for, but anti-Communist and acceptable as allies. It is a novel doctrine. Human rights are violated in totalitarian dictatorships and the U.S. government will protest firmly. The hideous abuse of human rights in authoritarian dictatorships is ignored, or smoothed over. Do the other Free World governments accept the Leader's line? They have made no public repudiation of this system of sub-dividing injustice. Perhaps we should stop calling ourselves the Free World and instead call ourselves the Free Enterprise World. More accurate, as that encompasses our "authoritarian" clients and cohorts.

Long before fear of the Soviet Union became the chief preoccupation of American governments, they sustained authoritarian dictatorships throughout America's traditional sphere of influence, the Caribbean, Central and South America. If hungry, oppressed people rebelled, send the Marines to establish order. If the people managed to elect a non-tyrant, who would care for their interests, destabilize that government. The tragic needs of the people of those countries were unimportant. The word *gringo* is not a joke; for the poor, who are most of the people, it is the name of the enemy throughout Latin America.

I went to El Salvador in stupefying ignorance. That winter I was in Mexico on a nostalgia jaunt, looking for remembered sun and sky, enchanted to see again the Mexican Indians who were a happy part of my life years ago. I had read about El Salvador but not properly understood the news; perhaps I did not want to. I imagined a little war in the hills, guerrillas ambushing army units, the army taking revenge on villages suspected of helping guerrillas. Civil war: clearly the business of Salvadorans, not the U.S. government.

As citizens, I think we all have an exhausting duty to know what our governments are up to, and it is cowardice or laziness to ask: what can I do about it anyway? Every squeak counts, if only in self-respect. Gloomily, because otherwise I would be ashamed of myself, I made the small effort of a detour to El Salvador.

Knowing nothing about the capital, San Salvador, I chose a hotel with a familiar name, the Sheraton. It is built in gardens on a hillside, a charming hotel, with pretty rooms and balconies overlooking the city. In this hotel's garden restaurant at breakfast, two American A.I.D. advisers and their Salvadoran colleague had been shot dead by Death Squad assassins. Apparently the reason for these murders was that the Americans were engaged in a cosmetic land reform program, part of the U.S. government's propaganda about improving conditions in El Salvador. A young American reporter checked in, left his luggage, went out and was not seen again until his body was returned to his family, a year or so later. Why the young reporter was killed remains a mystery. It could have been mistaken identity. When killing is so easy, general and never punished, there must often be casual errors.

The Sheraton, I learned, was considered unsound; but I liked the view and the sweet brown-skinned women who cleaned my room. Everyone else on the hotel staff was surly and hostile. The hotel was filled by a convention of Latin American Rotarians, or Chambers of Commerce, I forget which, all looking North American, prosperous and faceless.

I dumped my suitcase in the early evening and asked a taxi driver to take me to the center of the city, wherever people met. "Donde hay el paseo," I said, thinking of a Mexican square and the people ambling about, or chatting over drinks at sidewalk cafés. He stared at me as if I were mad and drove me to the Cathedral Square, where Archbishop Romero had been killed by a government sniper at the altar during Mass, and later the mourning crowds were fired on by the police. Not that I knew this. The driver told me not to stay long. Only minutes, he said. The square was poorly lit. A few stalls sold cheap candy by the light of kerosene lanterns. People were crowding into ramshackle buses to go home as darkness fell. They were dingily dressed, they looked tired. No one was talking or smiling. That was the first sign I had, and the first glimmer of understanding. Silent, grim Indian-mestizo people, hurrying to leave.

When the square was almost empty I started walking up a long street in a direction I thought led back to my hotel. The houses were stone, with doors and shutters closed, not a light showing, not a sound. The street lamps were scarce and dim. The street was empty. I heard fast footsteps behind me and two young men passed, almost running. Suddenly I was afraid, as if I had breathed fear from the air. There was no curfew in San Salvador but people did not move on the streets at night.

I have never been in such a frightening city. In Madrid and Helsinki and London, danger made a loud noise and came from outside. Here danger came without warning from anywhere. The police hunted at will, day and night. The U.S. government, paymaster of this diseased country, could not protect its own citizens. I was afraid for the people who talked to me. Those who should have hated me as an American were friendly and trusting. But I knew what they risked and was awed by their courage. Each one was alone against the police state, and the chosen weapon of this state is torture.

One afternoon I shared a bench in the backyard of the Diocesan offices with Pedro, the acting head of the Salvadoran Commission of Human Rights. By then the four founders of that group had been killed by the Security police or "disappeared." Pedro was a handsome and noble young man, part Indian, an ex-student of the University that the army closed and looted. We were selecting, from his files, sworn accounts of atrocity. A kid, late teens, came running to Pedro, breathless, his face scared under a lop-sided cap. I could not understand what he murmured to Pedro, who said to him, "Do not sleep at home. Move every night to another friend. Do not come here, we will let you know what happens." The boy nodded, Pedro patted his shoulder; he left the yard. Pedro said, "The Security police were asking about him at his house." That is all the people could do to protect themselves: hide and hope. I was afraid for Pedro for months and finally learned of a group of Americans in California, fine "bleeding hearts" who had contacts in San Salvador, wrote to them and in time heard that Pedro had escaped to Mexico. I hope it is true.

The rich Salvadorans, and they are very rich, are solidly protected by high walls around their houses, ten or twelve feet high, often topped with barbed wire. The doors in these walls are steel. Coming back to the hotel at dusk I would see patrolling plainclothes guards, with pistols showing under their loose shirts. The fear of the rich was a vague dread of Communists. Inside a well-sealed elegant house, I had a very different conversation with upper class ladies who assured me that only a few Communist agitators were causing the trouble. The talk about people being murdered was propaganda. If there were peasant refugees, they were fleeing from the Communists. As so many of their friends had departed to safe luxury in Florida, they were proud of themselves for staying here and leading their usual lives—work and play, dinner parties and dances at night in their homes; businesses were doing well. No, their sons were not in the army; the army was really for poor boys who learned hygiene and basic literacy.

Salvadoran peasants, Indians and part-Indian mestizos, bone poor in their villages, became destitute when forced to escape empty-handed to internal refugee camps. The government, which causes this pitiful exodus, gave no assistance, not a kilo of rice, not a blanket. Without the Church, courageous in El Salvador, the peasant refugees would starve. They survived in the worst conditions I have seen since Vietnam, in shelters built of cardboard, tin, scraps, with inadequate food and water, without medical care, in fear. The only secure camp was behind the large Catholic Seminary in San Salvador; the people were guarded by a building.

Generation after generation, the peasants remained illiterate for want of schools, a handicap that guarantees cheap labor. In the grounds of the Catholic Seminary, little groups of peasants were teaching themselves to read. They sat in study circles in the dust, in crushing heat. This self-education had been going on in villages throughout the country, perhaps started by their priests. Learning to read is the peasants' rebellion. Their primer is the Bible. They were called the People of the Word, and that made them subversives. Subversives are prey.

As we were talking, in that sad place, a whisper, a shiver ran through the crowd; women lowered their voices. They showed me a young man in an undecipherable blue uniform, walking like a cat along the top of the high wall that surrounds the football field and gardens of the Seminary. *Policia,* they said. No purpose in that cat walk except to frighten deeply

307

frightened people. "My friend Corazon," a woman whispered, "went outside to the dentist, she could no longer suffer the pain of her tooth. She has not come back, no one has seen her; we will never see her." The Catholic lawyer who had brought me said we ought to go; it was bad for the people if the police watched them talking to an obvious foreigner.

The U.S. Embassy is a gray cement stronghold constructed as if for attack by artillery and aerial bombardment. The turnstile entrance in the high link fence was guarded by armed Salvadoran soldiers; U.S. Marines guarded the interior. Authorized personnel escort you to your destination; too dangerous to let a stranger roam the premises. This nervy caution applied even to the foreign press stationed in San Salvador and well known at the Embassy. The briefing was held in a basement room, like a bomb shelter, where a conceited overfed American army officer, clearly an old Vietnam hand, patronized the young reporters with military-sounding rubbish. The news of the day was the capture of three guerrillas by the Salvadoran army; the captured weaponry, two shotguns and a pistol. (When asked what happened to the guerrillas, he smiled and shrugged.) Not exactly the weapons that President Reagan says are supplied by Cuba and Nicaragua. Those much-advertised weapons, which justify the enormous American military aid to the Salvadoran government, have never been found. Nor has anyone explained how these weapons could be delivered to isolated El Salvador, where the U.S. and Salvadoran governments have complete sea and air control.

The old-Vietnam-hand officer informed his respectful audience of young journalists that if only Congress would vote more money, El Salvador could get the equipment it needed and easily finish off this rebellion. Just like Vietnam. Since then, Congress has voted more and more of American taxpayers' money and that money has supplied Vietnam-style equipment. AC-47 planes, gunships known in Vietnam as "Puff the Magic Dragon"; Hughes 500 helicopters with Gatling guns; improved bombs; napalm and white phosphorus. The refugee population has increased.

I was given a runaround in a Salvadoran government office, calculated to insult. One stout well-dressed mocking official, seated behind his bare desk, sent me to another and another; finally the top man said of course I could visit Il-opango, the women's prison, all their prisons were model establishments, I was welcome to inspect. Of course I was not; I was stopped by an armed guard at the prison gate who got angry when I insisted and pointed his rifle and shouted at me to shut up and leave. But I had seen the thin weary women, in the clean faded cotton dresses that are their uniform, filing in with small baskets, bringing food to their daughters.

Suddenly I decided to get out; I could not stand another day in this fearful city. The callousness of those who owned and ran the country and the persecution of the poor made me sick, a state of nerves close to hysteria. I packed in a rush and drove to the airport; I would have taken a plane in any direction. The airport lounge was crowded and silent. People did not look at each other. They did not move; they stood or sat by their luggage. They waited as if holding their breaths. Planes are regularly overbooked in this part of the world; to be bumped off would have been bad enough but there must have been fear of being stopped by the police, for no reason, stopped and taken away. Yet these were the privileged who could get a passport and pay for a plane seat. I was the most privileged, with my splendid American passport and my travelers' checks, and I was frantic to leave.

The Contras' war on Nicaragua's northern frontier should be called Reagan's war, though it is organized terror raids, not war. Fomented and paid for by the C.I.A., evidently very dear to Mr. Reagan's heart, it mainly kills peasants—old men, women, children—and destroys the modest wood shacks that were new kindergartens and clinics. Hit and run in mountain territory. On the southern frontier, A.R.D.E., supplied but not directed by the C.I.A., does similar though lesser harm. I did not reach either frontier war zone, due to my lack of time, four-wheeled transport and superior leg muscles, not official obstruction or secrecy. The effect of this ugly little war is a drain on money and manpower, both of which are in very short supply in Nicaragua.

And of course, being human, Nicaraguans mourn the deaths, often atrocious. Clean killing was never the form of Somoza's guardsmen, the Contras, likened by President Reagan, in a flight of hyperbole, to the Founding Fathers of America. This is truly astonishing, since the Founding Fathers were not known to gouge out the eyes and mutilate the bodies of their enemies, or to commit other such unseemly acts. Combined with economic blockade, the undeclared American war by proxy is punishing the poor people of Nicaragua whose only crime is their will to be free in their own land, and free of gringos. You can understand their point. Gringo governments supported their tyrant Somoza for over 40 years; gringo Marines occupied their country, bolstering oppression.

Nicaragua is not a Communist state, no matter how often a gringo President says it is. The entire country is open for inspection by anyone, notably Americans, who wishes to visit, look, question. But Nicaragua, in desperate need, naturally and gladly takes help from wherever it comes. A multinational work force assists in everything from engineering to surgery, among them Cubans, Russians, Norwegians, Argentinians, Belgians, Britons, and many young Americans.

Thus far American public opinion prevents sending the 82nd Airborne, the Marines, the B-52s, whatever, to remove the Sandinista government by force. Sixty-three percent of Nicaraguans voted for the Sandinista government in a closely supervised election, whose honesty was confirmed by responsible foreign observers. It was not the sort of show election that the U.S. government promoted in Vietnam and now in El Salvador. Sixty-three percent is a sizeably larger popular majority than gave power to the present American or British governments.

The Sandinista leaders are inexperienced. Where would they have gained experience in government? They muddle and make mistakes, they are foolishly tactless. Perhaps people in Latin America are tired of being tactful to North America. It was terrible judgment as well as terrible manners to permit noisy rudeness to the Pope, the world's most appealing reactionary. The fact that the Church hierarchy in Nicaragua, very different from the Church in El Salvador, is hostile to the Sandinistas is no excuse. Far from being a highly organized police state, President Reagan's view, Nicaragua is highly disorganized, doing its best with inadequate means. But the Sandinista leaders have one major value. They are committed to the service of their people, who have always been wretchedly deprived; they intend to make life decent for the poor. As the foundation of a new life in Nicaragua, they abolished torture and execution which always before were the rule. For the first time, the state is out of the murder business.

The men in Washington seem unable to accept that there are more poor people than rich people in the world. They do not recognize that poor people, in the late twentieth century, cannot endure poverty and disease and ignorance forever. When minimal social justice is long denied, the poor will rebel. If rebellion can be crushed—as is perhaps possible in a very small country like El Salvador—it will rise again later. Nicaragua could be bombed flat, and then what? A success story like Vietnam?

The President, the Cabinet, the elected members of both Houses of Congress should read the Declaration of Independence of the United States of America, all of it, every day. It is a glorious statement of human rights, and does not date. "We hold these truths to be self-evident, that all Men are created equal, that they are endowed by their Creator with certain unalienable Rights, that among these are Life, Liberty, and the Pursuit of Happiness." Does that apply only to North American white men? And how about: "But when a long Train of Abuses and Usurpations, pursuing invariably the same object, evinces a Design to reduce them under absolute Despotism, it is their Right, it is their Duty, to throw off such Government, and to provide new Guards for their future Security." El Salvador and Somoza's Nicaragua in eighteenth-century prose.

Oh Yank, let's go home. Leave Central America to decide its own destiny. Americans should not be expected to quake in terror for the nation's safety because of two small underdeveloped countries south of its border. It is a ridiculous posture, like standing on a table and screaming with fear of a mouse. I prefer Edmund Burke to any panic speeches from Washington: "Magnanimity in politics is not seldom the truest wisdom; and a great empire and little minds go ill together."

Rule by Terror

July 1983

President Reagan once described the Vietnam catastrophe as "that noble cause." Recently he has called Somoza's guardsmen, again killing their compatriots in Nicaragua under CIA auspices, "freedom fighters." Now he speaks eloquently of "preserving freedom" in El Salvador for which more hundreds of millions of dollars are required. Salvadoran freedom is to be preserved in the tested Vietnam style. Lavish military aid, military training, land reform, elections and finally "pacification." Land reform and elections are meant to impress Americans. They are regarded in El Salvador with contempt as frauds.

Again U.S. policy knows what is best for others, in the U.S. national interest, while knowing nothing of the others, their history, culture, daily life and bitter needs. All Americans do not suffer from amnesia or worse. It took ten years for American public opinion to stop the Vietnam war; this time it is moving faster. Meanwhile President Reagan steps up his earnest rhetoric of deception and alarm and weapons and money flow to the Salvadoran government and Green Berets move into neighboring Honduras. A young Salvadoran lawyer said: "Reagan only prolongs the agony but we will win." Yes; but the agony is horrifying and to prolong it is a disgrace for the American people.

El Salvador is slightly larger than Wales and even more beautiful and mountainous, blessed with a benign climate, fertile soil, lakes, rivers and magical trees. A country like a garden, a rural

313

society, where most of the five million inhabitants live in destitu-
tion. For 162 years Salvador has been ruled by and for an oligarchy
of landowners and its allied military. The last collected statistics in
1971 show how this works. Eight percent of the top citizens
received 50 percent of the national income. Twenty thousand farm
properties occupied 75 percent of the land, leaving the rest for
330,000 small farms. Sixty-five percent of the rural population had
become landless seasonal laborers.

There was no peaceful way to change this permanent greedy
imbalance of wealth and opportunity. Elections were a sham, ballot
boxes invariably stuffed to suit the ruling caste, the swindle en-
forced by the military. Orderly protest marches ended in massacres
by the police. Strikes were broken by the army, strikers shot and
imprisoned. The majority of the Salvadoran people could live
without hope, or rebel. Misery is not a synonym for "communist
subversion." The true begetters of this civil war are successive
brutal Salvadoran governments.

By now there is no pretense of law. Salvador is ruled by terror
alone. The people have no protection except the Salvadoran Catholic Church, a moral and humanitarian support for which the
Church pays in the death toll of its clergy. Doctors, nurses, medical
students are murdered for giving their professional help to the
poor. Rule by terror threatens anyone and everyone apart from
those who use terror and rely on it. Nobody needs to tell you
"there is great fear in this country." You can feel it.

In Saigon, I doubted that the Embassy Americans and the
headquarters officers ever went anywhere, ever saw what real life
was like for the Vietnamese who were also having their freedom
preserved. Why didn't these privileged Americans visit the refugee
hovels and the hospitals full of women and children wounded by
American weapons and the orphanages and the *asiles* that sheltered
the starving aged, the shell-shocked insane and the abandoned
newborn? I had the same doubts in San Salvador. A few blocks
from the gray concrete fortress of the American Embassy, in the
shady backyard of the Diocesan office, there is a green-painted tin
shack, the home of the Salvadoran Commission of Human Rights.
It is a good place to get an overall view of what preserving freedom
means for ordinary Salvadorans.

You can read random selections from hundreds of sworn
accounts of atrocity. You can study photo albums of the murdered.

You can also have illuminating conversations with small sturdy brown-skinned women, instantly likeable in clean, faded cotton dresses with their black hair wobbed on top of their heads. The women are relatives of victims who come here, despite the hazard, to testify, to ask advice, to collect a weekly gift of flour, to talk. On my brief visit to Salvador, I was amazed by the trust of those who have most to fear.

For instance: I stopped a scrawny woman who was carrying a plastic bag of flour on her head. For her family? She has no family left except her mother and three of her brother's children. She is 47 years old and two years ago she had three brothers and an only child, exceptional here, a pregnant girl of 25. One by one they disappeared. She took me behind the shack to show me what had been done to her because she dared ask the police about her oldest brother, then her daughter. Her left breast was sliced down to the nipple, she had a deep stab wound on her shoulder and her head. "They all raped me. Afterwards they pushed a flashlight up me. I am broken inside. I walk badly." That was for her eldest brother. She lifted her dress quickly to reveal a long cut straight down her belly, other scars. "They thought I was dead, they left me for dead." That was when she tried to find out about her daughter. She had given no sign of self-pity, but said with sudden tears: "Imagine, a girl of 25, pregnant." When the second brother disappeared, her mother, unable to accept the loss in silence, returned to their village with her youngest son. Days later, her mother found the decapitated body of her last son seven kilometers from the village.

It was a chance encounter; she was no different from any of the other women collecting flour.

As wars go this one is minor so far, sporadic attacks with relatively light casualties on both sides. The guerrillas are destroying bridges, dams, pylons, factories, crops, striking at the wealth of the ruling caste. The real war is waged on the defenseless population by the government's security forces. Although the security forces have American planes, helicopters, bombs, mortars, machine guns, splendid rifles and unlimited ammunition, they are not very successful against the guerrillas, but hideously successful against the citizens—the Church estimates 35–45,000 unarmed civilian dead since 1979.

The National Police, the Treasury Police, the National Guard and the Army are the official security forces, unleashed on the people. A guess would be 12,000 men, maybe more. They are aided by an ominous body called ORDEN, some 100,000 strong, vicious peasant vigilantes paid to denounce, spy, provoke for reprisals, murder. "They wear sombreros and kill with machetes." The explanation for their treachery to their own kind is that they are rewarded with land, money, loot, and above all are safe from the security forces. There are also the unofficial Squadrons of Death, men in civilian clothes and cars, roaming at night, special murder gangs. Finally CAIN are the trained torturers who operate inside the National Police Headquarters. All these maintain rule by terror and none has been punished for violations of human rights.

Nobody accuses the guerrillas of using torture nor do they slaughter citizens in the towns they briefly occupy or in the countryside. Wisely the guerrillas have treated captured conscript soldiers well and set them free. According to the Human Rights Commission, their record is exemplary. In Vietnam also it was clear who won the hearts and minds of the people. The guerrillas are a merger of a dozen or more distinct groups from every occupation and background (high school students, market traders, peasants' union), with a dizzying range of initials to identify them. Only one of these is CP. The guerrillas and the Church and the small endangered humanitarian organizations demand "dialogue," a just political solution to civil war. The Salvadoran government, representing five rightist parties and the White House view of Communist subversion, refuses.

The young men and women, who form the Human Rights Commission, are wonderful kids, gentle, intelligent and heroic. They risk their lives to document exactly how terror works "for the eyes of the people and democratic governments of the world." The statistics of terror are hard to come by: to witness and report violations of human rights—the Salvadoran body count—is a subversive act. But reports are brought to the green-painted shack and to the Church: there must be a national grape-vine. I am using the Human Rights statistics, though they may well be incomplete.

Terror starts like this: in the city, at any hour day or night, anywhere, at home, at work, waiting at a bus stop, a Salvadoran can be seized by armed men, uniformed or not, tied up, blindfolded, bundled into a car and driven to police headquarters. The reason for arrest is suspicion of being "subversive." Subversion is not defined. Practically, it means less than complete approval of the Salvadoran regime. After arrest, the Human Rights Commission divides victims into three categories: Disappeared, Captured, Assassinated.

"Disappeared" is total Kafka. Witnesses—family, friends, passersby—watch a person dragged off by armed security men. The frantic family, as always, searches for him, or her, at the several police headquarters. The security forces then deny that they ever seized this person. He or she has disappeared, become a non-person, and is never found again. The dreadful assumption is that the "disappeared" has been tortured to death and the security forces took care to hide the body. They are not normally careful: they fling bodies on slum streets, on roads, on garbage dumps, anywhere. It would seem that the disappeared are the more important victims.

In February in the afternoon, armed men openly seized a doctor outside his surgery in a poor section of San Salvador. He was 35, father of three, universally admired as a man and a doctor, scheduled to be the next head of the dispersed, struggling medical school. An upper-class woman doctor said, "I know nothing of politics but that boy was of the most marvelous human quality." His work was at the Maternidad, the appalling public hospital and among the poorest women, who revered him. He had been a founder of the Human Rights Commission and a member of Amnesty. Latterly, he had helped the American Medical Mission who came to Salvador—sad irony—to learn why so many of their colleagues had disappeared. The American doctors persuaded Senators and the State Department to ask the Salvadoran government to find him. But Roberto Martelli, "of the most marvelous human quality," is lost without trace. This is one way to eliminate the generous minds that could lead and serve Salvador in the future. Disappearance began in 1966—outstanding students at first—and increased year by year. In 1982, 346 men and women were wrenched out of life, invisibly.

"Captured" is a weird form of habeas corpus. After the arrest, the security forces will admit to the searching family that yes, this man, woman, boy, girl is held in their custody. What happens next is routine: the "captured" are "interrogated," tortured, as people are routinely fingerprinted and photographed in lawful jails. The captured should theoretically reappear in the two political prisons.

In 1982, 766 people were captured, among them 104 students, 50 teachers, 18 professionals, three artists. I cite these numbers to underline the persecution of the intelligentsia, aptly defined by the Oxford English Dictionary as "the part of a nation that aspires to independent thinking." "If you think here, you can die," said a staff member of Christian Legal Aid. Though 766 men and women of all ages and occupations were captured in 1982, the men in Mariona prison reported only 280 new arrivals, the women in Ilopango prison reported 45 newcomers. Habeas corpus does not mean the body will be safe or returned.

I was promised entry to the women's prison and refused at the gate. Members of the American Medical Mission, to their surprise, spent hours interviewing the women prisoners from whom they learned the forms of "interrogation" for every woman there. They were stripped and pawed, threatened with rape or raped, subjected to electric shocks or burning with acids, hung by the wrists, forced to stand naked for days, beaten (pregnant women not excepted), nearly suffocated under rubber masks. The American doctors saw scars from acid and other tortures; one woman had open sores from branding with red hot irons. Among the women, nearly half are of the intelligentsia. The men prisoners described similar treatment. One old man had his testicles surgically removed after ferocious beating.

After torture, every prisoner signs an unread confession. None know what crimes they are supposed to have committed nor when, if ever, they will be brought to trial. This has been going on for four years. Women have given birth and are bringing up their babies in prison. The diet is minimal, unhealthy and unchanging; medical care is a token gesture. But these prisoners are the elite; they have been in the hands of the Salvadoran police, are alive and their families can visit them.

The families of victims are victims too. The families of anyone seized by the security forces gather up what they can carry at once and abandon their homes, taking refuge with friends or relatives. They fear reprisals f they stay where they can be found. This creates a class of concealed refugees, which by now numbers tens of thousands, living in worse than normal overcrowding, worse than normal poverty.

I talked to the wife of a "captured" man—call him Juan, aged

318

41, seized in his high school where he had taught for 21 years. He belonged to ANDE, the teachers union, the last though much depleted pre-terror union. Two hundred and sixty-two of their members have been assassinated since 1978. Juan's take-home pay was $100 a month, a sidelight on local economics. Now his tired, soft-voiced, frightened wife is penniless and homeless, with three children, hiding in a relative's house; two women, seven teenaged children in two pitifully bare rooms. "I can sew a little," she said.

Juan's "interrogation" was basic, almost a formality. For eight days he was kept alone, blindfolded, his hands tied behind his back, sleepless on a bench. He was kicked and hauled back if he fell from exhaustion. When they took off the blindfold his eyelids were stuck together and had to be medically opened. This does not count as torture. The interrogation began with beating: tied up, punched, kicked, or whipped and all the time taunted and mocked, pride broken by pain. After this, for three days, Juan was given electric shocks in the region of the heart and lungs, on the abdomen, the feet and ears. A heavy industrial machine is used, a sticky unguent is applied to the skin before attaching metal pads. Though I have read detailed descriptions in the Human Rights files, I cannot imagine the convulsed paralyzed body, the eyeballs burning, popping out, the screams. After six months, Juan still feels pain and noise in his ears. His wife says he is very thin, nervous and depressed.

"Torture in El Salvador has become customary as a method of work, considered natural and necessary by those who practice it." (Salvadoran Commission of Human Rights) The Gestapo introduced official torture into the modern world with great success. It has spread, poisonous filth, world-wide and made technical progress. The obscenities of CAIN surpass anything heard from Gestapo victims in Europe. Torture is the worst abomination of man and utterly condemns any government that sanctions it. El Salvador is a member of the United Nations and party to the Charter of Human Rights. Has the United Nations gone out of business? European officials rightly denounce psychiatric torture in the Soviet Union. Why keep obsequiously silent about El Salvador?

"Assassinated." In 1982, regarded as a good year, better than the preceding three, 5,840 mutilated corpses of men and women, boys and girls, were found, dumped everywhere throughout El Salvador. Of these, peasants were the majority. Few peasants were "captured," only eight "disappeared" in 1982. The method for peasants is immediate butchery in villages and fields. Peasant refugees tell how the army, or ORDEN, or the National Guard, came into their village, killing, before they stole the animals, looted and burned the houses. This is how refugees are made: an estimated 300,000 outside the country, 200,000 inside it, but the process is never-ending. Peasants are uprooted, killed, because they are Romero Catholics, *Catolicos*. They believe what their murdered Archbishop taught: misery is not decreed by God, but made by man. This is revolutionary Communism to the Salvadoran government. But then, Jesuit priests are considered Communists and live in danger.

Women, innumerable children, old men crowd into makeshift refugee encampments. They have all seen peasants assassinated. A sample: a pouter pigeon of a woman who has lived for two years with 1,200 other peasant refugees on the dusty playing fields of the Catholic Seminary. "It was ORDEN. We heard them coming. We ran to hide in the trees. But my daughter was eight months pregnant, she could not run fast enough. They caught her on the path. They cut open her stomach with a machete and pulled out the child and cut it in half. She was 17 years of age. I saw with my own eyes. With my own eyes. Then they stole everything we had worked for and burned our houses."

We learned that President Reagan was distressed by the photographs of the Phalange's victims in the Beirut Palestinian camps. He is morally obliged to see the Human Rights albums of assassinated Salvadorans. These people did not die quickly. Many faces are covered in blood below the eyes ("We think they do this with rifle butts.") Some have been strangled. Some are decapitated, the head beside the corpse. A naked boy, lying on his face, has long deep open stab slashes on his legs. A naked woman, also on her face, is riddled with bullet wounds through the lower half of her body; her nakedness presumes rape but that is commonplace for women. There is a gruesome statuary of eight entwined faceless bodies, burned down to nothing but smooth white fat. I studied specially the photos of those killed this January, the month when President Reagan certified that human rights reform in El Salvador warranted more military aid, although 672 Salvadorans were murdered in that month alone.

We free worlders elect our governments freely, so we are responsible for what they do in our name. If governments were better, wiser, more in touch with real life, citizens would not have to spend so much time educating and restraining them. Nadezdha Mandelstam, survivor of another tyranny, gave the best advice to citizens: "If you can do nothing else you must scream." Weary work but essential. We Americans have to scream our government out of El Salvador and well away from Nicaragua too. We really cannot become known in the world as a nation that interferes crazily and cruelly in the lives of small brown-skinned people who never harmed us.

"We Are Not Little Mice"

May 1985

In his ultra-sincere chocolate voice, President Reagan announces that Nicaragua is "a Communist tyranny." The Contras, America's hired killers, are "the true revolutionaries fighting for freedom." Clearly, the Sandinista government must go. Never mind that the Nicaraguans chose it, in their first ever honest general election. "The fate of freedom" hangs in the balance or is at stake, I forget which. The boyish old President might just be right on that one, but not in the way he means.

In March, I roamed around Nicaragua talking with strangers. It is a forlorn country; Managua, the capital, a sprawling mess, scruffy little towns, worse villages, thin brown-skinned people in worn-out clothes, mountains peeled bare of forest never replanted, great empty spaces for a few cattle. Nicaragua looks battered, misused. Yet everything grows here; there is enough land for everyone, even the rich. Nicaragua is half the size of Britain with only 3,200,000 citizens, half of whom are under 16. All Nicaraguans needed for decent prosperity was decent government. At long last, they have a chance.

Ten miles above Matagalpa, safe from the Contras' northern attacks, the barren landscape changes into tropical Bavarian Alps. Because coffee bushes need shade, the fine trees were spared. In this beauty spot, a sour well-dressed woman, a hereditary coffee magnate, owns a hotel. "I had no trouble with Somoza. I have no trouble with these Sandinistas. Of course I didn't vote. Nobody voted." That is, nobody like her, but 29 deputies represent the three parties of the right in the National Assembly.

Her land produces a quarter of a million pounds of coffee. "I have to sell to the government at a low price." For three months a year she employs hundreds of itinerant laborers to harvest the crop. "Only women and children now. The men are in the militia. No one wants to work." "Where do the women and children come from?" "Who knows?" she shrugged. "When they're finished they go back to their places."

"The farmers don't want to sell to the government, they only grow for themselves." Farmers' roadside stalls sell luscious high-priced fruit and vegetables; the same in Managua. "Anyway they're afraid to come to town for fear of being drafted." "How about fear of ambushes on the roads?" I asked. In the last six months of 1984, 129 civilians died, 69 were wounded in Contra ambushes, a daily danger. "Or fear of being kidnapped?" One hundred and sixty-three men, a strange way to recruit "true revolutionaries." The lady was only concerned with her personal fear, losing her land. All property of the Somozas and their cronies was confiscated, the land distributed to the peasants. "Have any of your friends been expropriated?" "Not yet." Not after five and a half years of Sandinista rule. "I make no profit from coffee, only from the hotel." I said, "You must have had richer guests before?" "There are plenty of rich people now. Industrialists. They're making money, they're doing very well."

The young man had the pale beauty wrongly attributed to poets and a terrible limp. We were talking in the small grimy office of the Frente Sandinista, the political party of the government. His right hip was out of line, the leg four inches shortened. He got this crippling wound as a student, fighting here in the streets of Matagalpa against Somoza's Guardia.

"We ran around with shotguns and petrol bottles, we didn't know what we were doing. Our army is better all the time. The boys have three weeks' training now. The Contras can make misery every day but they can't win. Our work? We go to the people, we listen to complaints, we explain the shortages, rising prices, why the boys must register for the draft, why we can't do more, faster. The people know there's a war but they don't see it. They only feel the economic difficulties. But if Reagan invades our country, it would take a long time to kill us all."

In Managua, the *barrios* are the slums, old and new. The old are narrow dark little houses like tunnels, built to last, with cement floors. The new are unsteady one-room boxes made of planks and corrugated tin, with dirt floors: homes of the refugees from the frontiers. Two middle-aged cheerful women sat on the steps of adjoining houses, old slums. They were cousins and had lived here for 20 years, each sewing 12 shirts a day for 180 cordobas, another aspect of local capitalism. Cordobas are meaningless; a short taxi ride costs 300 cordobas. The poor are protected by fixed-price rationed food in government markets. Private markets flourish as do small-time spivs who trade goods that fell off trucks.

When Somoza, in a parting gesture, ordered Managua to be bombed and strafed, a machine gun bullet broke the older woman's leg. That was past, the future is her 16-year-old son joining the army next year. She asked suddenly, "Was the war in Vietnam horrible?" Foreigners must know everything. "Very," I said, never forgetting it. "That is what Reagan would do to us here." Things were hard because of the Contras, "but our government belongs to us, we are not little mice anymore."

In a new slum, in this heat, a string-thin woman, almost toothless, barefooted, in grayish-black rags, was slapping tortillas and toasting them on a sheet of scrap iron over a wood fire. She supports her family—an old ailing husband, two young children— by selling tortillas to the neighbors. They are refugees from the Costa Rican frontier. "ARDE kidnapped my sons, two boys, 22 and 24. They hit them and tied them up and took them away." ARDE is the invasion force in the south, armed but not trained by the CIA. "We know the Contras, they are Somoza's men. But ARDE, those are the real traitors! They were on our side and now they attack us. They walk around with handfuls of dollars to show they are rich while we are poor. They come into villages and rob whatever they want, animals, chickens, furniture. They kill people and run away to Costa Rica. *Traitors!* For love of our country, we must fight them. We escaped at night, walking, with what we could carry. I pray I will see my sons again." They built their wretched shelter and dug a latrine like everyone else here. "There's a water tap across the street. The children go to school. We have a clinic nearby. The government helps me with very cheap dough." She does not complain.

Sandinista officials are too busy for stray visitors; their enemies have time and talk freely. Not much of a "Communist tyranny" where capitalists keep their capital, badmouth the government, and publish their scornful views in a big daily paper. Either President Reagan knows he is lying or he doesn't know he is lying; ominous, either way.

In the elegant headquarters of COSEP, the Nicaraguan equivalent of the CBI, a charming industrialist said, "Ninety-five percent of Nicaraguans were in favor of the Sandinistas when they came to power. Somoza was an obstacle to development. He had to go." It cost the lives of 60,000 other people to do that job. "We're not worried about taxes and profits, we're concerned about liberty." Sixty percent of the economy is in private hands but the government has passed five laws to regulate what is a war-time economy. COSEP decries these laws as an assault on liberty. Liberty is a free market economy.

Do the laws affect his business? "No, I have a small chemical industry, everything is small in Nicaragua. They think I am essential." His friends? "Not yet, but we feel very insecure." COSEP won't invest, won't co-operate, they are sitting on their hands: a novel form of sabotage by passivity.

"If you got power, what about social welfare?" Major Sandinista programs: a continuing campaign against illiteracy, a network of clinics in a country where tuberculosis, poverty's disease, is endemic. "Social welfare of course," said the charming man. "We say you cannot have prosperous businesses with poor people."

Meantime, to the end of 1984, U.S. taxes have paid for the murder of 3,954 harmless men and women and 3,346 children, the uprooting of 142,980 people now refugees, the destruction of 137 hopeful modest infant centers, clinics, schools, co-operatives, built by the Sandinistas for the peasants. If American taxpayers saw the photo record of this would they feel that their money was well spent? President Reagan's destabilization plan grinds on: torrential propaganda, strangling economic boycott, death and devastation at bargain rates. If the plan worked, resulting in chaos, suitable Nicaraguans would receive power on a plate from an American President, in the traditional style.

In 1823, the Monroe Doctrine established the claim that the U.S. had a backyard and the right to supervise it. Since 1909, when the U.S. ousted a popular Nicaraguan President, the American government has actively supported its own choice for President of Nicaragua, sending the marines if there was any sign of revolt. No American President denounced the long and real Somoza tyranny.

Nicaragua proves that a poor poeple can win the right to choose a government for itself. Nicaragua is setting a bad example to Latin America. This heady idea of national self-determination might spread to all the other poor people in the area. The fate of freedom does hang in the balance.

The Sandinista government can be overthrown only by direct U.S. military intervention. Easier than Vietnam, perhaps, but blood-soaked. And what would be the fine moral difference between the Soviet Union invading Hungary and Czechoslovakia, to teach those people obedience, and the U.S. invading Nicaragua?

CONCLUSION

In 1945, the U.S. had produced three nuclear weapons, the A-bombs; one tested, two used. After the Japanese surrender, the end of the Second World War, there was no need or excuse for more of these weapons. It was the moment to decide in favor of the human species and the planet earth: STOP NOW. Bulldoze Los Alamos, knock the installations flat, smash the machinery, burn the records, threaten anyone who might pass on information with high treason. Sow the place with salt for good measure. I like to believe that Franklin Roosevelt would have done it. He could have, with no complaints from the citizenry. Americans, whose war was particularly in the Pacific, hated Japan, but those bombs felt wrong, unnatural, too doom-laden, long before we understood just how different they were from all previous killing tools.

Franklin Roosevelt died in the spring, months before the two fateful August days and they, whoever they were—military, scientific, political advisers clustered around the novice Truman—decided to invest in better bombs and hide the know-how of nuclear destruction from our ally, Stalin. Secret executive decisions. In our freedom-loving democracies, we do not know what has been decided; in due course, we feel the results. Parliament, Congress, the Chamber of Deputies, whatever, may argue about executive decisions after they have been taken but are not consulted at the crucial moments; and they can be deceived just like the rest of us. We voters learn some of the secret decisions when they have turned out to be very bad

and reach the newspapers. Those two secret executive decisions, after the Japanese surrender, shaped the postwar world.

As soon as the U.S. alone had the means to wipe out
Moscow in a couple of minutes, Stalin ordered his physicists
and engineers to concentrate on producing a Russian A-bomb.
For forty-two years, the U.S. and the U.S.S.R. have had no
guiding foreign policy except mutual harassment and hostility,
with their allies trundling behind, and the wretched Third
World dragged in as proxies when convenient. In 1949, communist China became number-two enemy, sometimes neck and
neck with the Soviet Union, sometimes ahead, but now we are
all pals with China while at present the Soviet Union is not, so
that's all right. What a long mess it has been; what a waste; and
who has benefited?

But in 1945, though not in very good shape, we innocently
imagined we had survived the worst possible war and were
innocently unaware that something far worse, beyond imagination worse, was already being prepared. The U.S. had the
knowledge and machinery to make more nuclear weapons, but
none on hand; the Soviet Union was rushing to catch up. The
arms race began then. There are now some 60,000 nuclear
warheads in the world, 97 percent of them owned by the
U.S.S.R. and the U.S., front runner in the arms race. Since
1945, every government in the U.S.S.R., the U.S., Britain and
France bears part of the guilt for this criminal stupidity.

Chernobyl should concentrate all minds, even political minds,
even military minds. It does not require imagination, it is fact,
and shows what a minor nuclear explosion at ground level can
do to Europe. The force of the Chernobyl explosion was 0.1
kilotons, or 100 tons of TNT to make it clearer for those of us
who do not think in kilotons—1000 tons, the measure for the
power of nuclear weapons. Nothing like that flaming catastrophe, on April 26, 1986, had ever been known. The firemen who
tried to put out the flames died; then helicopters were brought
to bomb the flames with sand; then men tunneled beneath the
reactor to contain even worse disaster and covered the plant
above and below ground with a thick shield of concrete. There
it will stand forever, if there is forever, like the Great Pyramid
of Cheops, a tomb for poison.

One hundred thirty-five thousand Russians, within an 18-mile radius of the Chernobyl plant, had to be evacuated from their homes and resettled in safe locations. Their blood will be tested regularly for years to come. Water and soil are still monitored in the surrounding contaminated areas. Radiation sickness and cancers kept on developing in Japan, decades after the A-bombs exploded. Russians will live for decades in dread of the aftereffects of Chernobyl.

The wind picked up a cloud of radioactive dust from the burning Chernobyl plant and spread it erratically across Russia and Europe. Day after day the cloud moved, changing its shape, until by the eighth day it had dispersed all over Europe from east of Moscow to north and west in Finland and Sweden and south to Greece and European Turkey. Concentrations of radioactive particles in rainfall varied, the worst "hot spots" developed in southern Germany, northern Italy and Alsace. Or so they say. Children were given iodine against thyroid cancer in Poland. Iodine tablets sold out in Germany. Milk and green vegetables were suspect, cattle could not graze outdoors, foodstuffs from eastern Europe were prohibited. Governments, in total confusion, sent out conflicting information and instructions or none, until absurdly late. The French and British governments, devoted to the wonders of nuclear power, were lackadaisical.

In Britain, a small area judged to be in the "medium range" of the huge affected whole, a still smaller area was most at risk. On the second and third of May 1986, heavy radioactive rain from the Chernobyl cloud drenched parts of North Wales, Cumbria and Scotland. This is sheep farming country. The government in Whitehall soothed, nothing to worry about, until their scientists found high levels of radio-caesium in lambs. Two million sheep were exposed in Wales alone. From June 20, their movement and sale were restricted. The Welsh Agricultural Office began a thorough monitoring system which continues still. Sometime that summer in Wales, we were warned not to drink standing water as if we usually ran out and gulped from rain puddles. All our drinking water stands in great open reservoirs.

One year later and 1,400 miles from the Chernobyl explosion, 100,000 Welsh sheep remain contaminated and quarantined, and scientists testing new grass from the Welsh hills have found rising levels of caesium. Like almost everyone else, I am an illiterate beginner in this frightful subject and I know less about the radioactive make-up of the Chernobyl cloud than I know about Aramaic, but I read that caesium 137 was a major component. Research (by telephone to Lord Zuckerman) reveals that caesium 137 has a half-life of 30.5 years. This means, I gather, that half the poisonous radioactivity of caesium 137 seeping into the rainy ground deteriorates for 30.5 years, half of the remainder deteriorates for another 30.5 years and so on, ad infinitum, until the last caesium 137 particle has finally perished. Animals, feeding on radio-caesium tainted grass, fertilize the soil again with radio-caesium poison through their droppings; besides absorbing radio-caesium into their bones permanently. It is a circle of injury of a kind and a lastingness unknown before the nuclear era.

A Welsh farmer said, "I am apprehensive about the next one [the lambing season] in 1988, for then the Chernobyl lambs will themselves be lambing." No one has explained that the silent beautiful Welsh hillsides, where the rain fell, are an unmapped danger zone for an indefinite time. To February 1987, Welsh farmers had been paid £2,604,000 compensation for sheep they could not sell. They say bitterly that this does not cover their losses.

These conditions are true of Cumbria and Scotland where about 150,000 sheep are still tainted and quarantined. A Cumbrian farmer added an interesting piece of news: farmers are supposed to bury sheep dead of radiation sickness on their own land but he says he has no time to dig graves in rocky soil for five or six animals, soon the Lake District will stink of carcasses. The land, the crops, the cattle, the livelihoods of thousands and thousands of farmers in Europe have been impaired the same way, or worse. I guess the grimness of the outlook depends on how much caesium 137, and whatever else, soaked into how much soil from Norway to European Turkey. And everyone will be lucky if it is only a financial disaster. Estimates of cancers resulting from the passage of the radioactive cloud are too wildly different to make sense. Time unfortunately will tell.

The truth is that we have no idea of the long-term damage

to Europe from a single 0.1-kiloton nuclear explosion in western Russia.

Then: consider the weakest, least harmful weapon in our arsenal of battlefield nuclear weapons, a dinky toy compared to the big stuff, the missiles. It is an American 8″ artillery shell with the explosive force of 0.5 kilotons, 500 tons of TNT, five times stronger than Chernobyl. As it is designed to explode in the air, its blast, heat and radiation potential are far more than five times that of Chernobyl. Only nuclear power stations are ground anchored. This shell is fired from a standard self-propelled gun, like any normal shell. Shells are fired as fast as gunners can slam them into a gun breech, one round every minute. By published reports, our side has 3,000 of these nuclear shells while the Soviets have 4,000, presumably identical. A bombardment of super-Chernobyls is seriously contemplated as battlefield tactics in the center of Europe. Nothing makes clearer the infuriating madness of nuclear weapons. And the infuriating madness of all those who built the nuclear stockpiles, East and West.

But no, nuclear weapons are not madness. You're ridiculous to fuss about the fatal time bombs that lurk on the land and are whisked around the seas and the skies. You simply don't know what's good for you. Fancy calling it madness; it is called Defense. And we have provided even more Defense; we have invented and manufactured in avalanche quantities the most sophisticated deadly conventional weapons of all time. Of course we don't want war but we suspect the Other Side's intentions so we have all organized to fight a defensive war that will either annihilate the world or merely annihilate Europe. You will be defended from the cradle to the grave.

Statistics are heavy to read and often rigged in self-interest by governments. But they are also compact and if you use figures from the most trustworthy, eminent, non-governmental sources, they give a quick overall view of this weird enterprise, Defense.

Officially the world is at peace. Local wars do not count except to the victims. In 1986, the International Year of Peace, global military expenditure is reliably estimated at $900 billion. (Statistics are added up more slowly than money pours

331

out.) Compare the 1983 figures (the latest available) of global military expenditure—$728.3 billion—and global health care, $545 billion. One third less money for means to look after the ills of humanity than for means to inflict them. This is the regular pattern. The Third World spends more for its military requirements than for health and education combined. The Soviet Union, using its wealth to rival the other military Super-power, does the same.

In ten years to 1985, Third World governments ran up a debt of $240 billion for imported weaponry. At present eighteen armed conflicts spread across the Third World from the Middle East to Central America. Armed conflicts have been a tragedy for the poor people of the Third World every year since 1945, with a death toll calculated at 20 million and mounting. There has never been a census of co-related deaths from famine but we know that there are now millions of war-displaced semi-starved or starving refugees in Eritrea, Ethiopia, Sudan, Uganda, Angola, Mozambique and in and around El Salvador.

Weapon manufacturers, communist and capitalist alike, export their products without concern for their use and effect. Like heroin exporters. Arms exports were a $39.3 billion world business in 1983. That is the last official figure. The Stockholm International Peace Research Institute thinks that at least $50 billion, and perhaps much more, is the figure now, boosted by the Iran-Iraq war. Secret arms deals and barter for weapons make accuracy difficult. Fringe benefits increase the value of the arms export trade. Commissions, bribes, and straight graft. In February 1987, the U.S. Justice Department estimated that the U.S. Defense Department was swindled out of no less than $100 billion a year through fraudulent invoices, double-billing, and the sale of sub-standard equipment.* Formerly regarded as a dirty business fit only for dirty people, the merchants of death, governments now compete to sell their wares and proudly announce the weapons contracts won by their home industries. Heroin is trivial set against the massive casualties due to our weapons.

In 1984, 26,980,000 men and some women wore the

Newsweek, February 9, 1987.

military uniforms of 140 nations: global armed forces of nearly 27 million people. The number will not have decreased. A mammoth dead-end labor force which neither sows nor reaps but is a crushing expense for those who do.

Armed forces are administered by national Departments of Defense, by any name the same thing. Civilian employees in these bureaucracies everywhere outnumber public employees in all other national departments. Over one million civilians are employed in the U.S. Defense Department. In Britain, the Ministry of Defense employs one third of the total civil service personnel.

Armed forces must be housed, clothed, fed as well as equipped with transport and weapons, bombers to bullets. This creates vast civilian employment. It has been reckoned that altogether—armed forces, bureaucracies, scientific staff, suppliers, weapons manufacturers—100 million people are employed world-wide in preparing for war if not actually engaged in it.

Defense is like a giant man-made tapeworm feeding on the economy of the host country and weakening it. As proved by the three nations with the biggest Defense budgets. The Soviet economy is sorely ailing; the British economy is not in rosy health and the U.S. economy staggers under colossal debt for colossal Defense.

Economy is an abstract word and does not say enough. *We all pay* for this Defense, this greatest single industry on earth. We, who do not profit from it, support it. And what do we get for our money? Security? Who feels secure?

Defense is about enemies, a chronic disease of governments, which is why history is so lowering to read, those endless wars, old enemies exchanged for new enemies. Can you believe that 1,500 British troops are on permanent guard duty in Belize because the Guatemalan government claims to own Belize, as if owning somebody else's 8,876 square miles of overheated jungle would improve life for the cowed dirt-poor Guatemalan peasants. Micro-enemies or macro-enemies are irrelevant to two thirds of the world's population. They battle with their own genuine enemies year after year, always losing.

If a portion of the money and expertise used for Defense were used to assist them, it need not be a losing battle. That requires a mind shift in all governments, an enlightened definition of security.

International organizations such as UNICEF, the World Bank, the International Labor Organization, the World Health Organization, UNESCO estimate that: 700 million people, more than the entire population of western Europe, the U.S. and Canada, do not have enough food for normal healthy lives. 15 million children, 40,000 a day, die each year unnecessarily, for want of rudimentary health care and the meanest necessities. 90 million people are unemployed and as many as 300 million more underemployed, thus barely clinging to existence. 880 million adults cannot read and write and 715 million children who should be in school are not. And now there is AIDS, foreseen as a pandemic killer in Africa and an unlimited threat everywhere. Selections from a large catalogue. The Third World is the most afflicted, but we have a shaming share of that catalogue in our prosperous countries too.

The Superpowers' rivalry looks like an egomaniacal side issue. The real issue is this gigantic dangerous imbalance in human life. Do our governments think we can perch safely on top of our weapons while most of the world's people drown in misery below us?

After two generations of relentless propaganda war, a New Man emerges, from the Kremlin of all places, wearing a halo of common sense. He speaks in a calm rational tone about compromise and negotiation and ordinary people, like you and me and the neighbors and similar millions can hardly believe our ears, being so unaccustomed to good news; and we rejoice. Not so our leaders. Nor are the grim old leaders of the Warsaw Pact allies glowing with enthusiasm.

The New Man in the Kremlin has spread alarm among our Western leaders by proposing to do what they said they wanted. NATO men, the hard-headed Defense experts, realists, the powerful ones who know what's what, those who decide for us, troop across our TV screens sounding evasive, if not earnestly deranged. They advise us that non-nuclear Europe would be naked; we cannot sleep safely in our beds without nuclear protection. If Cruise and Pershing go, can the U.S. be far behind? Europe might then be abandoned to its interminably advertised fate: invasion by the Red hordes. Ours not to reason why the Soviets should be more suicidal than we are, nor recall the indelible Russian memory of the horrors of war. Our role is to shiver and tremble and have our brains washed in the old known way. The NATO men explain that disarmament is dangerous, to be handled with extreme caution and as slowly as possible. To that end they haggle and argue, find objections and whomp up a scare about inferiority in conventional weapons. Like the old Missile Gap, the Window of Vulnerability and other familiar scares. Meanwhile, to display strength and self-reliance, the British and French governments plan to increase their nuclear forces, ultimate waste and conceit. The NATO leaders cling to the ever imminent hypothetical war and to their cherished nuclear weapons.

The New Man in the Kremlin has shown that he recognizes the folly of the arms race, and Chernobyl may have helped to clarify Russian thinking in general. But hawks and hard-liners abide in the Soviet hierarchy as in ours and if the New Man fails to get firm co-operation from the West he is not guaranteed a free hand and indefinite job tenure. It is terrifying to think that our hawks and hard-liners could bungle and miss the first steps toward sanity since the history of mankind changed at Hiroshima and Nagasaki.

What can we do, we who only live here? Sit still? Think about something else? Pray? Hope for the best? Instead, anonymous citizens all over the so-called developed world, from Australia to Norway, decided to say NO. An international grass roots rebellion. People of all ages, all backgrounds, all political beliefs, all creeds and none, have joined in public opposition to nuclear weapons and militarism. The media named this the Peace Movement. Movement: "a body of persons with a common object." The Peace Movement has no central direction, no rules, no agreed plan of action. Peace groups in every country formed themselves spontaneously and do their own thing, whatever they see as most effective. Unity of purpose is their link. I wonder if anything like this ever happened before: a world-wide campaign that grew from individual conviction, organized itself, persists; but then nuclear weapons, which begat today's Peace Movement, never happened before either. By its existence, the Peace Movement denies that governments know best; it stands for a different order of priorities: the human race comes first.

Some peace groups are famous, like International Physicians for the Prevention of Nuclear War, founded by an American and a Russian doctor and now numbering 175,000 medical men and women from 55 countries, and growing. This group was awarded the Nobel Peace Prize in 1985. Or the Women of Greenham Common who have kept a brave protest vigil through five hard winters outside the sinister fence of the American base for Cruise missiles in Berkshire. There are 5,700 peace groups in the U.S., the heartland of the arms race. In Britain the Campaign for Nuclear Disarmament is the largest among many peace groups, with 84,000 national members and 250,000 regional members in small towns or sizeable villages throughout Scotland, Wales and England. One hundred peace groups in Scandinavia have merged in the Nordic Alliance. Holland has 47 national peace groups but no peace office is able to count or even estimate the total number of peace groups in western Europe. Huge demonstrations against nuclear weapons and war indicate their size. The Peace Movement has done well in its appointed task of educating and converting public opinion. No major political party can now ignore its effect; they concede the effect if only by hammering the hard sell on nuclear weapons, but the Peace Movement cannot rest.

Watching the Peace Movement grow in numbers and competence, I see it as talented citizenship. Citizenship is a tough occupation which obliges the citizen to make his own informed opinion and stand by it. And I am impressed by the friendliness in the Peace Movement, rare these days, and the way that friendliness naturally extends across the East-West divide: we do not hate and fear other people because of their governments any more than we wish to be hated and feared because of ours.

I hold to the relay race theory of history: progress in human affairs depends on accepting, generation after generation, the individual duty to oppose the evils of the time. The evils of the time change but are never in short supply and would go unchallenged unless there were conscientious people to say: not if I can help it. The Peace Movement splendidly confirms my relay race theory. As a senior citizen, I am exhilarated by the commitment of younger and much younger citizens to the Peace Movement, other generations of conscientious people. We have a wide range of evils in our time and a wide range of reformers determined to oppose them. The Peace Movement is a base for all reformers since the human condition cannot be bettered nor the natural world protected unless we ensure the survival of the planet.

We must always remember that we are not the servants of the state. As the British Attorney General said in his final speech at the Nuremberg Trial, "The state and the law are made for man that through them he may achieve a fuller life, a higher purpose and a greater dignity." The state has fallen down on its job: instead of a fuller life, the state has led man to a haunted life.

There has to be a better way to run the world and we better see that we get it.

Kilgwrrwg, Wales
July 1987